T0295370

Dead Labor

DEAD LABOR

Toward a Political Economy
of Premature Death

JAMES TYNER

University of Minnesota Press
Minneapolis
London

A previous version of chapter 3 was published as "Population Geography I: Surplus Populations," *Progress in Human Geography* 37, no. 5 (2013): 701–11 (journals.sage pub.com/doi/abs/10.1177/0309132512473924). A previous version of chapter 4 was published as "Population Geography III: Precarity, Dead Peasants, and Truncated Life," *Progress in Human Geography* 40, no. 2 (2016): 275–89 (journals.sagepub.com/ doi/abs/10.1177/0309132515569964). A previous version of chapter 5 was published as "Population Geography II: Mortality, Premature Death, and the Ordering of Life," *Progress in Human Geography* 39, no. 3 (2015): 360–73 (journals.sagepub.com/doi/ abs/10.1177/0309132514527037). Adapted by permission of SAGE Publications.

Published by the University of Minnesota Press
111 Third Avenue South, Suite 290
Minneapolis, MN 55401-2520
upress.umn.edu

Printed on acid-free paper

The University of Minnesota is an equal-opportunity educator and employer.

Library of Congress Cataloging-in-Publication Data
Names: Tyner, James, author.
Title: Dead labor : toward a political economy of premature death / James Tyner.
Description: Minneapolis : University of Minnesota Press, [2019] | Includes bibliographical references and index. |
Identifiers: LCCN 2018037429 (print) | ISBN 978-1-5179-0362-6 (hc) | ISBN 978-1-5179-0363-3 (pb)
Subjects: LCSH: Labor—Philosophy. | Premature death—Philosophy. | Labor theory of value.
Classification: LCC HD4904 .T96 2019 (print) | DDC 331.01/3—dc23
LC record available at https://lccn.loc.gov/2018037429

CONTENTS

PREFACE

On the evening of April 17, 2013, shortly before 8 p.m., an explosion at the West Fertilizer Company rocked the town of West, Texas, killing 15 people and injuring an additional 252.[1] In the aftermath of the disaster, the cause of the explosion was traced to an uncontrolled fire in a building that housed fertilizer-grade ammonium nitrate.[2] Alongside the destruction of the West Fertilizer plant, over 150 other buildings were damaged or destroyed, including a middle school, a high school, a nursing home, and an apartment complex.[3] An investigation by the Chemical Safety Board (CSB) concluded that, if the explosion had occurred, say, during a school day, the death toll would have been dramatically higher. It is quite possible that hundreds of children could have died. According to the U.S. Environmental Protection Agency (EPA), no schools *should* be built within a half-mile radius of hazardous materials. However, compliance with this regulation is voluntary, and indeed, like many states, Texas has no regulations about siting schools near chemical storage sites or other hazardous areas.[4] To this end, the CSB's investigation found that nearly half of the forty facilities in Texas that store fertilizer-grade ammonium nitrate are within a half-mile of a school.[5]

On the night of August 25, 2017, Hurricane Harvey made landfall near Rockport, Texas, with peak winds topping 130 miles per hour and torrential rains, with many areas recording upward of 40 inches, while Cedar Bayou registered a record-setting 51 inches. Flood waters associated with the hurricane inundated hundreds of square miles, resulting in the displacement of more than 30,000 people and the death of more than 40.[6]

Long after the storm made its way to the east, its flooding continued to impact the region. A week later, many areas still had no power. In Crosby, Texas, a small town twenty-five miles northeast of Houston, two explosions occurred at the Arkema chemical plant. Heavy precipitation had flooded the facility, setting off a chain of events that led to the blasts. Inundated with six feet of water, operations at the plant had to be shut down, including the cooling of chemicals stored at the site. Without refrigeration, the chemicals began to degrade, ultimately erupting. Rich Rowe, Arkema's president and CEO, explained that the resultant fires—with toxic smoke billowing above the facility—would not "pose any long-term harm or impact."[7]

Residents of Crosby were lucky: unlike West, they lost no lives.[8] However, the explosions called to question the underlying attitude of business executives toward the life of their laborers and others who live in the shadow of their companies. Investigative journalists, writing even as the flooding continued, uncovered a sordid history of congressional lobbying and backroom deals. In the aftermath of the disaster in West, then-President Barack Obama worked to raise safety standards for chemical plants. To this end, in a 2013 executive order, Obama proposed a massive overhaul of the EPA's Risk Management Program. The objective was to increase safety by strengthening existing regulations.[9] Under the revised regulations, Arkema's Crosby plant, which housed large amounts of toxic sulfur dioxide and flammable methylpropen, would have been subject to strengthened safety rules. It is not coincidental that Arkema, which operates six chemical plants in Texas, has received over $8.7 million in taxpayer subsidies and yet has also been fined multiple times for safety violations; in 2016 alone, the company was fined over $90,000.[10]

In a letter submitted to the EPA in May 2016, representatives of Arkema complained that the regulations "will likely add significant new costs and burdens to the corporate audit process."[11] The market logics of

capitalism prevailed, or more cynically, personal greed won out. Lobby-
ists of the American Chemistry Council, including members of Arkema,
successfully blocked the Obama-era regulations that were set to go into
effect toward the end of 2017. As Karen Graham writes, tens of millions of
dollars were poured into federal elections, primarily toward sympathetic
Republican lawmakers who received substantial campaign donations
from the chemical industry. And while the specific deregulatory efforts
of 2017 played no direct role in the hurricane-related explosions, Arkema
symbolizes a wider effort on behalf of the chemical industry to risk the
lives of its workers and those living in the surrounding communities in
an effort to amass ever-greater profits. Indeed, the proposed deregulations come on top of an industry *already* grossly underregulated. Studies
following the disaster in West concluded that "poor hazard awareness,
inadequate emergency planning, regulatory gaps, the proximity of the
facility to nearby homes and other buildings and limited regulatory oversight all led to the incident's severity."[12]

In the aftermath of Hurricane Harvey, I watched with both horror and
disbelief as spokespersons for the Arkema facility downplayed the seri-
ousness of the explosions and the subsequent toxic plume. I wondered
how many people might die *prematurely* not because of deliberate mal-
feasance, but simply because the political economy of America's chemical
industry was performing exactly as planned, according to a calculative
rationality that places profit before people. The fatal tragedy at West was
not, of course, an isolated incident. On March 23, 2005, for example, a
series of explosions at BP's refinery in Texas City resulted in 15 deaths
and 180 injuries, and on February 7, 2008, an explosion and fire at the
Imperial Sugar refinery near Savannah, Georgia, led to the death of 14
workers and injuries to 38 others.[13]

As Arkema's near-disaster played out live before a national audience,
the subordination of health and safety concerns to the dictates of capital were all too clear. "Even though chemical plant safeguards fail every
week," Greenpeace writes, "the chemical industry has largely refused to
make their plants safer and more secure."[14] Throughout the United States,
hundreds of thousands of people are at risk of injury or death; indeed,
according to Greenpeace, "one in three Americans could fall victim to
a similar poison gas disaster by virtue of living near upwards of 12,000
plants that store and use highly toxic substances."[15]

The deregulations proposed following the disaster in West and the subsequent potential loss of life posed by Hurricane Harvey's effect on myriad chemical plants and related industries highlight an underlying theme of this book: the fundamental biopolitical questions of who lives, who dies, and who decides. More precisely, it highlights an ever-more-important bio-*economic* question: is it still sufficient to consider the sovereign right to make life, take life, or let die, or must we instead confront the pecuniary issue of who profits from the death of another? In the following chapters, I present the argument that, under capitalism, death has been outside the realm of the biological *or* the biopolitical and that it continues to move further into the realm of the bioeconomic. Consequently, one's exposure to death is more and more conditioned by one's position in capitalism. Stated differently, the relations between labor and capital necessarily inform the relations between life and death. Inequalities that are manifest along the familiar axes of exploitation and oppression (ethnicity, gender, sexuality, and citizenship) materialize as inequalities to the exposure and occurrence of death.

Capitalism is a form of social organization that, on the surface, appears as a system of exchange: commodities appear on the market to be bought and sold through the intermediary of money. Accordingly, under capitalism, "commodity exchange plays an essential role in satisfying even the most basic human needs."[16] To this end, as Marx writes, "definite social relations" between real, living people assumes "the fantastic form of a relation between things."[17] Marx cautions against this fetishism of commodities and instead calls attention to the precise social relations inherent to capitalism.

Living labor conditions Marx's method and, as such, provides the pivot upon which to interpret capitalism critically as a form of social organization.[18] Here, "the category of living labor commands the creation of categories appropriate to their solution and the building of a theoretical system of capitalism as a historically determined mode of production."[19] However, Marx pairs "living labor" with "dead labor": labor that was expended in the past and embodied within a *thing*, expended energy that is reanimated in the production process. Marx writes: "In so far as labor is productive activity directed to a particular purpose . . . it raises the means of production from the dead merely by entering into contact with them, infuses them with life so that they become factors in the labor process, and combines with them to form new products."[20] Marx uses the term "dead labor" metaphorically to emphasize the previous social activities that went into the making of something, for the "product of labor which has been congealed in an object, which has become material."[21]

Don Mitchell asks geographers and other social scientists to consider dead labor in other-than-metaphorical terms.[22] Thus, in calling attention to the violence that surrounds the production process, Mitchell highlights the exploitative and oppressive working conditions of migrant farm workers, such as the dangers of prolonged exposure to pesticides and insecticides and the dangerous journey to the fields themselves. Indeed, the labor that is embodied in commodities, the living labor that reanimates dead labor, is frequently injured or killed in the labor process. In short, living laborers, through the transformation of dead labor, may become (quite literally) dead laborers. Mitchell forces us to think of the dead laborers that lay buried beneath the ground, those men, women, and children who died all-too-soon in the making of capitalism.

In *Dead Labor: Toward a Political Economy of Premature Death*, I acknowledge Mitchell's lead and consider how dead and dying bodies "work" for political and economic purposes. This is a robust field and has stimulated considerable debate and discussion.[23] My concern, however, is less with the symbolic work performed by corpses and more with how profits are increasingly realized through the material death of laborers.[24] Stated differently, my apprehension is that death has become and continues to be commodified under capitalism, not from the standpoint of buying and selling dead bodies, but rather from that of those conditions that facilitate death being increasingly recognized as sites of capital accumulation. Ongoing rounds of deregulation, the elimination of welfare and health care, and the greater ease with which tissues and organs are bought and sold are all indications of a fundamental shift within capitalism whereby life and death, living and dying, are blurred.

Workers, Friedrich Engels writes, labor "under conditions in which they cannot live . . . in which they can neither retain health nor live long."[25] To this end, I highlight several figures of dead labor, thus calling attention to the embodiment of premature death within capitalism. When we see dead laborers, whose lives have been truncated, we must recognize those social and structural relations that condition life itself, for prior exposure to oppression and exploitation are congealed in death itself.

More precisely, I construct a Marxist-inspired, historical materialist account of premature death. I do so not because I believe Marx to be the final arbiter of exploitation, oppression, and death, but rather because I follow Terry Eagleton in recognizing that the writings of Marx still provide the most cogent critique of capitalism and must therefore provide the foundation for any attempt to interpret the grave effects of unequal social relations inherent to capitalist society: "[Marx] dealt with the terrible condition of the human world. One need only think of the numerous famines in the midst of affluence, the tolerated environmental disasters and the worldwide persistence of social conflict to see that little has changed. . . . As long as capitalism is still in business, Marxism must be as well."[26]

However, I readily accede also to the claim of Frantz Fanon that, in the context of racism, for example, Marx's writings must be stretched. It is vitally necessary to work critically through Marx from the standpoint of feminism and antiracism. To this end, I concur with Julie Matthaei that the "theoretical merging of Marxism, feminism, and anti-racism allows the development of a more inclusive, and more liberatory, understanding of the economy."[27] By extension, it becomes possible to articulate more precisely the intersectional workings of class, sex, and "race" (among other axes of difference) within capitalism, to better articulate the political economic *conditions* of premature death. As Emma Laurie and Ian Shaw explain, here, "conditions are the very *geographies of being*: the existential resources that nourish and sustain, but also harm and violate."[28]

As deployed in the following chapters, "materiality" does not refer solely or even primarily to the physiology of death or to the politics of corpses.[29] Rather, in the sense in which I am using it, "materiality" calls attention to the understanding of death within a particular mode of production. Indeed, it is my argument that there is no essential conception of death; rather, the positing of death is conditioned by and constitutive of myriad social relations that comprise any given society. In this discussion, I retheorize the production of premature death within capitalism, arguing that death is imbricated with the real subsumption of labor to the market logics of capitalism (see chapter 2 for Marx on "formal" subsumption) and that one's exposure to death within capitalism is predicated on a particular valuation of life. For, as J. D. Taylor writes, "capitalism intrinsically negates individual and collective capacity for equal political representation, social rights, and quality of life, given that its base assumption is that the value of life is determined by its success in individually accumulating and trading wealth."[30]

My overall thesis is straightforward: There exists a contradiction between the demands of capitalism in the pursuit of profit and the requirements to sustain and reproduce life itself. More precisely, premature death is conditioned by the unequal commodification of living labor. This is seen, for example, in the acceptance of the potential and actual sacrifice of laborers (and first responders) rather than the sacrifice of compliance with safety regulations, in the selling of kidneys by the world's poor to extend the lives of those who have greater access to wealth, in the deaths of countless men, women, and children dispossessed and displaced by corporate greed, and in the portfolios of insurance companies that profit from the death of persons denied adequate health care.

In the following chapters, I argue that we are presently witness to a new political economy of premature death, an emergent *necrocapitalism* in which the valuation and vulnerability of life itself is centered on two overlapping criteria: productivity and responsibility.[31] Capital *values* those bodies deemed both *productive* (e.g., in a position to generate wealth) and *responsible,* with responsibility conceived of as the ability to participate fully as producers and consumers in the capitalist system while, simultaneously, not incurring a net loss to the system. Those individuals who are deemed nonproductive or redundant, based on an economic bio-arithmetic, are disproportionately vulnerable and increasingly disallowed life to the point of premature death.[32] In other words, our concern is necessarily with the "production of death, of dead bodies which undergird the very extension of market rationality."[33] Necrocapitalism is thus marked by a distorted morality in which mortality constitutes individual failure. Increasingly, those who are subjected to both direct and structural violence are judged by society to be responsible for their own suffering and demise—a perverted variant of blaming the victim. By extension, there is a corresponding indifference to the death of the other, a detachment from and disinterest in those persons who are perceived as "mis-fitting" into society and seemingly lacking the wherewithal to survive.[34] In short, I argue that a pervasive indifference to surplus or redundant bodies is matched only with a nascent preference toward the profitability of dying or dead bodies.

The Road Ahead

Hurricane Harvey offers insight into the bioeconomic conditions of a rapacious capitalism. Hurricane Maria demonstrates all too well the brutal indifference of necrocapitalism. On September 20, 2017, Maria devastated the island of Puerto Rico. In the immediate aftermath, the full extent of damage was unclear, although observers understood readily that the impact was severe. As Jesse Roman explains, "information and images unveiling a disaster of historic proportions slowly emerged through amateur texts, videos, and news releases generated from the island's capital, San Juan."[35]

The federal response to Harvey in Texas was, for the most part, robust and effective; the response to Puerto Rico was dismally and morally deficient.[36] Initially, the number of emergency personnel deployed was exceptionally low, far below the numbers sent to Texas in the aftermath of Harvey. The response of the military was similarly restrained: fewer air assets were deployed to Puerto Rico than were sent to Haiti (in response to Hurricane Matthew) or the Philippines (following super-typhoon Haiyan) under the Obama administration. President Donald Trump downplayed the severity of the Maria crisis and described his administration's response as "incredible" and "unbelievable."[37]

The violent conditions manifest on the ground in Puerto Rico spoke truth to power in light of President Trump's tepid response. Roman recounts that, ten days after the storm, "only 5 percent of the power had been restored on the island, only 11 percent of cell phone towers had been fixed, only half of the supermarkets were open, only 9 of 69 hospitals had been connected to the electric grid, and less than 50 percent of water services had been re-established."[38] It only made the problem worse when "supplies remained untouched in thousands of sealed shipping containers, and delivery of supplies to those in need remained hampered by the lack of trucks, fuel, drivers, and importantly, a clear, comprehensive, and implementable plan of action."[39]

Interruptions in health care, Ted Alcorn explains, "were a particular concern for vulnerable populations."[40] Indeed, emergency rooms were rendered inoperative and hospitals were forced to close surgical sites; clinics remained closed, and patients waiting for dialysis, chemotherapy, and transfusions were unable to receive treatment.[41] Compounding the problem, administrators in Puerto Rico are confronted with the prospect of massive budgetary cuts, including cuts to Medicaid. According to Ricardo Rivera-Cardona, former executive director of the Puerto Rico Health Insurance Administration, "either you reduce benefits or you take one million people out of the program—which creates a huge impact on the lives of close to a third of the population."[42]

Carmen Zorrilla writes that the impact of Maria "on morbidity, survival, adherence to treatments, and medical complications has yet to be documented."[43] The official death toll, as of December 2017, stood at sixty-four, and health-care practitioners warn that the actual number is considerably higher.[44] This is not surprising to the doctors who continue to care for patients long after the immediacy of the disaster, as thousands of men, women, and children suffer from preventable diseases rendered more deadly in the absence of federal assistance.[45] In effect, the people of Puerto Rico are being disallowed life to the point of premature death. As Ryan Kresge explains, the ongoing humanitarian disaster unfolding in Puerto Rico is exacerbated by the interplay of poverty, structural racism, militarism, and environmental degradation. Here, following Ruth Gilmore, we understand how "racism," when coupled with other social and structural relations, refers to the "state-sanctioned or extralegal production and exploitation of group-differentiated vulnerability to premature death."[46]

Dead Labor constitutes an explicit engagement with the political economy of premature death, an effort to catalogue and comment on those social and structural conditions that truncate life. As academics or activists, scholars or commentators, or simply citizens of a global community, we have the ability to promote—through our writings, our teachings, and our participation in the world around us—a different, less hostile and violent world. Such an ethics of care centers on a radical rethinking of life, death, and dying: not only a commitment to the prevention of taking life and the building of a nonkilling society but also a commitment to the elimination of those practices and policies that disallow life to the point of death. In other words, it is insufficient to simply not kill or to prevent others (including the state) from killing: we must also cultivate an ethic of not allowing others to die prematurely. To do so requires that we pry open the philosophical and ethical question of life and death from the standpoint of political economy and the moral underpinnings of killing and letting die. We must recognize that women and men who migrate from Mexico to the United States are not "criminals" and "rapists"; they are mothers and fathers who seek a better life for their children. They want what we all seek: a chance to live. Their decisions are made within a broader context of geopolitical and geoeconomic machinations, structural conditions over which they have little control and yet significantly, vitally, establish parameters for their everyday life. So too do the growing number of men and women who are forced because of poverty to "freely" sell their kidneys in the global biological marketplace, or the men and women who risk dismemberment or death working on assembly lines with inadequate safety regulations. Our actions (and inactions) will have a determining impact on whether these *human beings* live or die.

1. LIVING LABOR

An embodied historical materialism provides the foundation of my thesis. "The physical materiality of the body," Sébastien Rioux affirms, "is the most concrete and irreducible aspect of the human being and constitutes the fundamental premise of historical materialism."[1] Accordingly, the "body" must remain central to any discussion of premature death, but not simply because it is the living, embodied laborer that will inevitably die. Rather, the salience of an embodied perspective lies in the observation that, "in a world plagued by hunger, homelessness, exploitation, disease and violence, to recover the physical materiality of the body is one of the most banal yet politically charged theoretical openings."[2] As Linda McDowell argues, the body has become a major theoretical preoccupation across the social sciences, as well as an object for scrutiny and regulation by society as a whole.[3] However, as Reecia Orzeck explains, "a historical materialist theory of the body remains only partially articulated."[4] Notably lacking has been an explicit engagement with the death of the body. In other words, few scholars have considered in any detail those conditions that transform living laborers into dead laborers.

Life, the Body, and Historical Materialism

In *The Eighteenth Brumaire of Louis Bonaparte,* Marx states that "Men make their own history, but they do not make it just as they please; they do not make it under circumstances chosen by themselves, but under circumstances directly encountered, given, and transmitted from the past."[5] In *The German Ideology,* writing with Friedrich Engels, Marx develops this theme in greater depth. "The first premise of all human history," they explain, is "the existence of living human individuals."[6] On the surface, this tautological statement appears rather banal. And yet, this deceptively simple, almost throw-away line provides a context for a more nuanced understanding of society. According to Joseph Fracchia, Marx and Engels underscore that "the manifestations of human being are produced by humans living in specific sets of social relations and thus vary accordingly."[7] This is a point driven home by Marx in his "Theses on Feuerbach": "The essence of man is no abstraction inherent in each single individual. In its reality it is the ensemble of the social relations."[8] In other words, for Marx (and Engels), "the first fact to be established is the [corporeal] organization of these individuals and their consequent relation to the rest of nature."[9]

Historical materialism is grounded in human corporeal organization; it is a framework premised on the argument that "people's economic behavior, their 'mode of production in material life,' is the 'basis' of their social life generally."[10] But how are we to understand the "body" within such an approach? As Orzeck explains, "a historical materialist theory of the body remains only partially articulated."[11] In part, this incomplete understanding follows from the fact that "Marx never systematically elaborated the very corporeal foundations of human being in which he rooted his critique of capitalism."[12] To date, considerable effort has been directed toward resolving this dilemma. In the following two sections, I suggest that what is needed is a consideration not simply, following Marx and Engels, of the material conditions of life but also, as corollary, of the material conditions of death.[13] Indeed, this is a recurrent theme in the writings of Marx, most notably in his 1844 manuscripts. Here, Marx explains that, under capitalism men and women are reduced to mere workers, and accordingly, "as he has no existence as a *human being* but only as a *worker,* he can go and bury himself, starve to death."[14]

A historical materialist account of the *relational* body must begin by considering how individuals rooted in time and place obtain the basic necessities of life: food, water, clothing, shelter, and so on. Everything else follows from this, for as Marx and Engels explain, "by producing their means of subsistence men are indirectly producing their material life."[15] This is not to conclude, however, that "human needs are fixed and unchanging."[16] Indeed, both Marx and Engels readily understood that cultural practices and social institutions emanate from the satisfaction of the basic necessities of life. And yet, religion, marriage, and inheritance rights, for example, do not precede survivability or emerge separately from the attainment of the conditions of one's corporeal existence. Marx explains: "Neither legal relations nor political forms could be comprehended whether by themselves or on the basis of a so-called general development of the human mind. They originate in the material conditions of life."[17] Likewise, cultural understandings of death emanate from the obtainment of the necessities of life. However, as Fracchia sardonically writes, "we may admire the power of culture to elevate mind over body, but we should not forget that rejection of food because of cultural taboos will ultimately lead to the Pyrrhic victory of the body over mind—death."[18]

It is helpful at this point to consider, following Orzeck, the presence of two bodies within the framework of historical materialism.[19] On the one hand, there is the "natural" body, the living organism subject to death in the absence of food, water, and shelter. For Rioux, the importance of the natural body lies precisely in its foundational, transhistorical character, for it is the natural body that must inevitably die.[20] On the other hand, there is the "laboring" body, that entity "engaged in the social production of material life by metabolizing nature through labor in order to meet human needs and survive."[21] Importantly, the natural body and laboring body, according to this framework, should not be understood as oppositional. Instead, while the framework recognizes that the very existence of all living organisms is conditioned by biology, it also argues that the ways in which living bodies meet their physiological needs are socially produced.[22] In other words, all living laborers must *produce* those conditions necessary to survive. It follows, therefore, that any attempt to theorize life—and by extension, death—must be grounded in particular modes of production and, by extension, definitive social relations.

Marx's clearest exposition of the "mode of production" appears in his *Contribution to the Critique of Political Economy*: "Men inevitably enter into definite relations, which are independent of their will, namely relations of production appropriate to a given stage in the development of their material forces of production. The totality of these relations of production constitutes the economic structure of society, the real foundation, on which arises a legal and political superstructure and to which correspond definite forms of social consciousness."[23] Of immediate relevance is the argument that all social apparatuses, including but not limited to law and politics, are internally related to the dominant mode of production at any given time or place. In other words, by "mode of production," Marx means "relations of production *in their totality*."[24] As such, the mode of production encompasses myriad social relations that include but go beyond those commonly understood as making up the economic sphere of production. Consequently, any particular mode of production, following Marx and Engels, "must not be considered simply as being the reproduction of the physical existence of individuals": "Rather it is a definite form of activity of these individuals, a definite form of expressing their life, a definite *mode of life* on their part. As individuals express their life, so they are. What they are, therefore, coincides with their production, both with *what* they produce and with *how* they produce. Hence what individuals are depends on the material conditions of their production."[25]

This discussion has broad implications for the theorization of both dead labor and premature death, since it establishes a connection between dominant modes of production and life beyond the death of any individual. Indeed, it is a strange twist that "the death with which we are . . . confronted is always the death of others. . . . For the human becomes aware of itself as human only through anxiety in the face of death, which is what is brought back to life by the death of the other."[26] Death, we will see, is both relational and socially conditioned, and accordingly, as these social relations and conditions are transformed, so too will the occasion of death be transformed. David McNally writes: "The constants of bodily existence take shape through manifold and pliable forms of social life. This is what it means to describe the human body as an indeterminate constancy; and it's what it means to talk . . . about historical bodies."[27] For, just as labor is not transhistorical, neither is one's vulnerability to premature death. Thus, again turning to Orzeck, "we must consider not only how the always-hypothetical, single atomized body transforms and is transformed by nature, but how bodies transform and are transformed by the social relations of production they share."[28] In short, "every mode of production—that is, every social formation aimed at reproducing itself—produces bodies particular to it."[29] By this logic, every mode of production will produce *dead* bodies particular to it. Just as life is conditioned by the overall mode of production, so too is death.

So what exactly *is* the body? Are we, as embodied, corporeal beings, simply a collection of cells, tissues, and organs? Conversely, is there some part of "us" that exists beyond our carbon-based form? A soul, perhaps? Or a small homunculus pulling the levers in our brain? Alongside these metaphysical questions, we are confronted also with common sense. After all, we all have bodies. As Gillian Rose writes, "we all live through our bodies: we think, touch, feel, breathe, smell, dream and sleep with our body, and we constantly encounter other bodies."[30] And we are all born, and at some point we will all die.

Or do we? Well into the twenty-first century, we can no longer presume that all bodies undergo the same processes of life and death, fertility and mortality. There are, in other words, qualitative differences in the quantification of vitality. Since 1978, for example, it has been possible to be conceived via *in vitro* fertilization as opposed to *in vivo* fertilization. And in fact, worldwide, upward of five million babies have been conceived "outside" of women's bodies. The category of death likewise has undergone numerous transformations. In the United States, as a case in point, it is possible for two "bodies," each with identical vital signs, to be classified differently—one dead and the other alive—depending on where those bodies are located.

The human body, as it turns out, is not so straightforward; and neither, by extension, is our understanding of life and death. Indeed, the complexities posed by living (and dying) bodies have inspired much philosophical thinking and anthropological study. For example, a long-standing presumption (at least in Western thought) is the separation of the mind from the body. During the Enlightenment, it was argued that the mind was separate from the body and superior to it. It was the mind that made possible those processes that allow us to think, to reason, and to argue, and these constituted "active" or "voluntary" processes. Conversely, involuntary activities such as respiration and digestion were located in the body.[31] A Cartesian understanding of the body therefore holds that the body is inert, passive, and unthinking, in contrast to the active, thinking mind. Indeed, while the body is conceived as part of "nature," a material object consisting of organs, appetites, and biological functions, the mind is the locus of one's consciousness. It is the mind, separate from the fleshy, inert body, that is important. Feminists, and especially poststructural feminists, have challenged the perpetuation of the mind–body dualism.[32] They have argued, in part, that it is not possible to consider a mind or consciousness that is somehow prior to or separate from the material body. We cannot therefore take for granted the existence of a body, or even the death of the body. These concepts come into existence through practice. We may agree that a body exists, this concrete, material, animate organization of flesh, organs, nerves, muscles, and skeletal structure, but the meanings of such bodies—both living and dying—are discursive and, by extension, politically contested.[33]

To forward the proposition that the body is incontrovertibly produced in and through social relations is, therefore, to countenance the proposition that life and death are *not* transhistorical, but rather socially conditioned. Beginning with the mode of production thus directs attention to the fundamental social and spatial relations of society, which is a necessary step, given that one's exposure (or vulnerability) to death is conditioned by one's relationship to both the means and the relations of production. In short, an engagement with the conditions that "nourish and sustain, but also harm and violate" is to negate the seemingly apparent universality of death itself.[34]

Negating the Universality of Death

Despite its seemingly uncritical universality, death is a surprisingly ambiguous phenomenon.[35] And yet, for many social scientists, the definition of death (and, as corollary, the definition of life) often poses little problem. For example, death (and life) is most often located within the realm of biology. As Steven Luper explains, an "organism" is an entity that has a substantial capacity to maintain itself through particular vital processes, including homeostasis, metabolism, and reproduction, and this, in turn, forms a basic understanding of life.[36] James Bernat defines more precisely: "An organism is a complex life form composed of individually living subunits, including cells, tissues, and organs. Each subunit is organized in a functional group, and is not merely a random aggregation of components. Thus, cells form functional subunits of tissues that in turn form functional subunits of organs. The interrelationships of the numerous hierarchies of functional subunits within an organism create an integrated, coordinated, functioning and unified whole. This whole is the organism itself: the highest and most complex unit of life that subsumes all its living subsystems."[37] Consequently, when these vital functions cease, the "living" organism is said to die.

This constitutes the basic premise of a "biological" paradigm of death and is implicit to most historical materialist accounts of the body: essentially, when the ability to secure the basic material requirements of food, water, and shelter is unmet, death results. Accordingly, following Bernat, death is properly defined as "the irreversible loss of the capacity of the organism to function as a whole that results from the permanent loss of its critical system."[38] The definition and criteria of death are thus understood to fall within the province of biologists or physicians. However, recent technological advances have called into question the salience of the biological paradigm, and even within the medical community, there is now a startling amount of confusion about the determination of death.[39] For example, as Bernard Schumacher notes, "the recent technological discoveries that make it possible to transplant human organs and to keep a human being alive artificially with the help of machines have given rise to a heated debate revolving around the question of knowing when a human subject is really dead."[40] Indeed, these questions figure prominently in the debates surrounding abortion, euthanasia, and organ transplantation. For this reason, Luper cautions that, while it seems apparent that death is the ending of a life, in several respects the term "death" is unclear and ambiguous.[41]

To begin, philosophers frequently distinguish between death as "process" and death as "event." On the one hand, we may state that "death begins when something starts dying and ends when the dying process is over."[42] This is a process view of death, and it assumes different forms. For example, when we are shot, stabbed, splashed with acid, or poisoned, as Luper explains, the cells in our bodies are killed in a straightforward way: they undergo a form of death called *necrosis,* whereby cell membranes stop operating properly, causing them and some of their organelles to swell and burst. Consequently, more and more systems that are essential to cellular maintenance are destroyed, causing a chain reaction of system failure. This contrasts with *apoptosis,* whereby enzymes begin to digest cells, causing cells to shrink and organelles to break down into fragments that attract phagocytic cells that engulf and consume them. Both necrosis and apoptosis are distinguished from *senescence,* a process whereby somatic cells, the cells of which most of the body is composed, are no longer able to proliferate themselves; this, more commonly, refers simply to the aging of organisms.[43]

The forwarding of death as a process greatly informs our understanding of premature death. As Luper elaborates, "the fact that vital processes can decline before completely ending suggests that the process of dying occurs in degrees, and if the state of death is not just the final product of the process of dying, but also the intermediate product, then dying can put us into a state in which we are only partially alive."[44] Consequently, our conceptualization of premature death acquires a heretofore unexamined temporality. It thus becomes possible to speak alternatively of premature *dying* as an ongoing condition whereby the inability to secure water, food, and shelter place living bodies at risk. Stated differently, the vulnerability to premature death is more properly understood as the actual condition of premature dying.

On the other hand, death may be premised as a momentary event, and this premise likewise informs our subsequent understanding of premature death. Surprisingly, the issue at hand pivots on our conceptualization of momentary events. For Bernat, "death is an event and not a process," and this follows from his proposition that: "'Alive' and 'dead' comprise the only two fundamental underlying state of any organism. All organisms must be either alive or dead; none can be both or neither."[45] Thus, we may presume that death occurs only at the moment when the various physiological systems of the organism completely and finally cease to function as an integrated whole. This constitutes "denouement" death.[46] The biological paradigm of death, following Bernat, would hold that it is only this form of death that matters, for prior to this seemingly precise moment, the organism remains alive. However, Luper counters that it is possible to identify various "moments" of death. For example, the moment of death may be presumed to occur when an organism's vital processes fail beyond a point of no return, when death *becomes* irreversible, and this is termed "threshold" death. Historically, the cessation of the heart or the respiratory system or the failure of key organs such as the kidney would irreversibly, inevitably lead to death. However, Jeffrey Botkin and Stephen Post note that "contemporary technology has fostered confusion by forcing us to recognize the ambiguous nature of the moment of death."[47] Thus, as they explain, if we can restart functions such as breathing or heartbeat when once they would have been irreversibly lost, someone cannot really be considered dead.[48] Crucially, therefore, what constitutes "irreversible" differs according to the level of technology available at any particular time or place. This suggests that it is not simply the impact of technology on extending life; it indicates that premature death is also a function of one's access to life-extending technologies. This factor alone imparts an unequal geography to premature death and calls into question the salience of political economy. For those people living in impoverished areas, for example, where people do not have ready or affordable access to necessary medical and technological innovations, people will most certainly die who otherwise would not. We may therefore premise that, the more precarious one's life is, the greater the likelihood they will experience premature threshold death.

To summarize: Definitions and criteria of death are as much matters involving metaphysical reflection, moral choice, and cultural acceptance as they are biological facts waiting to be discovered.[49] However, from an anthropocentric viewpoint, the fact that we inevitably die (i.e., denouement death) is often held to be the most important fact about us. Indeed, from the most banal of activities (for example, eating, getting sick, or having sex) to the most spectacular (such as violence, war, and genocide), the apparent fact of death significantly informs how we live. Not only does death negate our mortal, material existence; the *awareness* of this inevitability is also profound. Zygmunt Bauman explains that "the fact of human mortality, and the necessity to live with the constant awareness of that fact, go a long way toward accounting for many a crucial aspect of social and cultural organization of all known societies."[50] Consequently, Marx's approach to political economy, and specifically his focus on the labor process, is foundational to our retheorization of premature death. Orzeck concludes: "By averring that humans, in procuring from their surroundings what they need to survive, change their own nature, Marx is confirming that bodies are produced through labor; but, by insisting that humans must be in a position to live before they can create history, Marx is also insisting that humans have basic, non-negotiable needs that they must and will pursue in order to survive."[51]

Precarity, Precariousness, and Premature Death

When scholars working in the social sciences or humanities write of premature death, they do so generally from an uncritical acceptance of death as simply the cessation of life, from an understanding of denouement death, which occurs when the dying process completes itself.[52] And yet, the biological and philosophical literatures have called to question the concept of death and, by extension, force us to rethink our understanding of one's vulnerability to premature death. Consequently, we need to take seriously the production of premature death as foundational to the conditions of precariousness and precarity.[53]

Judith Butler explains that precariousness and precarity are intersecting concepts.[54] She elaborates: "Lives are by definition precarious: they can be expunged at will or by accident; their persistence is in no sense guaranteed."[55] For Butler, precariousness is a condition of all life, in that all living organisms exhibit a shared mortality. As mortal beings, all humans will die. We share also in this condition, this shared mortality, the certainty of death. However, while all humans are vulnerable to a shared mortality at the species-being level (as living beings we will all die), at more refined scales, the experience and *condition* of death is far from equal. "The concept of precariousness," as Christopher Harker clarifies, "does not explain why certain subjects and populations experience a greater risk of death and injury than others."[56] Thus, for Butler, precarity "designates that politically induced condition in which certain populations suffer from failing social and economic networks of support and become differentially exposed to injury, violence, and death."[57] In other words, precarity is conditional upon one's position in the dominant mode of production. As Orzeck writes, "insofar as socially differentiated bodies perform different types of labor, and occupy different positions in the nexus of social relations, their corporeal differentiation is inevitable."[58] We understand from this that the laboring process constitutes a lived experienced; but inherent to this process is always and already a twofold

vulnerability to death. On the one hand, the inability to secure the basic
necessities of life—for example, because of *lack* of employment or insufficient wages—raises one's precariousness to the level of precarity. On the
other hand, the *condition* of one's employment (say, conditions of greater
danger) may also intensify one's precariousness to the point of precarity.
Orzeck effectively summarizes this condition:

> Different types of labor transform the body in different ways. Work-
> ers lose limbs, digits, fingernails, eyes; they develop repetitive strain
> injuries, respiratory diseases, skin diseases, diseases from exposure to
> asbestos, pesticides, and other hazardous substances. Equally material
> are the transformations of the body that take place beyond the work-
> place which owe their existence not to a type of work but to a worker's
> location within the nexus of social relations—relations which include
> uneven development and the division of labor as well as structural fac-
> tors such as racism and patriarchy.[59]

Living laborers are unevenly subjected to myriad social formations of
premature death. For example, as Kathryn Gillespie and Patricia Lopez
note, "racialized social relations in the United States, characterized by
uneven social and economic hierarchies of support and privilege, make
black bodies (and black *male* bodies, in particular) killable and disproportionately exposed to bodily violence, incarceration, and premature
death."[60] In short, there is a socio-spatial organization to (premature)
death, a geography that is conditioned both materially and discursively.
It is for this reason that we should approach living labor as a "subject
position."

Subject positions are conditioned by the dominant mode of production of any given society. As Jason Read explains, "materialism exceeds
the production of things and includes the production and productivity
of ideas, relations, and desires," and consequently, "a mode of production
is inseparable from the production of a particular social relation, and a
particular subjectivity, which it needs to reproduce itself."[61] However, as
Martha Fineman relates, throughout much of the world today, "dominant
political and legal theories are built around a universal subject defined
in the liberal tradition."[62] This has profound implications for our understanding of both premature death and the articulation of shared mortal-
ities. From the standpoint of the so-called liberal subject, Fineman explains, equality "is the expression of the idea that all human beings are by

nature free and endowed with the same inalienable rights."[63] In practice, the promotion of the liberal subject is predicated on the idea of a "sameness of treatment," whereby myriad classifications, such as race, gender, sexuality, religion, and national origin define individual legal identities and form the main axes around which claims for equal protection can be made.[64] From such a position, differential life expectancies are to be corrected through the equal applicability of law; all persons, regardless of "identity" are to have equal access to employment, housing, and so on.

There are numerous problems associated with the promotion of the liberal subject within the formal model of equality, and two stand out in particular. On the one hand, as Fineman writes, "['equality'] reduced to sameness of treatment or a prohibition on discrimination, has proven an inadequate tool to resist or upset persistent forms of subordination."[65] This stems in part from the recognition that many legal institutions, despite claims to equal universal treatment, fail to recognize the multiple forms of oppression that may intersect simultaneously in complimentary and contradictory ways and, subsequently, may reinforce inequalities and/or unevenly expose persons to harm or premature death. The legal concept of universal human rights, for example, is flawed in many respects, for as Berta Hernández-Truyol explains, it "has western, heteronormative, patriarchal, colonialist, racialized, [and] sexist foundations."[66] For instance, members of the LGBTQ community face many challenges that explicitly contribute to unequal exposure to premature death. Indeed, there are seventy-four states around the world where homosexual acts are criminalized, and in thirteen of these, the death penalty can be imposed.[67]

On the other hand, equality as applied to the liberal subject is "weak in its ability to address and correct the disparities in economic and social wellbeing among various groups."[68] As a result, the structural factors that underscore the unequal exposure to premature death are left in place, as attention is directed principally toward individuals and individual actions; the systemic aspects of existing societal arrangements are left out of the picture.[69] Furthermore, societal injustices are compounded through the precise configurations of the liberal subject. Fineman explains that, while the "liberal subject informs our economic, legal, and political principles," it does so from the standpoint "of autonomy, self-sufficiency, and personal responsibility, through which society is conceived as constituted by self-interested individuals with the capacity to manipulate their independently acquired and overlapping resources."[70] However, as Linda McDowell argues, we need to replace the ideal of "an independent individual fully participating in the labor market" with one of "solidarity and mutuality between networks of individuals in relationships of different forms of interdependence."[71] From this reasoning, we need to conceive of premature death not as an individual experience, but as a process embedded within myriad social networks and structural relations.

The liberal subject experiences a precarious existence and shares a universal vulnerability to harm and death. To address those who have been excluded from society, geographers and other social scientists have turned to the theoretical insights of Giorgio Agamben and, in particular, his formulation of *homo sacer*. Briefly stated, according to classical Roman law, *homo sacer* constitutes "bare life," a threshold position between *zoē* and *bios,* the former term designating "the simple fact of living common to all living things" and the latter representing a collective and qualified life: that which emerges when life enters the polis, or political space.[72] Notably, these terms (*zoē* and *bios*) merge easily with the aforementioned concepts of precariousness (i.e., a common fact of shared mortality) and precarity (i.e., a qualified vulnerability to death). One who has been reduced to bare life, the figure of *homo sacer*, occupies a liminal position, for this constitutes a person who could be killed with impunity and whose death would constitute neither homicide nor sacrifice. Agamben holds that "what confronts us today is a life that as such is exposed to a violence without precedent precisely in the most profane and banal ways."[73] Hosna Shewly elaborates: "Bare life is the life of homo sacer, who is subject to the law but is unprotected by the law. Extremely inferior to a politically qualified life, it is, rather, a life exposed to violence in an extralegal space and status."[74]

The insights of Agamben are instructive but incomplete. Notably, Agamben's inability to engage seriously with gendered and racialized differences, for example, forces him to collapse a qualified vulnerability to death into a shared mortality. We are not all *homines sacri,* for we occupy different and unequal relations within society. Because we are positioned differently within a web of economic, political, and institutional relationships, our vulnerabilities are conditioned and experienced in particular ways.[75] Those conditions that are productive of premature death are not universal, but instead materialize differently at different times and in different places. In other words, precarity is necessarily situated within specific and dominant modes of production. It is for this reason that Fineman seeks to replace the liberal subject with the "vulnerable subject," a strategic move that highlights the social relationships inherent to life and death. For example, many scholars have noted the fact that all humans, at some point in their lifetime, are highly dependent on others, thereby calling into question the idealized notions of independence, autonomy, and self-sufficiency.[76] For Fineman, models of interdependence provide an important critique of the liberal subject but, in certain respects, are limited. Dependency, for example, may be treated as a stage or phase in one's life, and consequently, proposed solutions may unduly focus on individuals' equal access to resources during these episodic moments in life, notably at birth and as one approaches death. The vulnerable subject instead acknowledges that harm and premature death are constant possibilities, that individuals within any given society are always and already placed in positions of dependency, and that the liberal ideology of autonomy, independence, and self-sufficiency are as fictitious as that of the free market.

Contemplating our shared vulnerability, Fineman postulates, "it becomes apparent that human beings need each other, and that we must structure our institutions in response to this fundamental human reality."[77] This premise brings us full-circle to the materiality of life: it is necessary to view the vulnerable subject *not* as a universal or transhistorical figure, but as one that is intimately produced within specific modes of production articulated across myriad spaces and scales. In medieval England, serfs experienced precarity in ways fundamentally different from those encountered by enslaved Africans in the antebellum United States, and so too is precarity experienced differently by unemployed factory workers in twenty-first-century Germany or by Syrian refugees crossing the Mediterranean Sea. Thus, it is useful to rearticulate the vulnerable subject, following Rosemarie Garland-Thomson, as a "misfit."

Developed in the context of disability studies, the figure of the misfit is a vulnerable subject that fails to conform to society. More precisely, "the concept of the misfit emphasizes the particularity of varying lived embodiments" and "clarifies the current feminist critical conversation about universal vulnerability and dependence."[78] Hence, for Garland-Thomson, the "utility of the concept of misfit is that it definitively lodges injustice and discrimination in the materiality of the world more than in social attitudes or representational practices, even while it recognizes their mutually constituting entanglement."[79] Persons confined to wheelchairs, for example, literally do not fit in many public places. Here, the materiality that matters involves an encounter between bodies with particular shapes and capabilities and the particular shape and structure of the built environment.[80] Accordingly, the misfit speaks to the argument forwarded by Nancy Duncan that "there can be no pure public spaces in which the liberal ideals of equality, impartiality and universality are achieved" and that those "marked by differences deriving from their sex, skin color, old age, sexuality, physical incapabilities or other variations from the posited 'norm,' do not qualify for full participation in the liberal democratic model."[81]

The liberal subject prefigures a shared mortality but, in the process, negates the lived experiences of the vulnerable subject. As Garland-Thomson writes, "vulnerability is universally inherent . . . but it is a potentiality that is realized when bodies encounter a hostile environment and is latent in a sustaining environment."[82] This suggests a decidedly more nuanced geographic configuration of premature death, a spatiality that includes but is not limited to our understanding of death or the exposure to death as measurable or mappable. Instead, such a shift necessarily grounds the vulnerability to premature death within definite place-specific structures and social relations, for as Louise Waite writes, "experiences of precarity should be seen as intimately connected to socio-spatial contexts."[83] For example, Laura Pulido explains that the devaluation of black (and other nonwhite) bodies has been a central feature of global capitalism and, in the process, has created a landscape of differential value that can be harnessed in diverse ways to facilitate the accumulation of more power and profit than would otherwise be possible.[84] More broadly, as Gillespie and Lopez argue, marginalized human bodies are continuously made vulnerable to premature death in service to capital accumulation—their bodies used, worn out, discarded.[85] By extension, the different valuation of vulnerable subject positions greatly informs a distinction between those lives considered grievable and those that are not, for as Butler writes, "the differential allocation of grievability that decides what kind of subject is and must be grieved, and which kind of subject must not, operates to produce and maintain certain exclusionary conceptions of who is normatively human."[86]

Conclusions

Throughout his writings, Marx expresses tremendous concern over the specter of premature death, over the radical inequalities of early death experienced by those men, women, and children consigned especially to factory work. As Rioux notes, "Marx was particularly attentive to the ways in which capital is inscribed on the bodies and in the flesh of laborers, documenting as he did how long hours of work, unregulated environment, and dangerous working conditions produced tired, diseased, maimed, unhealthy, overworked, stunted and injured bodies."[87] Hence, in response to the dismal working conditions endured by England's factory workers of the late nineteenth century, Marx writes: "[Capital's] answer to the outcry about the physical and mental degradation, the premature death, the torture of over-work, is this: Should that pain trouble us, since it increases our pleasure (profit)?"[88] Foreshadowing our contemporary engagement with the precarity of life, Marx declares: "Capital . . . takes no account of the health and the length of the worker, unless society forces it to do so."[89] I argue that premature death is an intrinsic, systemic condition of necrocapitalism. Political and economic decisions set in place those relations that consign some to a vulnerable subject position, making them more at-risk to premature death. Consequently, in the following chapters, I chart a path through the political economy of necrocapitalism to highlight the material transformation of living laborers into dead laborers. I begin with a discussion of the commodification of living labor.

2. COMMODIFIED LABOR

Throughout the writings of Marx, death was a constant. For, underlying his critique of both political economy and capitalism was a concern with life itself. His use of "mortal" metaphors, for example, is well-documented, as is his penchant for describing the horrors of capitalism in monstrous, violent, murderous terms.[1] David McNally observes that, as Marx "searched for a means of depicting the actual horrors of capitalism—from child-labor, to the extermination of North America's indigenous peoples, from the factory system to the slave-trade—he reworked the discourse of monstrosity that emerged with the rise of capitalism."[2] Most notably, Marx equated commodities with "dead labor": dead labor constitutes past labor power, the expended energy that is embodied within a thing, whether that thing is a linen coat, bushel of corn, or piece of plywood. Marx writes of workers reanimating past (dead) labor: "In so far as labor is productive activity directed to a particular purpose . . . it raises the means of production from the dead merely by entering into contact with them, infuses them with life so that they become factors in the labor process, and combines with them to form new products." [3] Here, "dead labor" serves as a metaphor, in opposition to the living laborer who expends his or her own energy reanimating the dead labor to serve a useful purpose.

Despite his penchant for metaphors, Marx never loses sight of the fact that actual living men, women, and children are vulnerable to premature death. Marx understands also that death, while at one level a universal condition (e.g., all living people will die), is conditioned by the particular social relations and structures of any given society, that there is a fundamental unevenness to one's vulnerability to disease and death that is not necessarily of one's own choosing. Marx concludes that, within the capitalist mode of production, "the capitalist can live longer without the worker than can the worker without the capitalist."[4]

Premature death is *not* a universal condition of life itself. Rather, one's vulnerability to disease, malnutrition, starvation, injury, or death is predicated on one's ability to secure, either individually or (more frequently) collectively, the basic necessities of food, water, and shelter. Thus, the capitalist mode of production must be understood first and foremost from the vantage point of waged labor. Capitalism is a particular mode of production in which all participants, both producers and consumers, depend on the market for their basic needs.[5] As a form of economic organization made possible by the exaltation of private property, capital's foundation is the social (class) separation of direct producers from the means of production. It is because of this social relation that workers, although formally free, are forced by material circumstances to sell their labor power to capitalists who own the means of production.[6]

These fundamental social relations make all the difference for understanding a political economy of premature death. Warren Montag writes: "The market reduces and rations life; it not only allows death, it demands that death be allowed by the sovereign power, as well as by those who suffer it. In other words, it demands and requires that the latter allow themselves to die."[7] Montag's point is simple yet far-reaching. As elaborated below, market relations set vital parameters on one's ability to participate in society and, consequently, one's ability merely to survive. Keeping them from alternative means of subsistence, capitalism requires that workers "freely" participate in waged labor through the formal labor contract. By extension, while informal labor is performed outside the formal waged-labor market, it is still also intimately associated with and included in that system precisely through the *exclusion* of those workers engaged in the informal labor market. Simply put, there would be no informal labor market without the corresponding existence of a formal labor market. The key factor is who is allowed to participate in the formal sphere of production. Moreover, it is because the informal market is both included in and excluded from the formal (i.e., legally recognized and sanctioned) labor market that informal workers are more highly exploitable.

Workers do not readily submit to premature death. They resist; they demand increased wages; they demand better working conditions; and most broadly, vitally, they demand access to food, water, shelter, and health care. The history of labor unions, strikes, protests, and social movements illustrates well that workers refuse to simply let themselves die. At this point, as Montag explains: "[The state] is called into action: those who refuse to allow themselves to die must be compelled by force to do so. This force, then, while external to the market, is necessary to its existence and function."[8]

In this chapter, I provide a class analysis of premature death. I follow Stephen Resnick's and Richard Wolff's approach to class as "a process in society where individuals perform labor above and beyond ('surplus' to) that which society deems necessary for their reproduction as laborers."[9] Hence, a class analysis "classifies individuals in a society in terms of their relationship to this surplus" and "asks who performs the necessary plus surplus labor power, how is this socially organized, and how does the organization of the surplus impact the larger society."[10] More precisely, I question how these social relations and one's position to the generation and distribution of surplus inform one's vulnerability to premature death. However, I remain sensitive to the charge that "one aspect of society is not the ultimate determinant of the others."[11] That is, a class analysis is necessary but insufficient. Capitalism and capitalist class relations appear in myriad forms, conditioned in part by specific histories and geographies of displacement and dispossession. As Resnick and Wolff explain, it is not possible to reduce society or history to the determinant effect of just one of its constituent aspects.[12] A Marxist analysis, therefore, "should always be slightly stretched"[13] to incorporate the intersectionality of gender, sexuality, race, and other socially perceived and socially construed factors that underscore one's vulnerability to premature death.[14]

The Commodity Fetish

Following the Second World War, the laissez-faire doctrine of governmental non-interventionism in the "free" market came under attack.[15] Myriad economic theories, including welfare economics and Keynesianism, held that systemic market failures required explicit state involvement in the form of governmental regulations and an overall hands-on approach to managing the economy. From the 1970s onward, however, various conservative economics, pundits, and politicians forwarded a radically different understanding of state intervention. Notably, these spokespersons held that it was precisely because of impartial and ineffective government interference that failures in the marketplace occurred. Sitting under the umbrella term "neoliberalism," economists such as Milton Friedman, Freidrich von Hayek, and George Stigler premised that minimum wages, welfare programs, higher labor standards, occupational safety measures, and environmental regulations all curtailed the efficiency of the free market and that, in contradistinction to governmental interference, the market should be left to function on its own. Supposedly freed from artificially imposed constraints, the free market is posited as a self-regulating market, an arena that is open to all potential buyers and sellers.[16] Unfettered by unnecessary encumbrances, the free market is portrayed as a level playing field, one where anyone, regardless of race, sex, gender, or any other such social factors can succeed, if only they are responsible, disciplined, and hardworking.

The notion of free markets today, Mark Martinez writes, "has become a caricature, largely a rhetorical device, employed by conservative politicians and media pundits who are unfamiliar with history, blinded by ideology, or both."[17] Simply put, the positioning of a free market devoid of state action does not hold. As Ha-Joon Chang explains, depending on which rights and obligations are regarded as legitimate and what kind of hierarchy between these rights and obligations is accepted by members of society, the same state action could be considered an intervention in one society or interference in another.[18] Indeed, in the modern era, Martinez observes, firms and industries have been regularly granted access, for example, to taxpayer dollars and state assistance on the premise that they are too big to fail.[19] Moreover, as Bernard Harcourt elaborates, the "rules and regulations surrounding our modern markets are intricate and arcane, and they belie the simplistic idea that our markets are "free."[20] He continues: "our contemporary markets are shot through with layers of overlapping governmental supervision, of exchange rules and regulations, of federal and state criminal oversight, of policing and self-policing, and self-regulatory mechanisms."[21]

The fetishization of the free market is crucial for our understanding of the political economy of premature death. Conservative rhetoric aside, the market is not a level playing field and not all participants are afforded equal opportunities. Capitalist exchanges are rife with racism, sexism, and other discriminatory and prejudicial beliefs and attitudes. And not only are these unjust principles (e.g., white privilege and patriarchy) manifest in unequal access to resources; they are also codified into the very same institutions use to protect the cherished ideal of the free market. So pervasive has been the attempt to protect neoliberalism that Harcourt warns of the emergence of neoliberal "penalty": "the government does not belong in the economic sphere, which has its own orderliness, but it has a legitimate role to play outside that sphere, especially in law enforcement."[22] Accordingly, neoliberal canon holds that government interference is to be avoided at all costs, unless of course one is speaking of a repressive intervention designed to protect the status quo: "The punitive society we now live in has been made possible by . . . this belief that there is a categorical difference between the free market, where intervention is inappropriate, and the penal sphere, where it is necessary and legitimate. This way of thinking makes it easier both to resist government intervention in the marketplace, as well as to embrace the criminalization and punishment of any 'disorder.'"[23]

Hidden by the flowery language of "liberty," "freedom," and "equality," neoliberal policies have portrayed the modern capitalist mode of production as the bastion of meritocracy, a stronghold of color-blind and gender-neutral opportunities that, if left to operate without undue state interference, ensure that material wealth is possible for all. As a consequence, according to David Roberts and Minelle Mahtani, "neoliberalism effectively masks racism [and other forms of oppression] through its value-laden moral project: camouflaging practices anchored in an apparent meritocracy, making possible a utopic vision of society that is non-racialized."[24]

Paradoxically, any effort to challenge this valued belief is set upon by a repressive state apparatus that is anything but color-blind or gender-neutral. This is seen for example in the ongoing racial profiling of "persons of color" and racially biased sentencing guidelines.[25] William Chin writes of a "racial cumulative disadvantage" whereby racial bias permeates both the criminal justice system and society as a whole.[26] More precisely, racial (as well as sexual and gender) cumulative disadvantage arises through myriad pathways, including but not limited to inequalities in criminal justice systems, educational systems, housing, health-care provision, and employment.

The categories we use to organize, understand, discuss, categorize, and compare, Harcourt explains, "have the unfortunate effect of obscuring rather than enlightening."[27] This statement strikes at the very core of Marx's conceptualization of the fetishization of the commodity, a concept that is vital to the understanding of the capitalist labor market: "A commodity appears at first sight an extremely obvious, trivial thing. But its analysis brings out that it is a very strange thing."[28] This strangeness arises from the observation that, under capitalism, ordinary, sensuous things are transformed into extrasensory things.[29] Marx explains:

> The mysterious character of the commodity-form consists . . . simply in the fact that the commodity reflects the social characteristics of men's own labor as objective characteristics of the products of labor themselves, as the socio-natural properties of these things. Hence it also reflects the social relation of the producers to the sum total of labor as a social relation between objects, a relation which exists apart from and outside the producers. Through this substitution, the products of labor become commodities, sensuous things which are at the same time suprasensible or social.[30]

Don Mitchell provides a particularly apt illustration of the mystical properties of the commodity. Strawberries, he writes, appear as sensuous, trivial things, and yet the surface appearance of the strawberry, its texture, shape, size, smell—in short, everything that we associated with the humble strawberry—belies a complex network of social relations and structural conditions that enable the strawberry to simply exist as an object of consumption: scientific advances in genetic engineering, the hiring and management of farm labor, the application of pesticides and herbicides, the physical transportation infrastructure.[31] Here we see that the fetishization of the seemingly natural, sensual strawberry disguises the reality that: "In every social form of production characterized by a division of labor, people stand in a particular social relationship to one another. In commodity production, this social relationship between people appears as a relationship between things: it is no longer people who stand in a specific relationship with one another, but commodities."[32] We speak of the exchange of commodities, of the flow of goods from place to place; we don't think about those very real people who make possible both the existence of the commodity and its movement.

Neoliberal dogma, with its emphasis on the free market, effectively fetishizes the social relations of production inherent in capitalism. This holds especially when one considers not just the commodification of berries but also the commodification of labor. For Marx, capitalism is predicated on two key conditions. The first is that "labor-power can appear on the market as a commodity only if, and in so far as, its possessor . . . offers it for sale or sells it as a commodity."[33] However, this condition holds only if a second condition is met: "The possessor of labor-power . . . [must] be compelled to offer for sale as a commodity that very labor-power which exists only in his living body."[34] It is through the satisfaction of these two conditions that workers *appear* free in a double sense: legally free and free to enter into the waged-labor market. Workers under capitalism, of course, are anything but free, and a repressive state apparatus ensures their compliance. As Jamie Peck writes, "in capitalist societies, the preparedness of workers to offer their labor on the labor market is largely secured by the systematic erosion of possibilities of subsistence outside the wage system."[35] It is, consequently, Marx's second condition that assumes prominence in our understanding of the political economy of premature death.

Labor as Commodity

Commodities have a dual character, being composed of both "use" values and "exchange" values. As products of human labor, commodities possess some useful quality for people, and one commodity may be exchanged for another commodity. The use value of a commodity stems from the qualitative properties that make it useful, while exchange value stems entirely from the social homogeneity of commodities, whereby they differ only quantitatively.[36] Marx explains, however, that, within capitalism (unlike, say, a barter system), commodities are not simply exchanged (e.g., a shirt exchanged for a bushel of corn). As Marx writes, these "are only commodities because they have a dual nature, because they are at the same time objects of utility and bearers of value."[37] Furthermore, as Marx elaborates, "the volume of the mass of commodities brought into being by capitalist production is determined by the scale of this production and its needs for constant expansion, and not by a predestined ambit of supply and demand, of needs to be satisfied."[38] Stated differently: under capitalism, the rationale for production is *profit*, not need or use in the abstract. There are many people in dire need of food, water, shelter, and medicine, but products that satisfy these vital needs are produced only to the degree that profits may be realized.

Marx argued also that commodities are not exchanged according to their degree of usefulness. Instead, there is a quantitative relation that appears in all commodities that facilitates their exchange. This common denominator, Marx concluded, was not money (itself a representation of value), but instead labor power. Such an argument is crucial in that it establishes a foundation by which life is evaluated within capitalism, for within the capitalist mode of production, the worker is but an objective factor, a source of labor power; any other human dimensions are largely irrelevant.[39]

Within the production process, capitalists combine the means of production (e.g., machinery and raw materials) with labor power (purchased on the labor market) in order to transform materials into commodities (use values) for exchange. The exchange value of the commodity, consequently, is composed of two parts: constant capital and variable capital. The valorization of capital (that is, the accumulation of profit) begins with the mobilization of labor power through the conclusion of the wage-labor contract: the capitalist buys the commodity labor power from the worker for a given period of time, and in return, the worker receives in wages the value of that labor power that is equal to the value of the material necessities (e.g., food, water, and shelter) necessary for the worker to reproduce him or herself as a worker.[40] However, it is a peculiar feature of the capitalist–laborer relation that the period of work time established by the contract will always be longer than this necessary labor time. Otherwise, as Joseph Fracchia explains, "there would be no gain for the capitalist and thus no reason to bother with the whole affair."[41] Workers, for

example, may produce enough value in six hours to offset their reproduction. And yet capitalists purchase labor power for a longer period of
time, perhaps ten hours. The remaining four hours, Marx argues, appear
as *absolute* surplus labor time: "The fact that half a day's labor is necessary
to keep the worker alive during 24 hours does not in any way prevent him
from working a whole day. Therefore the value of labor-power, and the
value which that labor-power valorizes . . . in the labor process, are two
entirely different magnitudes; and this difference was what the capitalist
had in mind when he was purchasing the labor-power."[42] In other words,
workers produce enough value to cover the costs of their wages in just a
part of the working day, and the labor performed for the remainder of
the day, therefore, does not have to be paid for—it is surplus labor that
produces "absolute surplus" value.[43]

The "free" worker, Fracchia sardonically writes, "is under no coercion—except by the fact that the only other alternative is unemployment."[44] Indeed, Marx and Engels well understood that, under capitalism, living laborers "live only so long as they find work, and [they] find
work only so long as their labor increases capital."[45] This vital condition
and its subsequent enforcement, according to Marx, signify the *formal*
"subsumption" of labor, constituting the earliest form of capitalism made
possible by the imposition of the wage on preexisting social and technological structures.[46] All else being equal, the lengthening of the working
day will result in greater profits for the capitalist. The prolongation of the
working day, according to Marx, "forms the general foundation of the
capitalist system."[47] It is also this feature of the valorization process that
underscores the historical contestation over the duration of the working day, with obvious implications for one's vulnerability to premature
death. Marx concludes: "In its blind and measureless drive, its insatiable
appetite for surplus labor, capital oversteps not only the moral but even
the merely physical limits of the working day. . . . It is not the normal
maintenance of labor-power which determines the limits of the working
day . . . but rather the greatest possible expenditure of labor-power, no
matter how diseased, compulsory and painful it may be. . . . By extending
the working day, therefore, capitalist production . . . not only produces
a deterioration of human labor-power by robbing it of its normal moral
and physical conditions of development and activity, but also produces
the premature exhaustion and death of this labor-power itself."[48]

The abstraction of absolute surplus value is an inherent condition of the wage-labor contract entered into, supposedly freely, by legally equal but socioeconomically very unequal partners.[49] As Fracchia explains, the contract effectively constitutes "an exchange in which the capitalist buys a commodity that is under contractual obligation to produce more value than it has cost."[50] It is necessary, therefore, to reconfigure the living laborer as a commodity consumed by the capitalist within the production process. Indeed, Marx explains that, "since the process of production is also the process of the consumption of labor-power by the capitalist, the worker's product is not only constantly converted into commodities, but also into capital, i.e. into value that sucks up the worker's value-creating power."[51] Thus, in a well-cited passage, Marx concludes: "Capital is dead labor which, vampire-like, lives only by sucking living labor, and lives the more, the more labor it sucks."[52] In other words, it is precisely the consumption of labor power that is at the root of premature death within the waged-labor market.

There are physical limits, however, on the extent to which capitalism can depend on the production of absolute surplus value. By reducing workers to mere physical bodies, capital not only maximizes its extraction of absolute surplus value but also reproduces itself at the cost of the life of the laborer.[53] Marx writes: "Within the twenty-four hours of the natural day a man can only expend a certain quantity of his vital force. . . . During part of the day the vital force must rest, sleep; during another part the man has to satisfy other physical needs, to feed, wash and clothe himself."[54] Consequently, the extension of the working day "produces the premature exhaustion and death of this labor-power itself."[55] The premature death of living laborers thus poses a *structural* problem to capitalism, in that the extraction of absolute surplus value is limited by the living laborer's own corporeality.

Contemporary studies support Marx's thesis that overwork significantly increases one's vulnerability to premature death. Dermont O'Reilly and Michael Rosato, for example, find evidence that working longer hours increases mortality risk, that employment relations or conditions of occupation are significant moderators of the relationship between long working hours and mortality risk, and that the stresses and physical health symptoms associated with long working hours are most apparent where there is little flexibility in the choice of overtime working or autonomy in terms of how many hours are worked and when they are worked.[56] Other studies have associated overtime and extended work schedules with an increased risk of hypertension, cardiovascular disease, musculoskeletal disorders, chronic infections, diabetes, fatigue, stress, depression, suicide, and alcoholism.[57] The fact that vulnerability to premature death is conditioned by social constructs such as race and gender within the waged-labor market should come as no surprise. In many countries, women's jobs in general tend to be poorer quality, offering them less autonomy, flexibility, and security.[58] When this is combined with insufficient access to preventive health care, pronounced differences in mortality are observed.

The mortal exhaustion of living labor may be tempered by reductions in the working day, but this is not necessarily the capitalist evincing concern over the plight of any given worker. Instead, if "the unnatural extension of the working day, which capital necessarily strives for in its unmeasured drive for self-valorization, shortens the life of the individual worker, and therefore the duration of his labor-power, the forces used up have to be replaced more rapidly, and it will be more expensive to reproduce labor-power."[59] For capitalists, however, the biological limits of life constitute just one contradiction among many to overcome. Indeed, other techniques to expropriate surplus value beyond the extension of the working day are subsequently introduced for the accumulation of capital. To this end, Marx introduces the concept of "relative surplus value." Unlike absolute surplus value, this value is generated not through the prolongation of the working day, but instead through the intensification of the labor process itself.

For Marx, it is not so much *necessary* labor time that is at the root of labor power's value, but rather *socially* necessary labor time, defined as "the labor-time required to produce any use-value under the conditions of production normal for a given society and with the average degree of skilled and intensity of labor prevalent in that society."[60] With an increase in the productivity of labor through, say, refinements of the division of labor or the introduction of machinery, the value of labor power falls and the portion of the working day necessary for the reproduction of that value will be shortened. For example, if a technical improvement in the conditions of production cheapens the consumer goods that workers buy with their wages, then the value of labor power has fallen; less time is required to reproduce labor power, and the portion of the working day devoted to necessary labor will fall, with the remaining hours of the working day appearing as surplus.[61] Capital thus "has an immanent drive, and a constant tendency, towards increasing the productivity of labor, in order to cheapen commodities and, by cheapening commodities, to cheapen the worker himself."[62]

Socially necessary labor time is fundamental to the extraction of relative surplus value. At an abstract level, the value of labor is represented by the value obtained by workers against the sale of their labor power, and this typically corresponds to the labor time socially necessary to produce the wage goods regularly purchased on average by the working class.[63] Competition among capitalists impels each of them toward the use of a labor process that is at least as efficient as the social average.[64] Individual capitalists that can produce more efficiently achieve greater relative surplus value, and those capitalists with inefficient production methods will not. This implies, as David Harvey writes, a perpetual incentive for individual capitalists to increase the rate of accumulation through increasing exploitation in the labor process relative to the social average rate of exploitation.[65] In general, any capitalist who invests in constant capital may gain a temporary advantage over his or her competitors and thus extract greater amounts of relative surplus value. Harvey clarifies that capitalists employing superior production techniques and with a higher than average productivity of labor can gain excess surplus value by trading at a price set by the social average when their production costs per unit are well below the social average. This advantage is ephemeral, since competitors will subsequently adopt similar production techniques or go out of business.[66]

Under conditions of competition, there exists a systemic incentive for capitalists to invest in constant capital at the expense of labor, to replace living labor with dead labor. Consequently, the organic composition of capital throughout society tends to rise over time because of the adoption of more efficient machinery and automation in an attempt to extract relative surplus value. Indeed, recent decades have witnessed an inexorable trend in production techniques whereby human labor is replaced by machines. This is occurring not only in the manufacturing sector but also in the service sector. Indeed, some predictions warn that almost fifty percent of current jobs are at risk of replacement by robotics and auto-mation technologies.[67]

As an abstract concept, socially necessary labor time transfers the level of argument from any individual capitalist to society as a whole. This is necessary because, as Ben Fine and Alfredo Saad-Filho explain, "produc-tion of relative surplus value depends critically upon all capitalists, since none alone produces a significant proportion of the commodities re-quired for the reproduction of the working class."[68] The extraction of rel-ative surplus value can occur only through a socio-structural relationship of competition.[69] Here, Marx explains that capitalist production properly begins when each individual capitalist simultaneously employs a com-paratively large number of workers and that, as a result, the labor process is carried out on an extensive scale and yields relatively large quantities of products.[70] This is seen most readily in the introduction of the assembly line, whereby the production process is decomposed into different partial operations. As Fracchia concludes, "[with] the co-ordination of several individual bodies working in a planned way, the system of production is very literally a materialized metaphor of the human body, a social body, a 'productive collective body' that magnifies the corporeal capacities of each individual."[71]

"With the production of relative surplus-value," Marx writes, "the form of production is altered and a specifically capitalist form of pro-duction comes into being."[72] More properly, the extraction of relative surplus value constitutes the *real* subsumption of labor by capital. It is important to note, though, that the relations established under the for-mal subsumption of labor do not disappear; indeed, the direct subordi-nation of the labor process to capital remains. However, on this founda-tion: "There now arises a technologically and otherwise specific mode of production—capitalist production—which transforms the nature of the labor process and its actual conditions. Only when that happens do we witness the real subsumption of labor under capital."[73] Marx continues: the "real subsumption of labor under capital is developed in all the forms evolved by relative, as opposed to absolute surplus-value. With the real subsumption of labor under capital a complete . . . revolution takes place in the mode of production, in the productivity of the workers and in the relations between workers and capitalists."[74]

Under conditions of real subsumption, labor power is "directly in-corporated into the production process of capital as a living factor; it becomes one of its components, a variable component, which partly maintains and partly reproduces the capital values invested."[75] And at this point, we see how capitalism imposes a differential quality to living labor's vulnerability to premature death. Marx writes that the division of labor in manufacturing is not merely a particular method of creating relative surplus value. It not only increases the socially productive power of labor for the benefit of the capitalist instead of the worker but also transforms the individual worker as new conditions for the domination of capital over labor are established.[76] Marx argues that, much as an animal is butchered into discrete parts, the individual living laborer within capitalism is "divided up," transformed into a "crippled monstrosity," becoming "a mere fragment of his own body."[77] As detailed in subsequent chapters, living laborers are literally disassembled as sellers of tissues and organs. And they are also disallowed life, as corporations garner profits through life insurance policies.

The Contract and the Subject

The capitalist labor market appears as a system whereby a person's capacity to work becomes a commodity that can be bought and sold on the market. In an oft-cited passage, Marx writes of this social space as "a very Eden of the innate rights of man . . . the exclusive realm of Freedom, Equality, Property and Bentham."[78] He continues:

> Freedom, because both buyer and seller of a commodity, let us say of labor-power, are determined only by their own free will. They contract as free persons, who are equal before the law. Their contract is the final result in which their joint will finds a common legal expression. Equality, because each enters into relation with each other, as with a simple owner of commodities, and they exchange equivalent for equivalent. Property, because each disposes only of what is his own. And Bentham, because each looks only to his own advantage.[79]

As this quotation illustrates well, many of our contemporary values and rights are grounded in one's position in or one's relationship to the waged-labor market. Consider, for example, the promotion of "freedom" in the

United States. It is frequently claimed (usually by those on the far right of the political spectrum) that participation in *the* labor market—one's right to sell his or her labor capacity—is a matter of free choice. This calls attention, therefore, to the dialectics of legal rights and waged employment. In most Western societies, for example, a distinction is made between "positive rights" and "negative rights." Positive rights permit or oblige action, whereas negative rights permit or oblige inaction. In other words, the promotion of positive rights is to actively intervene to create those conditions that allow one to participate fully in society. The promotion of negative rights, conversely, is to ensure that one is not denied the right to participate within society. Within the capitalist mode of production, there is no positive right to full and gainful employment. Instead, only the negative right to not be prohibited from working is guaranteed, which is a point made well by Engels: "No one guarantees [the worker] a subsistence, he is in danger of being repudiated at any moment by his master . . . and left to die of starvation, if the [capitalist class] ceases to have an interest in his employment, his existence."[80] As Joshua Barkan writes, "life, once politicized as necessary for the accumulation of capital, becomes expendable at that moment when it no longer assists in the circulation of value."[81]

In the United States, negative rights are promoted to the degree that all members are to be allowed to participate in the labor market. But this is not the same as a provision of equal participation, since this right indicates only that the state will ensure that no one is prohibited from participating. Stated bluntly, the state does not guarantee (full) employment; it guarantees (in principle) only that one is not prohibited from participating in the quest for employment. Struggles over the workplace therefore demonstrate clearly how the capitalist mode of production is marked by stark contradictions between the goals of the capitalist and those of the living laborer. This derives from the peculiar quality of labor-as-commodity. The goal of the capitalist is the maximization of surplus value, derived in the form of either absolute or relative surplus value; the goal of the worker is to increase his or her wages and to improve the conditions under which he or she labors.[82]

For Marx, the corresponding transformation of the relations of production created new relations of supremacy and subordination between the capitalist and the laborer. It is notable, therefore, that the worker enshrined in the wage-labor contract appears as a free subject. Indeed, capitalism as a mode of production evolved coincidental with the promotion of the "liberal subject," a character who features prominently in Western conceptions of law and greatly informs our economic, legal, and political principles.[83] As Martha Fineman explains, the figure of the liberal subject "is indispensable to the prevailing ideologies of autonomy, self-sufficiency, and personal responsibility, though which society is conceived as constituted by self-interested individuals with the capacity to manipulate and manage their independently acquired and overlapping resources."[84] Thus, as Jairus Banaji surmises, "the liberal conception of capitalism which sees the sole basis of accumulation in the individual wage-earner conceived as a free laborer obliterates a great deal of capitalist history."[85]

The Lockean idea of equality greatly informed the articulation of the free market by economists such as Adam Smith and David Ricardo. In the liberal model, "equality" is the expression of the idea that all human beings are by nature free and endowed with the same inalienable rights.[86] Consequently, as capitalism deepened, so too did the argument that individuals (as liberal subjects) were free to enter or exit the labor market at will. In the process, the liberal legalism that developed in the nineteenth century grounded the almost limitless subordination of the wage earner within the "anodyne fictions of consent."[87] Moreover, as Fineman explains, the legal metaphor encapsulating this vision of societal organization is that of a "contract." It is presumed, for example, that liberal subjects have the ability to negotiate contract terms, assess their options, and make rational, informed choices.[88] Marx disagreed, positing instead that capitalism is predicated on two key conditions that exist beyond the level of the individual. The first is that "labor-power can appear on the market as a commodity only if, and in so far as, its possessor . . . offers it for sale or sells it as a commodity."[89] In other words, capitalism, as a market-defined system, requires workers to obtain waged employment. Capitalism is predicated upon some women and men (waged workers) laboring for other women and men (owners). Given a choice, though, why would someone labor for another? According to the narrative advanced by Locke and Smith, a simple explanation might be that some individuals do not have the initiative or the desire; they just don't "have what it takes." Marx, not surprisingly, takes a different tact, for he proposes (as a second condition of capitalism) that "the possessor of labor-power . . . [must] be compelled to offer for sale as a commodity that very labor-power which exists only in his living body."[90]

Marx's reference to a person being compelled is significant. In slave societies, some men, women, and children are, through direct force or the threat of force, compelled to work for another. Likewise, in feudal societies, men, women, and children are required to work because of particular obligations. Within the "free" market of capitalism, how can it be reasoned that workers are compelled (i.e., forced) to participate? Indeed, the phrase "free market" suggests that workers are free to get a job if they want and that they are free to leave their job if they want. The market *appears* to be purely voluntary, and thus free of any extra-economic means of coercion outside of economics (e.g., material force).

For Marx, however, workers appear "free" in a double sense: as legally free to enter into the waged-labor market and as freed from the means of production. This "freedom" resulted from a series of practices that, over time, became codified in systems of criminal justice. Drawing on the example of England, Marx writes: "[The] process . . . which creates the capital-relation can be nothing other than the process which divorces the worker from the ownership of the conditions of his own labor; it is a process which operates two transformations, whereby the social means of subsistence and production are turned into capital, and the immediate producers are turned into wage-laborers." Marx terms this process "primitive accumulation" in reference to "the historical process of divorcing the producer from the means of production."[91] This concept will be developed in chapter 3, but for now, suffice it to say that the relatively recent appearance of the "free" market is manifest in concrete conditions that significantly alter one's exposure to harm, injury, suffering, and premature death.

Capitalism thrives on the illusion of freedom and choice; indeed, it is this illusory component that helps maintain order and stability. Because advocates *want* to believe that markets operate on their own, and thus are realms of equality and freedom, they too often fail to properly scrutinize how the workings of the market actually concentrate wealth in the hands of a few.[92] They fail to see that labor occupies a decidedly unequal position in the social relation of exchange, that the wage paid the worker is not equal to the value create by the worker's labor, but instead equal to the value of labor power. This is a crucial distinction because, as Arthur Schatzkin writes, the "difference between the value created by a worker in a day and the value of reproducing the necessities of life for that worker is the surplus-value which goes to the capitalist."[93] Exploitation is systemic to the social organization of production under capitalism.

The conditions of employment also always and already favor the capitalist. Within the United States, for example, governmental legislation demands only that workers are not discriminately prevented from participating in the waged-labor market; significantly, employment is not guaranteed. The privileging of employer over employee is codified in much legislation, notably the right to terminate employment "at will." As Jonathan Fineman explains, the at-will rule has been the basic foundation of American employment since the late nineteenth century. In effect, the at-will rule provides that each party to an employment relationship is able to unilaterally terminate the employment at any time and for any reason, thus positioning employer and employee as equal participants.[94] Indeed, at-will contracts are founded on the belief that employees are "individuals competent enough to understand and enter contracts of their own free will" and that they are therefore "free to enter into at-will employment relationships on equivalent terms with the employer."[95]

In practice, according to Fineman, "there are relevant and significant differences between the positions of and possibilities for employers and employees in terms of their ability to bargain with each other," as well as "in terms of their abilities to successfully respond to such things as economic dislocations, market fluctuations or distortions, and disruption of 'business as usual.'"[96] Fineman favors an epistemology whereby living laborers are positioned as "vulnerable subjects," but he notes that, as embodied subjects, our individual differences mean that we may experience vulnerability differently. Thus, while we are all vulnerable, for example, to morbidity and mortality, this shared vulnerability is not experienced equally. While, to a certain extent, antidiscrimination rulings that prevent employers from firing employees on the basis of race, religion, gender, or sexuality have ameliorated some aspects of differential vulnerability, the fundamental *structural* inequality of at-will contracts remains firmly in place. Simply put, as Fineman concludes, "with termination, an employee's access to and opportunities within employment are cut off and his or her ability to continue to build the resources necessary for resilience is impaired."[97] For example, termination may result in subsequent unemployment and underemployment and the diminishment of savings and other resources. Furthermore, unemployment affects the health of the family and its members, all of whom may experience depression, substance abuse, illness, and suicide. Diminished resources, in turn, severely impact one's response to these conditions.[98]

At-will contracts, as a material manifestation of the employer–employee relationship, codify fundamental inequalities within the waged-labor form of production. The employer has the unilateral ability to set pay, hours, and benefits; in other words, the ability to extract absolute surplus value simply through alterations to the employment contract. Furthermore, employers are able to unilaterally determine the form and nature of how work is performed, thereby facilitating the extraction of relative surplus value.[99] From capital's vantage point, this is the most desirable situation because it provides the highest level of flexibility for employers to control labor and labor costs.[100] It is for this reason that unions specifically and worker solidarity in general constitute the biggest threats to employer hegemony within the waged-labor market. Indeed, "many of the improvements in living and working conditions under industrial capitalism resulted from brutal class struggles won by the working classes."[101] Likewise, the establishment of workplace safety laws, such as the Occupational Safety and Health Act of 1970, came about from an empowered working class. For the capitalist, these struggles constitute a threat to their profit margins; for the living labors, these struggles constitute a threat to their very mortal existence.

Under capitalism, the formal waged-labor market emerged as and still largely remains the keystone for understanding the valuation of life as embodied by workers. Waged work, according to Kathi Weeks, "is not only the primary mechanism by which income is distributed, it is also the basic means by which status is allocated, and by which most people gain access to healthcare and retirement."[102] Reproducing people ready for waged work is the central goal of school, prisons, and the various welfare-to-work programs initiated in recent decades. Weeks writes: "Work produces not just economic goods and services but also social and political subjects. In other words, the wage relation generates not just income and capital, but disciplined individuals, governable subjects, worthy citizens, and responsible family members."[103] In short, it is through the promotion of waged work that values are instilled.

Accordingly, waged work "is not just defended on grounds of economic necessity and social duty; it is widely understood as an individual moral practice and collective ethical obligation."[104] It is also through the pivot between the waged work and unwaged work that gender and other social markers are produced. Feminist scholars, for example, have documented that, while women in the abstract have largely been relegated to selected tasks outside of the formal labor market (including the provision of food, care of the home, childcare, and nursing the sick, teaching), particular women did and continue to find (limited) waged employment, often in the "secondary" labor market. Unlike the primary (waged) labor market, which offers (in theory) jobs with relatively high wages, benefits, good working conditions, and employment stability, the secondary labor market offers jobs that are relatively low-paying, with poorer working conditions, little opportunity for career advancement, frequently harsh and capricious work discipline, and considerable employment instability characterized by high turnover.[105] Additionally, while women (as a generic category) operate within gender-restricted labor markets (both primary and secondary), racism and discrimination ensure that the position of women "of color" (and men) is even more restricted.[106]

In the end, however, even one's access to waged employment provides minimal assurance against premature death. As Jane Wills and Brian Linneker observe, we are increasingly likely to live in societies where large parts of the working population fail to earn the income required to sustain a decent standard of living.[107] Recent years have witnessed an expansion in the scale and scope of in-work poverty, whereby waged workers, despite working long hours, fail to earn sufficient income simply to live. Again, inequalities in one's vulnerability to in-work poverty are readily evident. Workers who are female, "of color," part-time, or on temporary or casual contracts are particularly vulnerable; so too are widows, divorcees, and young workers. And while many of these laborers may not be living in dire poverty, they are often one medical condition, accident, or other unforeseen event away from becoming destitute.[108]

From Production to Reproduction

Within the capitalist mode of production, Marx concludes, somewhat hyperbolically, "capital asks no questions about the length of life of labor-power": "What interests it is purely and simply the maximum of labor-power that can be set in motion in a working day. It attains this objective by shortening the life of labor-power, in the same way as a greedy farmer snatches more produce from the soil by robbing it of its fertility."[109] This is not entirely accurate. Schatzkin explains: "[A] certain level of physical and mental health is . . . necessary to maintain the maximum level of productivity. Below that level of health, the capacity to work falls off, and with it the amount of surplus-value that will be generated. The capitalist is simply not interested in the level of health beyond this, although the worker will be vitally interested from the point of view of quality of life, not of productive capacity."[110] In other words, capitalism is interested in the life of the worker only insofar as the worker stays alive long enough to return to work the next day.

Marx stresses that "every social process of production is at the same time a process of reproduction."[111] The living laborer, Marx writes, "is nothing other than labor-power for the duration of his whole life," while capital, "in its blind and measureless drive, its insatiable appetite for surplus labor, . . . oversteps not only the moral but even the merely physical limits of the working day."[112] Accordingly, the commodity of labor capacity functions unlike other commodities. Notably, the production and reproduction of the living laborer, who must "voluntarily" sell his or her labor-power, entails also a process of consumption. Marx explains that, "in taking food, for example, which is a form of consumption, the human being produces his own body."[113] However, as exploitation is systemic to the capitalist mode of production, the survivability of workers is called to question.

At a most basic, biological level, reproduction entails the day-to-day continuance of any given worker. The main rationale for a minimum wage, as a case-in-point, is to ensure the daily survival of the worker; to enable the worker to live (and work) from one day to the next. Of course, given the constant wear and tear on the worker and the biological fact that humans are mortal, capital requires a second form of reproduction, which is the generational replacement of one worker with another. In principle, the minimum wage (as opposed to a "living" wage) is to cover merely individual and generational replacement, a principle that has long been debated and contested.[114] As Marx and Engels charge, "the cost of production of a workman is restricted, almost entirely, to the means of subsistence that he requires for his maintenance, and for the propagation of his race."[115]

Biological and generational reproduction within capitalism are rife with myriad forms of oppression, not least of which is patriarchy. Marx's aforementioned reference to the fertility of soil is especially informative, for it is within the household—and specifically the female body—that capital is reproduced. Maria Mies explains that what the so-called house-wife produces in the family is not simply use value, but the commodity of labor power, which the (traditional) husband, as a free wage laborer, may then sell in the labor market. In effect: "The productivity of the housewife is the precondition for the productivity of the (male) wage laborer. The nuclear family, organized and protected by the state, is the social factory where this commodity 'labor power' is produced. Hence, the housewife and her labor are not outside the process of surplus value production, but constitute the very foundation upon which this process can get started. The housewife and her labor are, in other words, the basis of the process of capital accumulation."[116] Consequently, the *nuclear* family became the principle institution within capitalism by which labor power was to be re-produced, and in turn, the family came to be identified almost exclusively in terms of biological and generational reproduction. Heterosexuality likewise became the unquestioned norm, as the purpose of sex was re-duced functionally to procreation. The husband or father figure came to be identified as primary provider, protector, and disciplinarian, while the wife was constituted as both subservient and complementary, responsible for the care and nourishment of the present and future (waged) workers.

Thus, capitalism exhibits a third form of social reproduction, one that exists at the class level. To this end, capitalism requires simply that the class of laborers perpetuates itself, and here it does not matter if any individual laborer (or his/her children) sells his or her labor-power, as long as someone can replace the first worker. This follows from the real subordination of production to the dictates of capital, especially the on-going routinization and mechanization of production techniques. It is therefore feasible that, under capitalism, *some* laborers may die with no major disruption to the system as long as the class as a whole continues. This relates back to the idea of socially necessary labor time, in that "the sum of means of subsistence necessary for the production of labor-power must include the means necessary for the worker's replacements i.e., his children, in order that this race of peculiar commodity-owners may perpetuate its presence on the market."[117] Collectively, these three forms of social reproduction enable capitalism to reproduce itself, thus establishing a fourth and final form of reproduction.

Reproduction beyond the biological, generational, and class levels must exist at the level of the mode of production. And so, the capitalist mode of production must be reproduced continuously, therefore affording the context within which individual capitalists may function. We have seen that capitalism is an economic system in which: the material conditions of life are to be obtained nearly exclusively via the free market; wage labor is a defining characteristic; private ownership of the means of production is promoted; and the system as a whole is driven by certain systemic imperatives, by competition and surplus accumulation. We understand also that capitalism is predicated on two conditions that exist beyond the level of any one person: first, that labor power appears on the market as a commodity and, second, that the possessor of labor power must be compelled to sell as a commodity that very labor power which exist only in her or his living body.[118] That being said, according to Jason Read, "capitalism cannot be identified entirely with an unfettered development of production, [for] it too must reproduce particular economic, legal, and social conditions."[119] It is through this process that we witness more clearly the intersection of particular forms of racism and sexism within the capitalist mode of production.

Under capitalism, women's work increasingly became both invisible and naturalized; it became separated, materially and ideologically, from productive work.[120] These transformations redefined women's position in society and in relation to men, and the sexual divisions of labor that emerged from this not only fixed women to reproductive work, but increased their dependence on men, enabling the state and employers to use the male wage as a means to command women's unpaid reproductive labor.[121] Women were thus forced into a condition of chronic poverty, economic dependence, and invisibility as workers, features of the gendered division of labor that continue to impact most capitalist societies.[122]

Racism has also figured prominently in the reproduction of capital.[123] In the context of the United States, Evelyn Nakano Glenn explains, "where racial ethnic women diverge from other working-class women is that . . . their definition as laborers in production took precedence over their domestic roles."[124] She elaborates that, whereas the wife and mother roles of white working-class women were recognized and, to a degree, were accorded respect by the larger society, the maternal and reproductive roles of racial ethnic women were ignored in favor of their roles as workers. This has important consequences because, historically, racial ethnic women have been assigned distinct responsibilities for reproductive labor, thereby forming a key labor source for the reproduction of capitalism as a whole.[125]

It is inappropriate to view these four forms of social reproduction as mutually exclusive or isolated; rather, they are related dialectically. Moreover, reproduction is something more than mere repetition, since it presupposes certain relationships to remain in place. In other words, social reproduction always and already calls into question the conditions of living and, in turn, of dying. Capitalism, as is true of any mode of production, does not simply exist, but instead must be continuously brought into being.

The Wages of Health and Wealth

It is significant that both the reproduction of class relations and capitalism as a whole remain indifferent to the life of any particular person. A political economy of premature death, accordingly, recognizes that, under capitalism, "health" is positioned as the capacity of workers *in the abstract* to remain productive so as to facilitate the continued accumulation of wealth for capitalism.[126] More precisely, a contradictory relationship exists between capitalism, with its continual drive for profits, and the health needs of the masses of people in society.[127] Capital often appears more concerned with dead labor (meaning constant capital) than it is with living labor. Fred and Harry Magdoff write: "Capitalists take care of their buildings—factories, offices, and stores—and the various pieces of machinery and equipment are usually serviced and maintained regardless of business conditions. Workers, on the other hand, are disposable. Capital wants to obtain labor-power when needed, and lay off workers when they aren't needed. Treating labor as a disposable and/or easily replacement part of the production process promotes capitalism's central driving force—the never-ending drive to accumulate wealth."[128]

Capitalists cannot always consign their laborers to a premature death.

It often becomes necessary for both the state and the capitalist to limit the exploitation and degradation of the living worker, if only to facilitate the production of the next generation of workers in order to reproduce capitalism as a dominant mode of production. To this end, the social reproduction of workers as a social class is of considerable interest both to individual capitalists and to capitalism as a whole. And, while considerable practices of reproduction operate within the household, myriad apparatuses within the capitalist state have emerged to ensure, when necessary, the biological reproduction of living laborers. The provision of health care, for example, is part of maintaining labor power at the class level. However, it simultaneously represents to the individual capitalist part of the wages he or she must pay out, whether it is direct wages that buy food to keep the worker healthy or indirect "social" wages in the form of, say, medical services and insurance.[129] This begs the question of whether the provision of health care falls on the employer, the employee, or the state.

One position holds that health care should be a fundamental right; that is, if someone needs health care, society has a collective obligation to provide necessary services. A counter position holds that, if health care was universally provided, this would diminish the incentive of individuals and households to provide for their own health care—the so-called "free rider" problem. And yet, a follow-up question is whether, under the structural conditions inherent to capitalism, workers are positioned to provide health care for themselves and their family members. Are wages sufficient to afford health care? What of the work-related conditions of employment, such as the presence of safety regulations?

From the late nineteenth century onward, reformers in both the United Kingdom and the United States introduced legislation to improve working conditions in the factories and mills. In part, these efforts grew from the palpable fear that infectious disease epidemics in "slum" areas would spread. Also significant was the class struggle, meaning the demand among laborers for better working conditions. While these cannot be discounted, there was a more practicable, and indeed productive, reason for the reforms: capitalists were becoming concerned that workers were simply being worked to death.[130] In 1842, for example, Edwin Chadwick issued a *Report on an Inquiry into the Sanitary Condition of the Labouring Population of Great Britain*, in which he called attention to the necessity of maintaining the productive capacity of workers: "This de-pressing effect of adverse sanitary circumstances on the laboring strength of the population, and on its duration, is to be viewed with the greatest concern, as it is a depressing effect on . . . the bodily strength of the in-dividuals of the laboring class."[131] Consequently, the class struggle over working conditions offered common ground for both capital and labor, thereby ensuring that health would remain central to the (re)production of the capitalist mode of production.

Many early sanitation programs were subsequently viewed as a small price to pay for the reproduction of a healthy working class. One no-table example is the effort of the Rockefeller Sanitary Commission to eradicate hookworm throughout the American South. The Rockefeller public health philanthropies originated within the broader context of Western imperialism, in the application of medical sciences to tropi-cal regions. Throughout the late nineteenth and early twentieth centu-ries, various schools of tropical medicine were founded in France, the United Kingdom, the United States, and other colonial states. To these were added philanthropic institutions, such as the Rockefeller Founda-tion in the United States. Foreign public health programs promoted by the Rockefeller Foundation rested on four interlocking propositions: (1) U.S. control of the resources and markets, especially of nonindustri-alized countries, was considered essential to the prosperity of the United States; (2) increased development of economically "backward" countries was seen as necessary to the successful exploitation of their resources, markets, and investment opportunities by capitalist countries; (3) trop-ical diseases were believed to be obstacles to peoples of underdeveloped countries; and (4) it was thought that the application of biomedical sci-ences through public health programs would increase the health and working capacities of these peoples and, in turn, help induce them to accept Western industrial culture and U.S. economic and political dom-ination.[132] In other words, the promotion of public health campaigns was part and parcel of the formal subsumption of colonies into Western capitalism.

Within the United States, public health campaigns such as those for-warded by the Rockefeller Foundation operated under similar logics. As Richard Brown explains, "despite their humanitarian outward appear-ances, the major Rockefeller public health programs in the Southern

United States were intended to promote the economic development of the South as a regional economic, political, and cultural dependency of Northern capital."[133] In 1909, the Rockefeller Sanitary Commission for the Eradication of Hookworm Disease was founded with a startup of $1 million, and throughout its five-year tenure, it treated nearly 700,000 people for hookworm infection. On the surface, the campaign represents a laudable achievement, and yet, as Brown explains, the impetus of the program was a decidedly more pragmatic problem: efforts to expand southern agricultural productivity and to prepare southern whites and blacks for industrialization in largely northern-owned mills and factories were hindered by the physical condition of the rural population.[134] Consequently, health was articulated as the capacity to work and specific programs were to facilitate this capacity through the eradication of diseases mostly among working-age populations, as it was understood that "healthy, noninfected workers could produce sufficiently greater surplus-value per worker than infected workers so that maintaining healthy workers—even adding in the cost of the public health program—resulted in a lower proportion of total value created going toward the reproduction of labor-power."[135]

The conventional understanding of health as the capacity to work continued throughout the twentieth century, albeit waxing and waning according to the expansion and contraction of capital. In the United States, for example, from the Second World War onward, as capitalism expanded, "the full employment that resulted forced employers and the state to pay much more attention than previously to reproducing labor power and deflecting working class discontent."[136] "The postwar welfare state," Giuliano Bonoli writes, "protected well against the risk of being unable to extract an income from the labor market, be it because of sickness, invalidity, old age, or lack of employment."[137] Within this political climate, the provision of health care expanded rapidly, as labor was able to win the extension of employee health benefits and the socialization of costs for the aged and many of the poor.[138] Notably, many of these costs were shouldered by the federal government under the auspices of Keynesian economics. In 1950, health expenditures in the United States were 4.1 percent of the gross national product; this share increased to 5.2 percent in 1960 and 7.1 percent in 1970.[139]

To be sure, not all people benefited from the welfare state. Women, persons of color, and immigrants were often ignored, neglected, or simply discriminated against by many government programs. It is well worth remembering that, for many individuals, the welfare state provided little improvement in their day-to-day lives and, not infrequently, exacerbated already appalling conditions. Thus, for example, myriad welfare policies and practices served by design or default to reproduce racial divisions of labor, to disrupt household formations, and to augment forms of social control through increased surveillance and repression.[140]

Beginning in the 1960s, profitability in the major economies began to fall, and by the 1970s, the deepening crisis was accompanied by "intermittent periods of high unemployment, high inflation, and rising social expenditures, which led to large fiscal deficits and an expansion of government debt."[141] In general, Garry Leech explains, as "the rate of economic growth slowed in the Global North, resulting in capital experiencing a crisis of accumulation, it became necessary for capital to dismantle the Keynesian policy framework in order to resume expansion, this time under neoliberal globalization."[142] Here, neoliberalism is not merely a set of economic and social policies, but instead consists of an accumulation strategy, a mode of social and economic reproduction, and a mode of exploitation and social domination based on the systematic use of state power to impose, under the ideological veil of nonintervention, a hegemonic project of recomposition of the rule of capital in all areas of social life.[143] Notably, mass unemployment reduced labor costs and weakened the ability of trade unions (also under attack) to block reductions in wages and employment conditions.[144] Ultimately, as Peck writes, "although couched in the ostensibly apolitical discourse of free markets, competition, and flexibility, neoliberal attempts at deregulating the labor market have been associated with an unprecedented attack on the social and working conditions of labor."[145]

From the 1970s onward, we have witnessed ongoing efforts to cut the direct costs to corporations and to cut the indirect costs of social programs generally in the promotion of health care.[146] This was occasioned by the transference of responsibility for health promotion away from a social or collective enterprise to that of the individual worker.[147] The ascension of neoliberal globalization ushered in a conservative period of health promotion being centered on individual behavior and lifestyle: diet, exercise, substance abuse, sexuality.[148] Coinciding with a social, economic, and political climate in which the neoliberal subject is viewed as the appropriate focus for interventions to control health risk factors, an emphasis on personal responsibility in health campaigns glorified an individual's presumed rationality to control his or her own fate and to pursue private interests.[149] Nurit Guttman and William Ressler write that, "when personal responsibility is linked to causality one possible implication is that individuals should be held morally, and perhaps legally, accountable for their behavior," and by extension, "this notion of accountability can serve as the basis for the argument that society could be exempt from paying for health care costs resulting from behaviors considered irresponsible."[150]

"Such an individualist stance," Gavin Brookes and Kevin Hardy argue, "reflects the neoliberal approach to public health whereby the onus for well-being is placed firmly on the shoulders of the self-determining citizen, a corollary of which is to absolve the government of responsibility towards the health of its citizens."[151] In so doing, however, the neoliberal discourse of personal responsibility fails to articulate (1) the complicated genetic etiologies of health conditions and (2) the conditions of employment.[152] As Meredith Minkler writes, the programmatic emphasis on individual responsibility for health frequently was not accompanied by attention to individual and community response-ability, or the capacity of individuals and communities to build on their strengths and respond to their personal needs and the challenges posed by the environment.[153] Further, there was—and continues to be—a myopia regarding the structural conditions and relations inherent to the capitalist mode of production: the outsourcing of jobs, downsizing of firms, and the attack on unions. Under these techniques imposed to increase both rates of exploitation and profit, living laborers are placed in ever more precarious forms of employment. Indeed, through no fault of their own, countless workers, including those employed part-time or in low-wage full-time jobs, require assistance to maintain themselves: unemployment benefits, government-supported welfare, childcare, and monetary supplements to pay for rent, utilities, and food—in short, the basic requirements of life itself.[154]

The brutality of precarity became startlingly clear in 2007–2008, as the United States and other countries experienced a recession of monumental proportions. In the United States in 2008, an estimated 39.8 million people lived in poverty, up from 37.3 million in 2007, the poverty rate (13.2 percent) was the highest since 1997, and over 15 million Americans lived in "extreme" poverty, defined as having an income less than half of the poverty line or, in other words, earning less than $10,000 a year for a family of four.[155] Moreover, such income inequalities have come at a steep price. While the United States ranks first in the world both in gross domestic product and in health expenditures, the country is eighteenth in the world in the percentage of children in poverty, twenty-second in the world in low birth-weight rates, and twenty-fifth in the world in infant mortality.[156] The National Center for Children in Poverty calculated that approximately 21 percent of all children in the United States lived in poor households, defined as having income below 100 percent of the federal poverty level, which, in 2015, was set at $24,036 for a family of four. Of these children, more than one third lived in households in which neither parent was employed.[157]

Poverty translates directly into prospects for life and death. In 2008, an estimated 17 million households (14.6 percent of all households) were food insecure, and about one third of these households exhibited very low food security. Consequently, these households relied extensively on government programs, such as the Supplemental Nutrition Assistance Program (SNAP, formerly known as the Food Stamps Program), the Special Supplemental Nutrition Program for Women, Infants, and Children (WIC), and the National School Lunch Program.[158] In fact, for impoverished households, these social programs literally meant the difference between life and death.

Income inequality and poverty are themselves unequally distributed throughout the American body politic. A recent study released by the Pew Research Center found that the median wealth of white households was twenty times that of African American households, and eighteen times that of Hispanic households. In addition, the disparities are increasing for America's nonwhite population. From 2005 to 2009, for instance, inflation-adjusted median wealth fell by 66 percent among Hispanic households and 53 percent among African American households, compared with just 16 percent among white households.[159] These figures relate directly to life and death: a white male infant born in the United States in 2009 has a life expectancy of 76.2 years, whereas an African American male infant has a life-expectancy of just 70.9 years.[160]

In the decade following the Great Recession, inequality has only worsened. Global wealth, for example, is becoming increasingly concentrated among the elite.[161] Deborah Hardoon documents that, "in 2014, the richest 1 percent of people in the world owned 48 percent of global wealth, leaving just 52 percent to be shared between the other 99 percent of adults on the planet."[162] Moreover, a scant eighty men and women in the world had a collective wealth of US$1.9 trillion, equal to the amount of wealth shared by the bottom half of the world's population. In other words, eighty individuals accounted for an amount of wealth equal to that of 3.5 *billion* people.[163] According to a 2016 study by Richard Florida, Charlotta Mellander, and Isabel Ritchie, in 2015: 1,826 billionaires made up just 0.00003 percent of the world's population but accounted for more than US$7 trillion of the world's total wealth, comparable to Japan's entire economy; the world's fifty wealthiest billionaires controlled USD$1.6 trillion, more than Canada's economy; and the top ten controlled US$556 billion, roughly the economic size of Algeria or the United Arab Emirates.[164] And yet globally, according to Gholam Khiabany, one in nine people do not have enough to eat and more than one billion people live on less than US$1.25 per day.[165]

In the United States, inequalities in wealth are substantial and increasing: currently, the top 0.1 percent of the population holds approximately 22 percent of the country's total wealth.[166] It is perhaps self-evident that such inequalities significantly influence one's vulnerability to premature death. David Grusky and Alair MacLean surmise that "those at the bottom of the income distribution are now doubly disadvantaged: it is not just that they have less money (relative to others), but it is also that access to goods, services, and opportunities increasingly requires precisely the money that they do not have."[167] This follows because of the incessant dismantling of the welfare state and the concomitant real subsumption of society to the market logics of capital. Consequently, inequalities in life expectancy have similarly widened. Data for 2014 in the United States, for example, reported: "Men in the bottom 1 percent of the income distribution at the age of 40 years had an expected age of death of 72.7 years. Men in the top 1 percent of the income distribution had an expected age of death of 87.3 years, which is 14.6 years longer than those in the bottom 1 percent. Women in the bottom 1 percent of the income distribution at the age of 40 years had an expected age of death of 78.8 years. Women in the top 1 percent had an expected age of death of 88.9 years, which is 10.1 years longer than those in the bottom 1 percent."[168]

It is also hardly surprising that, in the United States and elsewhere, widening income inequalities among racial groups and between genders have been accompanied by significant differences in mortality.[169] Indeed, since the early 1970s, a period marked by the ascension of neoliberal policies, low-income African American and Hispanic families have experienced absolute declines in family incomes and these trends have been associated with worsening health conditions, including increases in mortality and a widening disparity of life expectancy of persons of colors compared to the white population. As a case in point, David Williams and Chiquita Collins report that, during the 1980s, the gap in life expectancy between African Americans and whites widened from 6.9 years to 8.3 years for males and from 5.6 years to 5.8 years for females.[170] More recently, Jo Phelan and Bruce Link document that the African American median household income is three fifths that of whites, that African American family wealth is less than one sixth that of whites, and that African Americans are more likely than whites to hold services occupations and less likely to be employed in managerial occupations.[171] Accordingly, African Americans (and other persons of color) are confronted with significant disadvantages. Structural racism manifests in unequal opportunities in education and employment and limited access to and quality of health care, all of which contribute to a distinct health disadvantage among socially marginalized groups, including higher rates of mortality.[172]

Conclusions

Historically, capitalists have shown little or no interest in the health of their workers or their general quality of life unless forced to do so by the mobilization of workers, by legislation, or by profit considerations.[173] Marx is clear on this point: "Capital . . . takes no account of the health and the length of life of the worker, unless society forces it to do so. Its answer to the outcry about the physical and mental degradation, the premature death, the torture of over-work, is this: Should that pain trouble us, since it increases our pleasure (profit)?"[174]

Marx's point is not simply that capitalism is violent. Rather, his critique lies in the assertions that, as long as capitalism exists, structural violence is both necessary and unavoidable and that capitalism causes unnecessary and avoidable premature death.[175] That these structural conditions are not considered criminal is, therefore, a reflection of how crime and violence are also historically and morally determined. For, as Marx recognized, the standards of "right" and "wrong" and of positive and negative duties are not transhistorical, but rather conditioned by the dominant economic (and hence legal) relations of society. Within the capitalist mode of production, the exploitation of workers—the reduction of life to that which is socially necessary—is not considered criminal. Within capitalism, "the lowest and the only necessary wage-rate is that providing for the subsistence of the worker for the duration of his work and as much more as is necessary for him to support a family and for the [class] of laborers not to die out" is considered a "free" and "equal" condition of existence.[176] This, ultimately, is the point raised by Engels toward the conclusion of his magisterial *The Condition of the Working Class of England*:

> When one individual inflicts bodily injury upon another, such injury that death results, we call the deed manslaughter; when the assailant knew in advance that the injury would be fatal, we call his deed murder. But when society places hundreds of proletarians in such a position that they inevitably meet a too early and an unnatural death, one which is quite as much a death by violence as that by the sword or bullet; when it deprives them thousands of the necessaries of life, places them under conditions in which they cannot live—forces them, through the strong arm of the law, to remain in such conditions until that death ensues which is the inevitable consequence—knows that these thousands of victims must perish, and yet permits these conditions to remain, its deed is murder just as surely as the deed of a single individual; disguised, malicious murder, murder against which none can defend himself, which does not seem what it is, because no man sees the murderer, because the death of the victim seems a natural once, since the offence is more one of omission than of commission. But murder it remains.[177]

3. SURPLUS LABOR

Greg Abbott, governor of Texas, described the scene as "a heartbreaking tragedy." On July 23, 2017, a tractor-trailer was found parked in a Walmart parking lot in San Antonio, Texas. Inside were dozens of men, women, and children, suffering from heat stroke or related injuries. Eight people were already dead, their lifeless bodies slumped inside the trailer, and two other people would later die from their injuries. Many of the survivors will likely suffer from irreversible brain damage.[1]

Authorities believe that upward of one hundred men, women, and children had been packed inside the trailer. They are but the latest victims of a so-called migration "crisis," for the victims and survivors were "undocumented" migrants smuggled into the United States from Mexico after paying traffickers exorbitant and debt-inducing fees for the possibility to work and carve out a better life. Every year since the late 1990s, from two hundred to five hundred people have died along the border between the United States and Mexico. The total number of deaths in the past twenty years is estimated between five and eight thousand, but in reality there is no accurate count of the people who have lost their lives trying to cross the border.[2]

The deaths along the southern border of the United States are but a fraction of the hundreds of thousands of other men, women, and children who risk death every day to cross international borders. According to estimates provided by the Missing Migrants project, in 2016, nearly eight thousand people died trying to move from one country to another.[3]

Government officials (sometimes) acknowledge these deaths as tragic but too often fail to concede the underlying structural problems that contribute to these fatal crossings.[4] Indeed, the so-called migration crisis and the attendant refugee crisis that have garnered international headlines from 2014 onward continue to deflect attention from the systemic structures and inherent exploitation of capitalism itself. The goal of governments across the globe "is to render invisible the innumerable consequences this sociopolitical phenomenon has for the lives and bodies of undocumented people."[5] And yet, as Susan Ferguson and David McNally explain, the distinct national spaces within the world market in labor are linked together as elements of a complex social whole constituted by racialized forms of citizenship and nonmembership and differentiated domains of security and precarity, all governed by an overriding logic of control and exploitation of labor.[6]

For, despite ongoing efforts to fortify borders around the world, and despite the increased militarization that patrol and police these borders, the object is not to prohibit border crossings, but instead to regulate these crossings through fear and intimidation. The neoliberal phase of capitalism has involved a significant reorientation in global labor migration. Not only are the dominant capitalist countries systematic importers of surplus labor generated elsewhere, they have also constructed an array of coercive immigration regimes designed to cheapen migrant labor by restricting its social and political rights.[7] In fact, one of the main features of the new global architecture of capitalism, Raúl Delgado Wise writes, is the assault on the labor and living conditions of the majority of the global working class, and in particular the undocumented migrant workforce, which is among the most vulnerable segments of this class.[8] It must be acknowledged that so-called undocumented migrations are "preeminently labor migrations" and, accordingly, are understood only through "a critical theoretical consideration of labor and capital as mutually constituting poles of a single, albeit contradictory, social relation."[9] As Gholam Khiabany relates, "it is in fact impossible to comprehend the current crisis without taking into account the increasing social inequalities at national and global levels, the financialization of global capitalism, the rapid environmental degradation, as well as increased imperialist interventions in the Middle East and Africa, as a major source of forced migration and staggering levels of displacement."[10]

One of Marx's most profound insights into the functioning of capitalism, Prabhat Patnaik explains, was that "the system could not do without a reserve army of labor."[11] Michael McIntyre concurs, noting that, for Marx, the creation of an industrial reserved army was not an aberration; it was an ordinary product of capitalist accumulation.[12] More precisely, the existence of surplus populations is systemic to the reproduction of capitalism, but it is detrimental to the reproduction of life itself. Currently, the global reserve army of labor comprises an estimated 2.4 billion people. This figure stands in stark contrast to the 1.4 billion people employed in the active labor force.

Collectively, this surplus labor population is made to work to facilitate ongoing rounds of capital accumulation.[13] It is ironic indeed that such "work" often materializes in the form of underemployment and unemployment. In this chapter, I engage first with Marx's concept of surplus populations and, second, with efforts to extend Marx's writings to account for the premature death of hundreds of thousands of men, women, and children who die needlessly in search of a better life. Marx's writings provide a powerful conceptual framework upon which to build a critical political economy of premature death and, consequently, to interrogate the concepts of vulnerability, precarity, and survivability. More precisely, this affords the opportunity to question the political and legal contexts of surplus populations, especially the pivotal role that citizenship plays within neoliberalism. For, a crucial determining factor for one's vulnerability to loss of life itself is the construction and documentation of multiple subject positions that, ultimately, condition one's access not only to employment but also to health and medical care.[14] In other words, it is precisely the articulation of a precarious citizenship that renders vulnerable populations—living laborers—disproportionately susceptible to premature death.

Surplus Populations and Primitive Accumulation

In volume 1 of *Capital,* Marx argues: "It is capitalist accumulation itself that constantly produces, and produces indeed in direct relation with its own energy and extent, a relatively redundant working population, i.e. a population which is superfluous to capital's average requirements for its own valorization, and is therefore a surplus population."[15] Marx's statement has received considerable empirical attention over the years, and these debates need not detain us at this point.[16] What is most relevant for our immediate purpose is how the concept of surplus populations informs our understanding of the political economy of premature death. For, such an engagement helps us understand the political-economic negotiation of life, of how both its existence and its vitality are linked to the regulation and contestation of who has priority to live and flourish and who might be left to wither and die. To this end, it is imperative that we heed the call of Michael McIntyre and Heidi Nast for a "reexamination of Marx's notion of surplus populations in light of contemporary capitalism and a world marked by tremendous global shifts in fertility rates, almost unprecedented rates of outmigration to hegemonic nation-states and enclaves, heightened levels of investment in (and hyper-exploitation of) formerly colonized nations, and massive degradation of the environment."[17] Such global flux requires that we consider those who live under the specter of precarity not as a by-product or residue of contemporary political economic practices, but instead as being constituted by and constituting the contemporary terrain of capitalism.

Surplus populations do not constitute a monolithic or homogenous group, but instead may be differentiated by their position within the capitalist mode of production. Marx observes that "relative surplus population exists in all kinds of forms" and that every "worker belongs to it during the time when he is only partially employed or wholly unemployed."[18] More precisely, Marx classifies surplus populations into three categories: floating, latent, and stagnant. The "floating" population consists of those workers cycling in and out of the labor force, those who are unemployed due to fluctuations in the accumulation process. Capitalism does not proceed uniformly, but instead is reflective of recurrent periods of expansion and contraction. This follows from the inherent contradictions within the capitalist mode of production. Thus, in times of economic growth, surplus workers enter the ranks of the formal waged-labor sector. Unemployment levels decrease, but this is only temporary. Subsequent economic slow-downs result in massive lay-offs, and hence a replenishing of the surplus population. Also included are those individuals made redundant as a result of technological innovations.[19] The "latent" population includes those with insecure employment. Notable in this regard are those in agriculture and artisanal industries who are made redundant under processes of real and formal subsumption. The dispossession and displacement of subsistence farmers, for example, constitutes a principle means by which latent surplus populations are produced. As Marx writes, "as soon as capitalist production takes possession of agriculture . . . the demand for a rural working population falls absolutely, while the accumulation of the capital employed in agriculture advances."[20] As noted above, this remains a key element of neoliberal globalization. Finally, the "stagnant" population is composed of those workers who are only rarely employed. It is the stagnant population in particular that forms the massive ranks of the "inexhaustible reservoir of disposable labor-power."[21] This population includes those workers engaged in part-time, casual, or informal labor, with the largest part to be found in domestic industries that consist of "outwork" done through the agency of subcontractors and are dominated by "cheap labor," primarily women and children.[22] To these three categories of surplus populations Marx adds a fourth: the *Lumpenproletariat*.[23] Distinguished *morally* from the working-class proletariat, this "lowest sediment" of society includes vagabonds, criminals, prostitutes, and those who either are able to work but do not (e.g., paupers) or are unable to work because of particular incapacities.[24] This last subset (the disabled) is composed of "people who have lived beyond the worker's average life-span; and the victims of industry, whose number increases with the growth of dangerous machinery, or mines, chemical works, etc., the mutilated, the sickly, the widows, etc."[25]

For Marx, the production of surplus populations is systemic to capitalism. Marx identifies a tendency within capitalism to overproduce workers, a paradoxical condition that exists alongside but apart from biology.[26] Marx writes: "Independently of the limits of the actual increase of population, [capitalism] creates a mass of human material always ready for exploitation by capital in the interests of capital's own changing valorization requirements."[27] How this occurs is a crucial question, one that has garnered considerable attention both within and beyond Geography in recent years.

Fundamentally, a Marxist perspective begins from the standpoint of "primitive accumulation," itself a term subject to much debate. Part of the confusion with the concept of primitive accumulation stems from difficulties in translation. As Werner Bonefeld explains, in the original German, Marx did not necessarily mean "primitive" accumulation, since the term used, *ursprünglich,* while loosely translated into English as "primitive," includes a variety of other meanings, such as "initial," "unspoiled," and "beginning."[28] Moreover, while these words appear synonymous, none effectively capture the essence of *ursprünglich.* Indeed, the term itself is suggestive not of causality, but of constitution. Bonefeld writes: "The systematic character of primitive accumulation is constitutive. It does not refer to a specific chronology but is rather a process of continuously reconstituted new 'beginnings.' It posits the principle constitution of capital, a principle which capital has to reproduce on an expanding scale and to which capital has always to return in order to posit itself as capital."[29]

In general, primitive accumulation is the historical process of separating workers from the means of production. This is not, however, a one-time occurrence, but rather a process marked by constant social struggle. Stated differently, the conditions of subsumption must be imposed continuously in order to reproduce capitalism. So-called primitive accumulation is therefore an ongoing process systemic to the (re)production of capitalism, but a process that remains a permanent condition of capitalism itself. Hence, Marx used the word *aufgehoben* to describe this condition of permanence. Usually translated as "suspended," *aufgehoben* also includes different, indeed contradictory, meanings. As Bonefeld explains, the term "has three main meanings: 'to lift up' or 'to raise'; 'to make invalid' or 'to cancel/eliminate'; and 'to keep' or 'to maintain.'" He elaborates that, in the context of primitive accumulation, this "means that the historic form of primitive accumulation is raised to a new level where its original form and independent existence is eliminated (or cancelled) at the same time as its substance or essence is maintained."[30] In other words, the separation of people from the means of production is necessarily the essence of capitalism. As Marx writes, "it is in fact this divorce between the conditions of labor on the one hand and the producers on the other that forms the concept of capital, as this arises with primitive accumulation, subsequently appearing as a constant process in the accumulation and concentration of capital, before it is finally expressed here as the centralization of capitals already existing in a few hands, and the decapitalization of many."[31] Simply put, primitive accumulation engenders two fundamental classes marked by struggle: those who own the means of production and those who are denied access to the means of production and are thus compelled to "freely" enter into the waged-labor market.

The coordinates of primitive accumulation are varied, conditioned in part by specific histories and geographies of displacement and dispossession and by particular social processes, including "the commodification and privatization of land and the forceful expulsion of peasant populations; the conversion of various forms of property rights (common, collective, state, etc.) into exclusive private property rights; the suppression of rights to the commons; the commodification of labor power and the suppression of alternative (indigenous) forms of production and consumption; colonial, neo-colonial, and imperial processes of appropriation of assets (including natural resources); the monetization of exchange and taxation, particularly of the land; the slave trade; and usury, the national debt, and ultimately the credit system."[32] Nor is the process of primitive accumulation uniform historically or geographically. Harry Cleaver explains: "In some cases the creation of waged labor was entirely marginal. Capital often either reinforced existing forms of social control and production (e.g. indirect rule) or transformed existing societies into new forms that did not use wage labor yet were well integrated into capital (e.g. sixteenth-nineteenth century slavery; sharecropping after the Civil War)."[33] Jim Glassman agrees, writing that "the process of proletarianization seems much more a contingent outcome of specific class struggles than a predetermined trajectory of capitalist development."[34] Glassman elaborates: "In some contexts, capitalists can benefit not only from garnering cheap resources but from turning precapitalist workers into wage laborers in the process. In such contexts, however, workers themselves may struggle against this process of proletarization with greater or lesser effect. In other contexts capitalists can benefit from maintaining a large non-proletarianized labor force that contributes indirectly to capitalists' ability to formally exploit wage labor."[35]

That primitive accumulation is experienced as a constant or permanent condition of capitalism arises from the fact that individuals do not necessarily want to relinquish their ties to the land in exchange for waged labor. In other words, the forcible separation of workers from their means of subsistence must be continually reproduced. As Cleaver notes, "the struggle between the emerging classes was about whether capital would be able to impose the commodity-form of class relations, that is, whether it had the power to drive peasants and tribal peoples from the land, to destroy their handicrafts and culture in order to create a new class of workers."[36] However, the "expropriation of the land . . . was not enough to drive people into the factories, as many preferred vagabondage or a life of 'crime' to the oppressive conditions and low wages of capitalist industry."[37] Many individuals actively resisted the onset of waged labor. On this point, in the *Grundrisse*, Marx explains: "They must be forced to work within the conditions posited by capital. The propertyless are more inclined to become vagabonds and robbers and beggars than workers."[38] Consequently, a bourgeois legal system—a "bloody legislation"—was imposed that effectively criminalized those people forcibly dispossessed and displaced from their land and livelihoods.[39] Marx writes: "Legislation treated them as 'voluntary' criminals, and assumed that it was entirely within their powers to go on working under the old conditions which in fact no longer existed."[40] I will cite but two examples. The first is a 1547 English statute: "If anyone refuses to work, he shall be condemned as a slave to the person who has denounced him as an idler. . . . If the slave is absent for a fortnight, he is condemned to slavery for life and is to be branded on forehead or back with the letter S; if he runs away three times, he is to be executed as a felon."[41] Second, an English law dated from 1572 likewise counseled: "Unlicensed beggars above 14 years of age are to be severely flogged and branded on the left ear unless someone will take them into service for two years; in case of a repetition of the offence, if they are over 18, they are to be executed, unless someone will take them into service for two years; but for the third offence they are to be executed without mercy as felons."[42] "Over and over," Cleaver writes, "we see how the key to capitalist colonial expansion, beyond the initial rape of local wealth, lay in its ability to separate labor from the land, and other means of production, and thus create a working class, both waged (working in the factories, on the plantations, etc.) and unwaged (working to reproduce itself as a reserve vis-à-vis the waged)."[43]

History illustrates that resistance was and remains ever-present in opposition to the expansion of capital. It is not by accident that Marx describes the history of capitalism as being "written in the annals of mankind in letters of blood and fire."[44] Indeed, as Marx writes, "the discovery of gold and silver in America, the extirpation, enslavement and entombment in mines of the indigenous population of that continent, the beginnings of the conquest and plunder of India, and the conversion of Africa into a preserve for the commercial hunting of black skins, are all things which characterize the dawn of the era of capitalist production. These idyllic proceedings are the chief moments of primitive accumulation."[45]

Central to the imposition of capitalism, therefore, is the requirement that the means of production come to be completely controlled by a ruling class, thereby excluding workers from subsistence production. However, the capitalist mode of production, Jason Read contends, "is founded on an abstract subjective potential, the indifferent capacity to do work, and it is this capacity that must be simultaneously produced and contained."[46] In other words, capital is exceptionally flexible in its quest for labor. This accounts both for the inherent disposability of labor within capitalism and for the ability of capital to seek out (indeed produce) surplus labor at a global level. Capitalist firms are footloose not simply because technological advances make the international division of labor possible. Equally important is that capitalism is able to substitute abstract labor in one location for abstract labor in another location. It makes little difference to the owner of a garment factory whether labor is hired in Cambodia or the Philippines. And if conditions warrant it, such as demands among its workers for better conditions or wages, the firm is always able to relocate in search of other sources of ever more exploitable labor.

In effect, on the one hand, capitalism must develop the flexibility, cooperative networks, and potentiality of the subjectivity of labor, while on the other hand, it must reduce the possibility of conflict and antagonism. This, according to Read, constitutes the "antagonistic logic of capital" in that "the assertion of the needs and desires of living labor and the demands of capitalist valorization continually impose themselves on each other."[47] A dialectic is established whereby the necessity of capitalist expansion through the exploitation of living labor interacts with the necessity of living laborers to satisfy their own conditions of survivability. As Andrea Fumagalli writes, "the transition from the formal to the real subsumption changes the relationship between labor-force and machines, or between living and dead labor, that is, between constant and variable capital."[48] But this transformation also imparts a change that quite literally marks the difference between living and dead laborers.

The real subsumption of society by capital therefore imparts a transformation of social relationships, including a transformation of the knowledges, desires, and practices constitutive of social relations.[49] This in turn is marked by a shift in the appearance of primitive accumulation and a transformation of violent practices. Marx writes that "the advance of capitalist production develops a working class which by education, tradition and habit looks upon the requirements of that mode of production as self-evidence natural laws," whereupon "the organization of the capitalist process of production, once it is fully developed, breaks down all resistance."[50] Marx elaborates: "The silent compulsion of economic relations sets the seal on the domination of the capitalist over the worker. Direct extra-economic force [i.e., direct violence] is still of course used, but only in exceptional cases."[51] Here Marx notably overstates his case, for it is simply not accurate that, within mature systems of capitalism, workers no longer resist. However, the historical transformation of social relations embedded in and stemming from practices of primitive accumulation does point toward a general transformation of violence.[52] This marks the moment whereby living laborers become dead laborers, not necessarily through direct violence, but through a systemic process of letting die.

The "need for an ever extended market," Marx writes, constitutes an "inner necessity" of the capitalist mode of production.[53] However, as John Foster and colleagues explain, this inner necessity "took on a new significance . . . with the rise of monopoly capitalism in the late nineteenth and early twentieth centuries." They elaborate: "The emergence of multinational corporations, first in the giant oil companies and a handful of other firms in the early twentieth century, and then becoming a much more general phenomenon in the post–Second World War years, was a product of the concentration and centralization of capital on a world scale; but equally involved the transformation of world labor and production."[54] Consequently, the previous decades have witnessed a global shift in employment: between 1980 and 2007, for example, the global labor force grew from 1.9 billion to 3.1 billion, a rise of 63 percent, and of this growth, 73 percent was located in the global south.[55] In turn, this has led to the disproportionate growth of a global reserve army of labor that absorbs between 57 and 63 percent of the global labor force, also located predominantly but by no means exclusively in the global south.[56] As Ferguson and McNally conclude, these trends constitute a "stunning increase in dispossession and proletarianization—and one that has been utterly crucial to the neoliberal reorganization of the capitalist world economy."[57]

Myriad factors have contributed to the rapidly growing oversupply of labor. On the one hand, the incorporation of China, India, and countries of the former Soviet Union into the global economy has dramatically increased the number of waged workers. As Richard Freeman describes, the entry of these countries into the global system of production and consumption from the 1980s onward effectively doubled the size of the world's workforce. However, he further notes that these additions, 1.47 billion workers, brought little capital with them. Consequently, the global labor market witnessed an overall decline in the capital–labor ratio that shifted the balance of power in markets away from wages paid to workers and toward capital, as more workers competed for working with that capital.[58]

Secondly, from the 1970s onward, as corporations within the global north replaced living labor with constant capital, a parallel response has been to increase the rate of exploitation through expansion of production activities in the global south. Here, the overall goal of capital's new course is enhanced profitability through greater flexibility on all fronts: to hire and fire workers, to obtain low-cost labor, to decrease worker and citizen benefits, to invest and market abroad, to repatriate profits, and to gain access to needed raw materials.[59] Delgado Wise explains that, "in the neoliberal era, the capitalist world system revolves around the monopolization of finance, production, services and trade" and that, "in expanding their operations, monopoly capitalism's agents have created a global network of production, finance, distribution, and investment that has allowed them to seize the strategic and profitable segments of peripheral economies and appropriate their economic surplus."[60]

The quest to find and exploit cheap labor has been crucial to these trends. Indeed, as Delgado Wise and David Martin show, a new form of imperial expansion has emerged in which multinational corporations are increasingly relocating their productive, commercial, and financial activities around the globe to take advantage of existent wage gaps. For example, in 2012, the average hourly compensation for manufacturing workers in the Philippines was just US$2.10, compared to wages in excess of US$35 in the United States or US$55 in Germany.[61] In is therefore little surprise that "leading U.S. multinationals, such as General Electric, Exxon, Chevron, Ford, General Motors, Proctor and Gamble, IBM, Hewlett Packard, United Technologies, Johnson and Johnson, Alcoa, Kraft, and Coca-Cola now employ more workers abroad than they do in the United States."[62] The result has been the increased proletarianization, often under precarious conditions, of much of the population of the global south.[63] In short: "Underdeveloped countries find themselves with massive population reserves, members of which are unable to find decent working conditions in their countries of origin for ensuring personal and family reproduction. This is the direct result of reduced accumulation processes derived from their asymmetrical relationship with developed nations."[64]

Consequently, international migration has acquired a new role in an era of neoliberal globalization.[65] Delgado Wise writes: "Mechanisms of unequal development produce structural conditions, such as unemployment and inequality, which catapult the massive migration of dispossessed and marginalized people. Compelled by the need to have access to means of subsistence or at least minimal opportunities for social mobility, large segments of the population are in practice expelled from their territories to relocate within their own country or abroad."[66] In short, patterns of contemporary migration are reflective of "a plundering, parasitic, rentier, and predatory phase of global capitalism."[67]

Thus, the construction and enforcement of political borders works in tandem with the management of human mobility. As Iosif Kovras and Simon Robins explain, the "most important innovation of the border is that it serves as a tool of inclusion ... but at the same time excludes the rest of humanity."[68] This imparts, in Saskia Sassen's particularly apt phrase, a "savage sorting" of men, women, and children into myriad bureaucratic boxes that greatly inform one's ability to live.[69] Crucially, a "range of specific labels is ascribed to living migrants, such as 'illegal,' 'undocumented,' 'minor,' and 'asylum seeker,' which drive policy approaches." These labels in turn have considerable material purchase.

Marie-Andrée Jacob details how documents generate "form-made persons."[70] On job applications or loan applications, college admission forms or driver's licenses, work-permits or passports, we exist within the rigid confines of predetermined *and legally binding* boxes. We become "male" or "female," "Caucasian" or "black," "citizen" or "refugee." And these so-called choices render us into manageable bodies.[71] As Jacob elaborates, while documents "answer the bureaucratic needs for efficiency and for comparability of documents," they also "make political subjects visible."[72] In turn, these subjects may more readily be "archived, classified, measured, compared, and controlled on a mass scale."[73] So-called undocumented migrants, for example, are constituted not in order to physically exclude them, but instead to socially include them under imposed conditions of enforced and protracted vulnerability.[74]

Sassen argues: "Migrations do not just happen; they are produced. And migrations do not involve just any possible combination, they are patterned."[75] By extension, the so-called migration crisis did not just happen randomly; rather, it is the end result of specific and multiple factors that have impelled or expelled people from their homes and livelihoods. Ongoing processes of accumulation by dispossession generate untold numbers of lives made vulnerable to premature death. Thus Delgado Wise and Humberto Márquez Covarrubias forward the argument that contemporary "migration" is best understood as forced displacement: "Given the massive oversupply of labor and the growing deterioration of living and working conditions for the bulk of the working class, migration . . . has become a necessity and not merely an option for family subsistence."[76] Migration-as-forced-displacement has four main characteristics: (1) these population movements take place primarily on a national and international level and move mainly from deprived peripheral regions toward relatively more advanced areas in peripheral or core economies; (2) they primarily affect the vulnerable poor and marginalized; (3) they generate an oversupply of cheap and disorganized labor, exploited by employers and corporations interested in keeping costs down; and (4) they fuel mechanisms of direct and indirect labor exportation among both low- and high-skilled workers.[77]

In the following section, I consider the political economy of premature death along the border between the United States and Mexico. Considerable research has been directed toward this topic and greatly informs my overall thesis.[78] Precisely, my intent is to critically interrogate those calculated, form-made bodies that become the object and target of governmental interference, those surplus populations that produce and are literally made to work in response to the uneven expansion of capitalism. In the United States, the history of labor migration, but especially the establishment and enforcement of the Mexico border, reveals the need to ensure a reliable yet flexible source of cheap labor. However, this history is also marked by increased "criminalization policies and practices, racialization, and race- and gender-based discrimination, which not only increases vulnerabilities and risk, but also often endangers life itself."[79] The repressive functioning of the global political economy, in short, provides a necessary context to understand the political economy of premature death among racialized and gendered populations on a planetary scale, since the criminalization of immigration is fundamental to the transformation of living laborers into dead laborers.

Death and Deportation along the United States–Mexico Border

The border between Mexico and the United States, Douglas Massey reminds us, is not just a line on a map.[80] Rather, "in the American imagination, it has become a symbolic boundary between the United States and a threatening world." The perception of its southern border as a last line of defense is not a static feature of American politics, but in recent years, calls especially among conservative politicians have increased in both vehemence and intensity. It has become *normal* for "politicians and pundits to call federal authorities to task for failing to 'hold the line' against a variety of alien invaders—communists, criminals, narcotics traffickers, rapists, terrorists, even microbes."[81] Moreover, the perceived failure of the federal government to stem the tide of this so-called foreign invasion has been marked by the rise of countless militia organizations and a rise in a violent form of vigilante justice. The hardening of the political divide between Mexico and the United States translates, therefore, into very real material conditions of people on both sides of the border.

The border with Mexico has a relatively short history. Following the Mexican–American War of 1846–48 and the signing of the Treaty of Guadalupe Hidalgo, the Mexican government ceded territories that would become California, Arizona, New Mexico, Nevada, Utah, Colorado, and parts of Wyoming and Oklahoma to the United States. Mexico likewise dropped all claims to Texas. In return, the United States' government paid a token US$15 million for what amounted to nearly half of Mexico's territory and three fourths of its natural resources.[82] The newly established border, however, was for the most part unregulated, and movement was largely unhindered.[83] In part, the porosity of the border was encouraged as a regional political economy took shape throughout the American Southwest. As Nicholas De Genova explains, mining, railroads, ranching, and agriculture relied extensively on the active recruitment of Mexican labor.[84] Indeed, during much of the latter half of the nineteenth century, both governments actively facilitated and encouraged the movement of workers across the border.[85] This is not to suggest, however, that the border was insignificant or unregulated. Rather, the relatively free movement of Mexican citizens stands apart from the gradual hardening of the border in the face of Chinese and, later, European workers.

Border management regimes are often explicitly or implicitly discriminatory, meting out different treatment to people based on nationality, "race" and ethnicity, gender, sex, and religion.[86] Beginning in 1875 with the Page Law, followed by the more restrictive 1882 Chinese Exclusion Act, laborers from China were increasingly prohibited from entering the United States, with enforcement falling on U.S. border officials, known as "Chinese inspectors." Within this context, Mexico became a conduit for smuggling Chinese workers into the United States, as demand for cheap labor remained. Furthermore, as U.S. immigration legislation prohibited more and more nationalities, the porosity of the Mexico border assumed ever greater importance. In 1921, Congress passed a temporary immigration act that represented the first quantitative immigration law based on national origin. The system was made permanent in 1924 with the passage of the Johnson-Reed Act. Heretofore, immigrants of any nationality were limited to just two percent of the 1890 population of that nationality, as counted by the U.S. census. The intent was to limit, if not entirely curtail, immigration from southern and eastern Europe. Consequently, a clandestine system to smuggle illegal Europeans through Mexico into the United States was established.

Economic transformations within Mexico, including the expansion of U.S. business interests, contributed to the growing movement of people. By 1920, for example, U.S. corporations controlled 80 percent of Mexico's railroads, 81 percent of its mining industry, and 61 percent of total investment in Mexico's oil fields.[87] Labor demands were met by drawing on a growing surplus population within Mexico, as the consolidation of the hacienda system displaced and dispossessed countless households from their traditional and communal system of land tenure.[88] By 1910, approximately 96 percent of all Mexican farming families were landless. These conditions continued throughout the twentieth century. Between 1940 and 1980, for example, 20 percent of Mexico's arable land was controlled by just two percent of the population; the remaining lands were distributed among a handful of subsistence farmers.[89] Denied access to land and livelihood, many Mexicans were impelled to look northward for employment opportunities. Indeed, from 1910 to 1930, approximately one tenth of Mexico's total population relocated north of the border.[90] And in the United States, a plethora of American business interests welcomed these landless workers. As a reserve army of labor, Mexican immigrants could be paid less than American (that is, "white") workers and could be leveraged strategically against unionized workers.[91]

In 1924, the U.S. Border Patrol was created and, as De Genova writes, it is not insignificant that the agency initially operated under the auspices of the Department of Labor.[92] A critical function of the Border Patrol was to curtail the inflow of "illegal" migrants from prohibited countries. With respect to migrant workers from Mexico, however, the policing of the border was more complex. On the one hand, for many U.S. employers, strict controls against Mexicans crossing the border were widely perceived as neither viable nor desirable.[93] As other supplies of migrant workers were barred, Mexican migrant labor became an indispensable necessity for capital accumulation.[94] The rapid expansion of agriculture throughout the American southwest, for example, necessitated larger numbers of workers, many of whom were recruited from Mexico. Hence, between 1901 and 1920, there were 268,646 Mexicans admitted into the United States.[95] On the other hand, a system was established whereby border enforcement coincided with the seasonable labor demand of U.S. employers, thereby instituting a "revolving door" policy whereby mass deportations would be concurrent with an overall, large-scale importation of Mexican migrant labor.[96] As De Genova concludes, "during this era, the regulatory and disciplinary role of deportation operated against Mexican migrants on the basis of rules and regulations governing who would be allowed to migrate, with what characteristics, how they did so, as well as how they conducted themselves once they had already entered the country."[97]

As a reserve army of labor, Mexican workers were increasingly viewed as expendable. As Patricia Zamudio writes, American corporations preferred to hire these workers via temporary employment contracts, a system that was intentionally flexible enough that Mexicans could be used in times of need and discarded during economic downturns.[98] During the Great Depression, for example, upward of half a million Mexicans were deported, including permanent residents and U.S. citizens of Mexican descent.[99] Indeed, it was during this period that "the more plainly racist character of Mexican illegalization and deportability became abundantly manifest."[100] As De Genova writes, "Mexican migrants and US-born Mexican citizens alike were systematically excluded from employment and economic relief, which was declared the exclusive preserve of 'Americans,' who were presumed to be more 'deserving.'"[101]

America's entry into the Second World War precipitated a significant change in U.S. policy concerning the Mexico border vis-à-vis labor. In 1942, a mass labor importation program known as the Bracero Program was institutionalized as an administrative measure to regiment the supply of Mexican migrant labor for American capitalism.[102] Under the purview of the U.S. Department of Agriculture, the Bracero Program codified the precarity of waged employment within the United States. As Ronald Mize explains, the threat of deportation was usually enough for workers to conform to grower expectations.[103] Indeed, living with the fear of immediate removal, migrant workers would engage in practices of self-policing. As De Genova concludes, "this legalized importation of Mexican labor meant that migrant workers, once contracted, essentially became a captive workforce under the jurisdiction of the U.S. federal government, and thus, a guarantee to US employers of unlimited 'cheap' labor."[104]

Throughout the life of the Bracero Program (1942–64), approximately five million temporary labor contracts were issued to Mexican citizens.[105] However, the demand for braceros surpassed the number legally allowed by the program. Equally important, however, is that U.S. employers often preferred to hire undocumented workers. As De Genova explains, "employers could evade the bond and contracting fees, minimum employment periods, fixed wages and other safeguards required in employing braceros."[106] In turn, to facilitate the every-growing demand for cheap labor, the U.S. government initiated numerous programs that would "legalize" these workers, thereby guaranteeing ready access to a pliable workforce that ebbed and flowed according to the changing tides of U.S. politics.[107]

The Bracero Program epitomized the Janus-faced approach to American immigration policy. While permitting both legal and undocumented workers into the United States, the U.S. government simultaneously launched a massive deportation campaign known as Operation Wetback. Vocal segments of American society, most notably labor unions, charged Mexican workers with depressing wages and displacing "American" workers. Consequently, U.S. authorities apprehended and deported over one million undocumented Mexican workers.[108] And yet, "as early as 1949, US employers and labor recruiters were assisted with instantaneous legalization procedures for undocumented workers, known as 'drying out wetbacks.'"[109] In effect, the "apparent contradictions of immigration policies surrounding the recruitment and deportation of Mexican workers demonstrate how immigration policy became embedded in formally regulating labor supply in the interests of US employers."[110]

The Bracero Program was officially terminated in 1964. However, as Zamudio explains, the legacy of the program remains especially virulent. During the life of the program, for example, Mexican migrants gained invaluable knowledge about border crossings and how to acquire jobs, key social networks and organizations were established to facilitate cross-border movements, and consequently, a significant movement of undocumented workers developed.[111] Furthermore, the "illegal" nature of the post–Bracero Program movement benefitted both U.S. employers and the federal government. On the one hand, employers capitalized on the undocumented status of Mexican workers. Lacking legal protection, undocumented laborers were less likely to organize or to complain about low wages or poor working conditions. On the other hand, the federal government was no longer seen as being complicit in a work program that supposedly "stole" American jobs.[112]

The official cessation of the Bracero Program was followed immediately with the establishment of the Border Industrialization Program. In 1965, the Mexican state focused development along its northern border, both to promote industrialization and to abate the high unemployment in the region, resulting in part from the termination of the Bracero Program.[113] Broadly stated, Mexico adopted a macroeconomic policy aimed at favoring, almost exclusively, the growth of the export sector.[114] In part, this was predicated upon Mexico's own precarity within the global economy. Beset with a balance of payment deficit and mounting debt, the

Mexican government was subject to heightened intervention by external institutions, such as the International Monetary Fund and the World Bank. Citing both the "South Korean miracle" and the "Brazilian miracle," officials of these agencies concluded that economic growth could materialize only through a strategy of export-oriented industrialization.

U.S. manufacturers were encouraged to move their factories south across the 2,000-mile-long border to take advantage of lower wage rates, tax exemptions, inexpensive energy, and restrictions against union formation and strikes. Concurrently, Mexican federal subsidies were used to provide necessary infrastructure, including state-of-the-art industrial parks, roads, and sewage systems.[115] Foremost among U.S. business calculations was the reduction in labor costs. For example, shifting capital to Mexico enabled U.S. firms to purchase labor at as low as nine percent of the cost in the United States.[116] Within a matter of years, Mexico's northern border emerged as a leading site for export-processing industrialization, as U.S. firms such as General Electric, RCA, Zenith, and General Motors relocated their machinery, infrastructure, technology, and design and organization schemes to northern Mexico in order to take advantage of cheap labor and other fiscal incentives.[117] By 1979, nearly 500 maquilas (assembly plants) were in operation, employing upward of 100,000 (mostly female) workers.[118]

The asymmetric regional economy intensified throughout the last quarter of the twentieth century as the United States began promoting neoliberal structural adjustment policies in Mexico, based on privatization, deregulation, and liberalization strategies.[119] Foremost was the passage of the North American Free Trade Agreement (NAFTA). Signed in 1994 by the United States, Mexico, and Canada, NAFTA was intended to simultaneously open the border to the flow of capital goods and close the border to illicit goods—including commodified but undocumented workers. As Joseph Nevins explains, the paradox of an open *and* closed border reflected the belief among U.S. officials that the "implementation of stronger immigrant enforcement measures and the development of a relatively barrier-free boundary to goods and capital would lead to greater levels of prosperity for people on both sides of the boundary."[120] As is often the case, reality does not necessarily live up to rhetoric. Throughout Mexico, neoliberal policies have contributed to widespread dispossession and displacement.

Overall, the export-led model of economic growth has demonstrated a low capacity to create employment within the formal sector; indeed, the informal labor market has accounted for approximately half of the growth in employment in recent years.[121] Delgado Wise summarizes well: "[The] export orientation of the Mexican economy demands certain macroeconomic conditions that are obtained by squeezing internal accumulation: in particular, reduced public investment expenditure, the state's withdrawal from strictly productive activities, privatizations, budget deficit controls, and interest rates that are attractive to foreign capital but that, in contrast, depress domestic activity within the economy. This further heightens social inequalities and generates an ever-growing mass of workers who cannot find a place within the country's formal labor market."[122] Moreover, NAFTA guaranteed that the Mexican government would not interfere with the activities of foreign corporations operating in Mexico and the agreement contained no binding protection for unions, wages, or displaced workers.[123]

The consequences of unequal trade agreements were predictably devastating, as "free trade" zones and increased trade with the United States undermined Mexico's manufacturing and agricultural sectors, displacing many workers and farmers and promoting domestic inequality.[124] In the industrial sector, approximately 40 percent of Mexico's clothing manufacturing went out of business, unable to compete with foreign corporations that were able to import cheaper fabrics from Asia. Other industries, such as toy and footware manufacturers, were also adversely affected. Overall, an estimated one million jobs were lost in Mexico as a result of NAFTA.[125] Likewise, in the agricultural sector, millions of small farmers have been displaced, as trade liberalization and imports from American-dominated agribusinesses undercut local producers. Indeed, within a decade, over 1.3 million small farmers in Mexico were forced into bankruptcy.[126] In turn, large numbers of dispossessed agrarian producers have moved both within and beyond Mexico in search of employment.[127]

Regional integration in the form of neoliberal economic policies has contributed to vast inequalities throughout society. On the one hand, between the early 1980s and the turn of the twenty-first century, purchasing power for most wage earners in Mexico declined by 75 percent and conditions for those in the informal sector were proportionately worse.[128] Accordingly, during this period, the number of households registering at either the poverty level or the extreme poverty level rose from just under approximately 13 million to approximately 16 million.[129] In short, the growing numbers of urban poor have been hit particularly hard by shrinking wages, growing unemployment, stagnation in the level of formal employment, and decreasing public funding for social expenditure and subsidies previously aimed at basic foodstuffs and urban services.[130] On the other hand, what economic growth did occur was disproportionately concentrated into the hands of a few. For example, the richest 10 percent earned 55 percent more in real terms in 1992 than in 1977, while concurrently, the bottom 40 percent of Mexico's population experienced a loss in real income over this same period.[131]

As Ferguson and McNally explain, a "central feature of the neoliberal era has been the *globalization of primitive accumulation*" whereby "unrelenting, large-scale processes of dispossession have dramatically swelled the size of the global labor reserve, while also rendering it more international than ever before."[132] In other words, the historical production and reproduction of processes of displacement and dispossession, manifest in myriad forms, is an enduring feature, but a feature that has been augmented in recent years by neoliberal policies. Consequently, far from creating a free trade pattern that benefits both nations, regional integration has resulted in new relations of production that involve an unequal system of exchange in which Mexico has become a specialized provider of surplus labor, whether in the form of maquiladoras or that of migrant workers.[133] Consequently, upward of 90 percent of the annual new entrants to Mexico's labor market was confronted with two options: to work in the informal sector or to migrate to the United States.[134] The wage gap between Mexico and the United States, coupled with continued demand among U.S. employers, made the second option decidedly more attractive, as precarious employment conditions and declining wage levels throughout Mexico made migration to the U.S. an ever more viable alternative.[135] Thus, as Delgado Wise and Márquez Covarrubias conclude, the present dynamics of Mexican migration into the United States must be viewed as "a response to the productive internationalization strategy employed by the large USA corporations, which is linked to the transnationalization and precaritization of labor markets brought about by neoliberal policies of structural adjustment."[136]

Regional economic policies and the resultant dispossession and displacement of Mexican workers have also negatively affected the condition of workers in the United States. For example, as U.S. corporations were transferring their manufacturing operations to northern Mexico and other offshore locations to take advantage of lower labor costs and greater tax breaks, American labor markets were devastated. In cities such as Pittsburg, Buffalo, Akron, Cleveland, and Detroit, companies closed factories or otherwise fired or relocated workers. Barry Bluestone and Bennett Harrison estimate that between 32 and 38 million jobs were lost during the 1970s as the direct result of private disinvestment in American manufacturing.[137] NAFTA compounded these woes: between 1995 and 2005, U.S. manufacturing jobs decreased by 17 percent, from 17.1 million to 14.2 million. Consequently, the impact of capital shifting to Mexico, Delgado Wise and James Cypher write, fell on the U.S. labor force, particularly organized labor.

The migration "crisis" associated with the Mexico border is not a crisis of unregulated flows. Rather, it is precisely the regulation of a precarious surplus population that is at issue. As Delgado Wise and Márquez Covarrubias write, "what matters is that this dynamic and the qualitative changes that accompany it are linked to the role played by Mexican workers, who act as a reserve and source of cheap labor to be employed by the US economy."[138] To this end, Delgado Wise and Márquez Covarrubias call attention to the transnational precaritization of labor on a binational level: "[The] productive restructuring led by the US economy has propitiated the reassignment, or spatial and sectoral redistribution, of the labor force."[139] Nicola Phillips develops this theme well, arguing that "the particular form of accumulation by dispossession associated with migration processes is enacted through a dual mechanism by which the labor force is disciplined by the increased and sustained favoring of migrant labor."[140]

The first part of the equation, Phillips writes, relates to the disciplining of migrants themselves. Often denied legal and civil rights, migrant workers, including both authorized and unauthorized migrants, constitute a highly vulnerable population subject to a repressive police apparatus that operates according to the dictates of capital accumulation. Migrant workers, but especially undocumented workers, are often confined to those occupations considered dirty, demeaning, and dangerous; they often endure poor working environments and receive low wages and few, if any, benefits. Moreover, their lives are conditioned by an overriding political vulnerability, the end result being a docile, pliant workforce that is less likely to demand, either individually or collectively, better conditions. The second part of the equation relates to the effect of migrant labor in disciplining domestic workers in the United States. On the one hand, "shifting production to Mexico made credible the threat of further production transfers, thereby weakening all U.S. labor and particularly organized labor."[141] On the other hand, the influx of Mexican workers has had an adverse effect on wage increases in the United States. Measured in constant 2000 prices, the minimum wage in the United States fell by 38 percent between the 1970s to the turn of the twenty-first century, from US$11.70 to US$7.20 per hour.[142]

In receiving countries such as the United States, the use of migrant labor constitutes a strategy of maintaining high levels of profitability. Unlike investitures in constant capital, firms utilize hyperprecarious populations to reduce labor costs, and in this way, greater levels of absolute and relative surplus value are accrued through the hyperexploitation of workers, and thus firms are able to enjoy higher rates of profit. Instead of replacing living labor with dead labor (e.g., machines and robots), living labor is replaced with other laborers more susceptible to premature death. This premature death materializes in the form of dangerous migratory journeys, oppressive working conditions, and wages often far below the legal minimum wages stipulated in the destination society.

Racialized discourses occlude the intentional porosity of international borders such as that between the United States and Mexico. That border, as Mathew Coleman explains, is often portrayed as "an unruly landscape of uncontrolled migration."[143] Such a political representation is necessary in order to "affect the state's ability to protect industry and to ensure its own political legitimacy."[144] As noted, since its inception, the Mexico border has served to regulate labor in a way that has facilitated the accumulation of capital for American business interests. But this regulation is always a delicate political-economic balance.[145] Since the 1970s, "undocumented migration, and Mexican migration in particular, has been rendered synonymous with the U.S. nation-state's purported 'loss of control' of its borders and has supplied the pretext for what has in fact been a continuous intensification of militarized control on the U.S.-Mexico border."[146] Border enforcement policies of the United States are rhetorically crafted around "national security." This discourse, however, masks the underlying function of the border: the regulation of surplus labor according to the demands of capital accumulation.

The conditions of labor supply and demand, Massey writes, did not change following the cessation of the Bracero Program. Consequently, neither did the broad coordinates of mobility between the United States and Mexico cease. Indeed, "by the late 1950s a massive circular flow of Mexican migrants had become deeply embedded in employer practices and migrant expectations and had come to be sustained by well-developed and widely accessible migrant networks."[147] Thus, once opportunities for legal entry were terminated, migrant farmworkers continued under undocumented auspices.[148] Accordingly, patterns of migration were remarkably similar to those that existed prior to the termination of the Bracero Program. As Douglas Massey and Karen Pren conclude, "illegal migration rose after 1965 not because there was a sudden surge in Mexican migration, but because the temporary labor program had been terminated and the number of permanent resident visas had been capped, leaving no legal way to accommodate the long-established flows."[149]

The termination of a legal migrant-labor program and the subsequent increase in undocumented workers coincided with the broader deindustrialization of the U.S. economy. Bluestone and Harrison estimate that somewhere between 32 and 38 million jobs were lost during the 1970s as the direct result of private disinvestment in American businesses.[150] That these economic hardships occurred during a period of profound social change should not go unmentioned. For moral conservatives, the social movements of the 1950s and 1960s were held accountable for a perceived breakdown of society. Both conservative politicians and pundits feared and decried divorce, abortion, homosexuality, drugs, sexual promiscuity, and civil and women's rights. It is within this context that the "Latino threat" narrative made its appearance.[151]

Increasingly, conservatives blame undocumented workers from Mexico for America's purported economic and social decline. As Susan Fiske explains, feeling individually deprived may alert a person to feeling collectively deprived, and this collective feeling in turn contributes to the blaming of out-groups for all that is wrong.[152] For example, "perceived threat to in-group economic status correlates with worldviews that reinforce a zero-sum, dog-eat-dog perspective" and "economic conservatism results."[153] In turn, this leads to the rise of extremist attitudes and the endorsement of right-wing authoritarian views.[154] Rhetorically, much of this angst is directed toward Mexicans. Since the majority of these migrants were now "illegal," and thus "criminal," a new opening for politicians opened up to cultivate a politics of fear, framing Latino immigration as a grave threat to the nation.[155]

Beginning in the 1970s, U.S. administrations supported an increasingly militarized and defensive southern border, as the presidential administrations of Gerald Ford and Jimmy Carter introduced new technologies to purportedly halt the influx of undocumented migration from Mexico and other Central American states. These efforts intensified, albeit selectively, under the presidency of Ronald Reagan. Motivated by fears of uncontrolled migration, purported medical risks, and fiscal burdens, in 1986, Congress passed the Immigration and Reform Control Act (IRCA), a legislative maneuver that ostensibly would "close the border to undocumented migration and eradicate the underground worker economy."[156] Materially, IRCA imposed employer sanctions, provided amnesty programs, and increased monies for detention facilities, ground and aerial surveillance hardware, fencing, roads, and border policing practices.[157] In practice, as Gilberto Rosa writes, Latinos, all too often regardless of their citizenship, and other brown bodies, became suspect. He concludes, "these dynamics articulate a 'dark' legacy of the IRCA, namely a collapsing of certain racial and criminalising anxieties that infiltrate policy and post-IRCA immigrant policing practices."[158]

Paradoxically, anti-immigrant sentiment continued to increase, although the actual number of entries, either documented or undocumented, did not rise appreciably. Rather, as Massey and Pren find, "the rise of illegal migration, its framing as a threat to the nation, and the resulting conservative reaction set off a self-feeding chain reaction of enforcement that generated more apprehensions even though the flow of undocumented migrants had stabilized in the late 1970s and actually dropped during the late 1980s and early 1990s."[159] Rhetoric, however, is often more powerful than reality, as U.S. officials used the Latino-threat narrative to justify ever more border enforcement strategies. Throughout the 1990s and into the twenty-first century, U.S. officials initiated a series of military-styled border enforcement policies. The first was Operation Gatekeeper, launched in 1994 as a means of securing a sixty-six-mile stretch along the California–Mexico border. Operation Gatekeeper, which would later be expanded into Yuma, Arizona, was followed by other border enforcement campaigns, including Operation Safeguard

(Nogales, Arizona), Operation Hold the Line (initially in Texas, later expanded into New Mexico), and Operation Rio Grande (also in Texas). Combined, these military-based operations constitute the centerpiece of a broader strategy to supposedly secure and regulate the border. Consequently, the border has become a highly militarized landscape. All manner of high-tech surveillance equipment has been installed, including underground heat sensors, infrared night scopes, encrypted radios, computerized fingerprinting equipment, and Black Hawk helicopters, and hundreds upon hundreds of miles of steel and concrete fences have been erected.

Contemporary border-management doctrine along the political divide between the United States and Mexico is marked by a strategy of prevention through deterrence.[160] By disrupting traditional routes and methods of clandestine entry, the intensified border-control campaign has transformed the relatively simple act of border crossing into a more complex system of dangerous, criminal practices.[161] Border crossings have shifted away from relatively benign, often urban, locations and toward remote areas that render the journey less appealing, more dangerous, and ultimately, more lethal.[162] In other words, border-control policies have produced the violent conditions that intensify the vulnerability of men, women, and children, thus augmenting risks of premature death. As Jeremy Slack and colleagues write, "border enforcement strategy has centered on the development of a militarized logic and a strategic plan for enforcement that emphasizes pain, suffering, and trauma as deterrents to undocumented migration."[163] Such a strategy, however, is not intended to eliminate all border crossings. Men, women, and children (indeed, entire families) continue to cross the border, but largely out of sight of the general public, thereby giving the impression that the U.S. government is actively working to prevent the unauthorized in-migration of workers. In actuality, between 2000 and 2008, the number of undocumented migrants in the United States is thought to have increased by 40 percent, from an estimated 8.4 million to 11.9 million people.[164] A key outcome of a doctrine of prevention through deterrence has not been a decrease in undocumented migration, but rather an increased loss of human lives. [165] Indeed, the number of migrants dying from dehydration, heat stroke, hypothermia, and drowning has increased sharply since 1995.[166] As Maria Jimenez writes, death accompanies migrants with every new path carved

in isolated, inhospitable terrain in order to circumvent stepped-up resources and fencing around population centers.[167] In effect, U.S. immigration policy has contributed to what Nevins describes as a "shifting
geography of migrant fatalities."[168] Moreover, such a strategy constitutes
also a vital form of labor regulation, in that the very real possibilities of
potential laborers dying introduces a more brutal form of disciplinary
control that extends beyond the lethality of the actual border crossing.
It is important, therefore, to recognize that the "increasingly militarized
border does not actually achieve its purported objective of reducing migration into the USA," but it does contribute to increased productivity
among the migrant workforce.[169]

As Massey and Pren write, not only did the massive enforcement effort
fail to prevent the entry of unauthorized persons, it actually accelerated
the net inflow in an unanticipated way. They explain that migration from
Mexico during the Bracero Program and into the 1970s was predominantly circular. Even "permanent residents" tended to circulate back and
forth.[170] The militarized border enforcement strategies radically altered
these dynamics. Hence, as "the costs and risks of unauthorized border
crossing mounted, migrants minimized them by shifting from a circular
to a settled pattern of migration, essentially hunkering down and staying
once they had successfully run the gauntlet at the border."[171]

The doctrine of prevention through deterrence, coupled with broader
national economic policies, has effectively captured a highly vulnerable
surplus population within the legal and territorial confines of the United
States. Ferguson and McNally hit the nail on the head. Neoliberal globalization, they argue, has "promoted continental flows of both capital
and labor, one liberalized and the other punitively policy."[172] They elaborate that "the deliberate thrust of US immigration policy in the NAFTA
era has been to simultaneously criminalize border crossings by Mexican
workers while methodically increasing the unemployment of unauthorized Mexican labor—and thereby to construct what has rightly been
called a *crimmigration* system."[173]

Yolanda Vázquez explains that, in immigration law, a noncitizen is defined as an "alien." And while this term has acquired a pejorative meaning, it refers legally to a condition in which noncitizens are afforded fewer
protections than U.S. citizens. In essence, noncitizens are "on probation"
and may either be granted full membership (citizenship) or be physically

removed from the community.[174] Historically, in the United States, the term "illegal alien" was used to describe individuals who entered without inspection or without documentation.[175] As noted above, however, following the termination of the Bracero Program and coincident with economic, political, and social shifts during the 1970s, the terminology mutated even as unauthorized migration was encouraged. Specifically, "American politics and societal attitudes began to see the increasing numbers of unauthorized Latinos as a serious threat to American norms and values, refusing to construct Latinos as "desirable" candidates for membership in U.S. society."[176] Migrants, but especially unauthorized persons from Central and South America, have increasingly been portrayed as criminals, rapists, drug traffickers, and terrorists and subject to immediate arrest, detention, and deportation. And yet, as De Genova explains, "migrants subjected to detention, very commonly, are literally 'guilty' of nothing other than their 'unauthorized' (illegalized) status, penalized simply for being who and what they are, and not at all for any act of wrong-doing."[177]

Robert Castro writes of a "language of illegality."[178] He argues that the ascription of legality onto migrants brands them as "criminal," and thus subject to exclusion, detainment, and deportation. Consequently, a language of illegality shifts the narrative from a labor struggle to a law-enforcement problem. Material solutions (as detailed below) are thus more often than not predicated on a repressive state apparatus, rather than on the transformation of structural conditions that precipitate border crossings. Media attention is turned away from unequal economic relations, as manifest for example in NAFTA, that underscore the movement of people from Mexico (and other Central American states) to the United States. Indeed, this linguistic slight of hand obfuscates the historical recruitment and hiring of workers, as well as the fact that American farms and businesses have long encouraged (and continue to encourage) both documented and undocumented workers. Indeed, enforcement is premised, as Nicole Trujillo-Pagán writes, on immigration policies that expand the definition of "illegality" in ways that simultaneously subordinate labor and promote capital.[179] So-called "illegal aliens," Vázquez explains, constitute "a large percentage of the work force in janitorial service, construction clean-up, agriculture, and other low-skilled and minimum-wage jobs" and yet continue to be accused "of 'stealing' jobs from hard working Americans, contributing to the decline of the economy, lowering wages, and, contradictorily, emptying the coffers of the federal and state treasuries in their attempt to receive social services and public benefits."[180]

The criminalization of migrants has wide-reaching consequences. Once one is labeled as illegal, all other features of one's identity disappear, subsumed by a singular, hegemonic descriptor. Once established, the mis-descriptor serves a semiotic function in which the initial label (i.e., "undocumented" or "illegal") signifies other (usually more degrading) attributes. Thus, the status of "illegal" becomes a sign for other forms of illegality and illicit activity: as rapists, as murderers, as pedophiles. The danger, Bridget Hayden warns, is that such a linguistic move begins to exclude the undocumented from the category of "human being."[181] The undocumented person no longer appears as a father or mother, brother or sister, son or daughter; the "undocumented" becomes an aberration, an outsider—no longer a person. They are dehumanized, reduced to bare life, subject to a social death that may ultimately culminate in actual death. Indeed, coupled with the militarization of the border and a broader militarized society, undocumented migrants are transformed into enemy combatants, their deaths dismissed as collateral damage.[182]

"The legal production of 'illegality,'" De Genova writes, "provides an apparatus for sustaining Mexican migrants' vulnerability and tractability—as workers—whose labor-power, inasmuch as it is deportable, becomes an eminently disposable commodity."[183] And as a disposable commodity, undocumented workers are especially vulnerable to premature death. As Ruth Campbell and colleagues summarize, in the United States, undocumented immigrants are considered to be a vulnerable population at higher risk of disease and injury than documented immigrants, refugees, and native citizens. On the one hand, undocumented persons frequently arrive bearing a disproportionate burden of undiagnosed illness and commonly lack standard immunizations and other basic preventive care, and on the other hand, they often enter the country under adverse circumstances and live in substandard conditions, factors that exacerbate poor health.[184] As Montserrat Gea-Sánchez and colleagues explain, despite international laws, policies and institutions that state that health is a fundamental human right, in practice, there are several barriers, especially in the United States, that limit health-care access to undocumented migrants, mainly resulting from the context of migration associated with situations of greater social vulnerability.[185] Paramount among these conditions is the threat of deportation, "a means to intensify the profound vulnerability of workers who live with the knowledge that they are inherently deportable."[186]

As Marcel Paret writes, the day-to-day experience of so-called illegality consists of a number of exclusions, from denied access to public spaces and services to the absence of various legal protections. However, Paret further notes that the most important effect is perhaps the perpetual possibility of deportation. For, even if the undocumented migrant is never deported, he or she must live and work under the surveillance of immigration officials and the threat of removal.[187] Essentially, as Ferguson and McNally note, "the purpose of inhumane and punitive border enforcement is not principally to deport undocumented workers, but to deepen their condition of *deportability.*"[188] In this way, the threat of deportation "can be wielded to repress migrant workers without necessarily compromising their ability to labor."[189]

The United States has a long and notorious history of deportation. What is distinct about contemporary patterns and practices is the increasing conflation of criminal law and immigration law. Most notably, since the creation of the aggravated-felony provision in the Immigration and Nationality Act, myriad shifts in immigration legislation and enforcement have expanded the criminal grounds for deportation and limited the scope of judicial review.[190] As Ruth Gomberg-Muñoz explains, until recently, "illegal entry and reentry had largely been treated as civil violations—offenses that could result in deportation (though frequently migrants were 'repatriated' with no formal order of removal), but not typically in criminal convictions."[191] As Alissa Ackerman and Rich Furman elaborate, according to federal law, the crossing of the U.S. border and entering without proper documentation is an administrative violation, in the same category of offense as, for example, filing taxes late.[192] However, this changed within the U.S. justice system as illegal entry began to be prosecuted as a criminal misdemeanor and illegal reentry as a felony, both with mandatory prison sentences prior to deportation.[193]

Immigration law reform "significantly enlarged the category of crimes which could count as aggravated felonies—a specific class of crimes committed by non-citizens, applicable only in the context of immigration law, and warranting deportation."[194] Coleman neatly summarizes these changes: individuals could be identified as deportable aggravated felons without an explicit conviction for an aggravated felony; convictions both postponed and suspended by the courts were to count as grounds for deportation; aggravated felony charges could be applied retroactively without limit; convictions would entail a permanent bar on reentry to the United States; mandatory and indefinite incarceration for those charged and awaiting deportation were imposed; and lengthy jail terms for aggravated felons caught reentering the United States were also codified.[195]

As a matter of practice, the aggravated felonies of which noncitizens are increasingly arrested, detained, and deported are neither felonies nor aggravated in the commonly understood senses of the words.[196] Rhetorically, though, changes in immigration legislation and enforcement are presented as part of a broader effort to secure the Mexico border by preventing from entry, or removing, dangerous felons and convicts. Indeed, throughout the presidential campaign of Donald Trump, anti-immigrant fervor was stoked by repeated references to Mexican gang members, drug dealers, rapists and other nondescript criminals. In reality, the vast majority of deportations did not involve criminal elements as represented in anti-immigrant discourse. In 2015, for example 235,413 men, women, and children were deported from the United States. Of these, 41 percent were removed for immigration violations, such as overstaying a visa. But what of the remaining 59 percent? Technically, these persons were convicted criminals.[197] And yet, the majority were deported for minor offenses: traffic offenses, bribery, counterfeiting, gambling offenses, petty larceny. The point is not to minimize the importance of these crimes; it is to emphasize the disconnect between political rhetoric and the economic reality of expanded immigration enforcement.

The growth of "crimmigration" practices, scholars note, has resulted in an economic windfall to private prison corporations. As of 2014, for example, the United States was home to approximately 250 immigration detention facilities, more than triple the number in 1996.[198] The vast majority of these detention centers are privately owned by either the Corrections Corporation of American (CCA) or the GEO Group. Profits resultant from the apprehension and detainment of unauthorized persons arise in two main forms. On the one hand, the simple warehousing of men, women, and children awaiting deportation translates into obscene profits. Since it began operations in 1983, for example, CCA has grown exponentially, housing over 75,000 inmates in over 60 facilities and recording a net worth of approximately US$1.4 billion.[199] This growth has been strategic, resulting not from any increase in criminal activities on behalf of noncitizens, but because of a symbiotic relationship between the U.S. Congress, the criminal justice system, lobbying groups, and private corporations. As Gomberg-Muñoz writes, "private corporations spend tens of millions of dollars on political lobbying and have been major campaign contributors to immigration hard-liners."[200] In turn, corporate giants such as CCA have secured lucrative contracts with: the Federal Bureau of Prisons; the U.S. Marshals Service; Immigration, Customs, and Enforcement; and countless U.S. state and local municipalities.[201] Congress, for its part, mandated that 34,000 people be kept in immigration detention, including children, every day.[202] On the other hand, profits result from the "leasing" on inmate labor. Thus, as localized labor shortages emerge, especially in the agricultural sector, following the arrest and detainment of undocumented workers, growers have sought to utilize prison labor. Ironically, as Gomberg-Muñoz finds, as increasing numbers of migrants are imprisoned because of a lack of documentation, they may end up doing the same work they performed as undocumented workers—only now as prison inmates with even fewer rights and for even lower wages.[203]

The extensive militarization of the Mexico border, a doctrine of deterrence, a language of illegality, the threat and actual practice of deportation, and the profitability of detainment all coalesce into a political economy of premature death that affects primarily, but not exclusively, surplus populations who exist in the form of undocumented workers. It is necessary to understand that nativist and populist rhetoric of security obfuscates the realities of labor mobility. To use Josiah Heyman's word, the legal vulnerability of undocumented workers renders them "super-exploitable."[204] For Trujillo-Pagán, the legal production of illegality and the related threat of detention and deportation ensure a ready supply of exploitable and disposable workers.[205] These workers, in turn, frequently live in substandard conditions, are confined to dilapidated and segregated neighborhoods, receive pitifully low wages, and have limited access to health services.[206] The accumulated stresses of economic hardships coupled with the fear of deportation contribute to a precarious existence that renders these people and their families every more vulnerable to illness, injury, and death. Ultimately, undocumented workers make up a symbolically dead surplus labor population that is disproportionately subject to premature death, as structural and institutional factors "reinforce deeply racialized forms of precarity under which migrant laborers comprise a 'permanent labor force of the temporarily employed.'"[207]

Conclusions

Whether the wording used to characterize such life is "bare life," "wasted lives," "humans-as-waste," "abandoned lives," "disposable lives," "precarious lives," or any of the other myriad terms currently being introduced, what is meant is that some populations are legally relegated to the realm of surplus and, thus, rendered expendable. Marx identifies a mechanism intrinsic to capitalism that transforms people into surplus populations: "a mass of human material always ready for exploitation by capital in the interests of capital's own changing valorization requirements."[208] In turn, these living laborers are rendered ever more vulnerable to premature death. Our current rendition of neoliberal capitalism is "characterized, at the top of the world system, by the domination of monopoly-finance capital, and, and the bottom, by the emergence of a massive global reserve army of labor," and "the result of this immense polarization is an augmentation of the 'imperialist rent' extracted from the South through the integration of low-wage, highly exploited workers into capitalist production."[209] The mobility of capital to so-called peripheral locations, such as Mexico's border region with the United States, ensures that absolute and relative surplus value is made not necessarily through the exploitation of workers in the global north, but instead via the hyperexploitation of displaced and dispossessed surplus populations in the global south. Within this context, the deliberate use of dispossessed and displaced surplus labor from the global south, but especially of undocumented labor, constitutes a strategy of maintaining high levels of profitability within the global north. Rather than invest in constant capital, firms and corporations utilize hyperprecarious populations to reduce labor costs. In this way, greater levels of absolute and relative surplus value are accrued through the superexploitation of workers. Instead of replacing living labor with dead labor (constant capital), living labor is replaced with

expendable, surplus laborers who are even more susceptible to premature death. This premature death materializes in the form of dangerous
migratory journeys, oppressive working conditions, below-minimum
wages, debt bondage, and inadequate access to shelter, nutritious meals,
and health care. However, if the new imperialism has its basis in the superexploitation of workers in the global south, it is also a phase of imperialism that in no way benefits the workers of the global north, whose
conditions are also being dragged down.[210]

Historically, it is understood that "a reserve army makes an extensive
welfare system necessary."[211] It was realized by early capitalists, Robert
Albritton reminds us, that capitalism passes through cycles and that
workers who die off now may be needed in the future when capital is
more expansive.[212] As Fred and Harry Magdoff explain, "because workers have only one way to live under capitalism—by selling their labor
power—a reserve army necessitates some mechanisms for maintaining the unemployed and those earning poverty wages in a state in
which they are available and ready to work when capital fails."[213] Consequently, various forms of state interventions (i.e., "safety nets") were
introduced, including state-supported retirement benefits, health benefits, and minimum wages, to maintain a indispensable supply of labor
held in reserve. Collectively, these forms of welfare contributed to the
de-commodification of labor power, a necessary concession to labor, so
that capital could ensure that prolonged and widespread labor shortages
would not occur.[214] And yet, the mobility and disposability of the hyper-
vulnerable temper the need to maintain even the most basic conditions
necessary for survival. On this point, capital remains indifferent to the
social reproduction of living laborers. It matters little whether workers
are home-grown, so to speak, or brought in as surplus workers from afar.
In this way, the hyperexploitation of a global surplus population enables
capital to recommodify local labor markets through recurrent attacks on
welfare. The increased vulnerability and precarity of commodified laborers in the global north is conditional upon the increased exploitation and
oppression of displaced and dispossessed laborers from the global south.

4. REDUNDANT LABOR

In writing of "redundancy" in contemporary society, Zygmunt Bauman explains: "[Redundancy] whispers permanence and hints at the ordinariness of the condition. It names a condition without offering a ready-to-use antonym. It suggests a new shape of current normality and the shape of things that are imminent and bound to stay as they are. . . . To be 'redundant' means to be supernumerary, unneeded, of no use—whatever the needs and uses are that set the standard of usefulness and indispensability. . . . To be declared redundant means to have been disposed of—just like the empty and non-refundable plastic bottle or once-used syringe."[1]

Redundancy suggests, but is not reducible to, excess or waste. Some waste products, for example, are repurposed into particular use values and, by extension, afforded exchange value. Similarly, redundant populations are not necessarily disposable. Here, disposability carries two distinct yet often interrelated meanings with respect to excess and waste. On the one hand, it may refer to something created for disposability that, following its immediate use, is treated as excessive or as waste matter (e.g., disposable cameras). On the other hand, something "disposable" can be something available for use in excess of need, such as disposable income or spare time.[2]

It is necessary to take seriously the nuances of terms such as "disposable," "redundant," "surplus," and "expendable," for they are not readily interchangeable and the shades make all the difference in consideration of the political economy of premature death. In the context of labor, for example, migrant workers are disposable, as potentially dead laborers, in the sense that they may be utilized for temporary purposes and subsequently discarded. However, it is possible also to consider surplus populations, including for example those people on welfare, as a valuable resource. Here, surplus bodies are disciplined to work, for their presumed idleness is perceived as lost potential. In this way, surplus populations are not necessarily redundant, since they collectively hold the potential for the valorization of capital. A modicum of investment is required to reproduce this population for the simple reason that their labor may be required to facilitate the accumulation of capital. By extension, investment in surplus populations is not to be wasted: even unemployed workers are to remain productive so as to not waste time or investment. This is the underlying rationale behind various work-fare policies.

But what of those disposable people who are no longer perceived even to hold the potential for productive activities. Are they, the truly expendable people, not worthy of investment, to be discarded as excess waste? Not quite. For, the infinite malleability of capitalism ensures that even waste products may be commodified into exchange values. Ironically, well into the twenty-first century, we see can see that, if capitalism is unable able to turn a profit not through investment, it can still do so by disinvestment: by letting die those persons deemed disposable, it is able to derive profit. As will become clear in subsequent sections, I term this "derivative violence," for it is not simply a matter of who lives, who dies, and who decides; it has become a matter of who profits from the death of living labor. Quite simply, in an age of precarity, living laborers are exploited not only in life but also in death.[3]

Finance Capital

According to David McNally, money has "always exercised grotesque powers in capitalist society, literally capable of determining who shall live and who shall die."[4] For example, the imposition of minimum wages determines in large part who lives and who dies, as does one's access to health care. Outside of the (formal) labor market, however, it is possible to understand the epistemology of abstract violence when, under so-called advanced forms of capitalism, it *appears* as if profits can be secured outside of the social relations of production and reproduction.

Marx well understood that not all profit was derived through the purchasing of the means of production in order to produce factories.[5] There are two ways in which money can be used as capital: on the one hand, when it is loaned with the intent of realizing interest as profit, and on the other hand, when it is invested in the means of production to realize surplus value.[6] A primary function of banks, for example, is to loan money, money that is to be repaid with interest. In the process, therefore, these institutions seemingly accrue profits in a manner distinct from those capitalists who take out loans in order to build the factories that house the workers who produce the commodities. For the capitalist factory owner, surplus value occurs through exploitation, while for the banks, it would appear that it originates outside of the production process.

In the third volume of *Capital,* Marx postulates that, "with the progressive decline in the variable capital in relation to the constant capital, this tendency leads to a rising organic composition of the total capital, and the direct result of this is that the rate of surplus-value, with the level of exploitation of labor remaining the same or even rising, is expressed in a steadily falling general rate of profit."[7] In other words, it is possible that a situation may arise whereby rates of exploitation remain steady, or even increase, and yet the overall rate of profit declines. This observation led to Marx's formulation of the law of the tendential fall in the rate of profit: "The progressive tendency for the general rate of profit to fall is . . . simply the expression, peculiar to the capitalist mode of production, of the progressive development of the social productivity of labor."[8] For Marx, this "law" was "the most important . . . of modern political economy," in that it demonstrates how the "growing incompatibility between the productive development of society and its hitherto existing relations of production expresses itself in bitter contradictions, crises, spasms."[9] More to the point, he continues: "The highest development of productive power together with the greatest expansion of existing wealth will coincide with depreciation of capita, degradation of the laborer, and a most straitened exhaustion of his vital powers."[10] Marx's premise is significant because it directs attention to the broader structural transformations of capitalism and, by extension, establishes parameters within which individual capitalists make investment decisions. Indeed, it is the rate of profit that capitalists use in their everyday calculation.[11]

Coincident with this shift toward flexible production has been the actual replacement of industrial production with financial capital. The increased role of finance in overall economic activity and the increased proportion of profits that are realized via financial channels, Geoff Mann writes, are the two main empirical indicators of a process called "financialization."[12] More precisely, for Mann, financialization can be understood in both a general and a technical sense. On the one hand, financialization describes the increasing role of financial motives, financial markets, financial actors, and financial institutions in the operation of domestic and international economies, while on the other hand, it is a pattern of capitalist accumulation that relies increasingly on profit-making through financial channels, even for capitalists that are not themselves financial firms.[13] Simply stated, the "ascendancy of finance capital has since increasingly subsumed capital accumulation under the logic of finance, channeling larger shares of corporate profits to the financial sector and making the activities and profits of non-financial corporations increasingly financial in nature."[14]

Financialization reflects a growing asymmetry between production and circulation during the last three decades.[15] In the 1950s and 1960s, for example, the financial sector accounted for 10 to 15 percent of total profits in the U.S. economy; by the turn of the twenty-first century it accounted for more than 40 percent of total profits.[16] According to Costas Lapavitsas, "a telling aspect of the transformation has been the rise of profits accruing through financial transactions, including new forms of profit that could even be unrelated to surplus value."[17] Historically, the functions of finance capital were to allocate capital to socially useful purposes by connecting people who have money to invest with people who need money to build factories, homes, farms, businesses, and so on. Increasingly, however, investments are no longer explicitly or directly tied to production, but instead are made on a purely speculative basis.[18]

"Money capital," according to Marx, constitutes a form of "fictitious capital." Here, the fiction is the apparent "fact" that interest-bearing capital is divorced from the production process. In the well-known formula "M-C-M'," for example, it is possible to see how surplus value is derived from the exploitation of workers. Here, money (M) is expended to produce commodities (C) that are sold to derive surplus value (M'). Fictitious capital, however, seems to magically appear, in the guise of "M-M'." Banks lend money (M) to capitalists and, in return, receive money with interest (M'). As McNally explains, "in this pure fetish of money-capital . . . we encounter a fantastic bourgeois utopia where capital endlessly gives birth to itself without entering the mundane world of labor and material production."[19]

However, as Marx was fond of explaining, appearances are illusory. Today's fetishization of financial capital—stocks, bonds, hedge funds—is particularly notable. Indeed, there exists a common misperception that financial capital is separate from the more traditional forms of accumulating surplus value. Lapavitsas, for example, explains that "production creates value; its motive is profit (surplus value) derived from the exploitation of labor." Financial capital, conversely, occurs when profits accrue through financial transactions, "including new forms of profit that could even be unrelated to surplus value."[20] The implications of such fetishization of fictitious capital for the study of premature death are many, not least of which is that the deleterious effects of societal inequalities become ever more distanced from the structural and institutional conditions that reproduce inequalities. McNally elaborates: "Paper-assets—not only bank-loans (which are assets for banks because they draw interest), but stocks, bonds, promissory notes or any other form of *fictitious capital*—look as if they possess an inherent capacity to metamorphose into material assets. In truth, fictitious capitals merely represent 'future claims on surplus value and profit', claims which become literally fanciful should the borrower default in the event of failure to generate adequate profits."[21] In other words, when we focus on so-called postindustrial capitalism, we fetishize the exploitation and oppression of those men, women, and children who continue to toil in the factories and fields producing commodities. It is necessary, following Mazen Labban, to recognize that, under current conditions, finance capital, long an intermediary in the process of capital accumulation, has become a somewhat autonomous and "privileged site of accumulation," while financial logic and the power of finance capital permeate all areas of economic activity and, on a deeper level, have greatly transformed everyday life.[22]

Much of the recent expansion of finance capital has been due to the growth of the speculative derivative market. According to Geoffrey Ingham, thirty years ago, the global value of derivative trades was less than US$10 million, but by the early twenty-first century, trading on these markets was estimated to be over US$400 trillion. Derivatives are anticipatory financial instruments that developed out of techniques such as "forward contracts" and "futures contracts," which were designed to reduce exposure to losses in commodity markets where supply and prices were subject to unpredictable fluctuations. Such financial instruments were and are exceptionally common within the agricultural sector, where the vagaries of weather may wreak havoc on anticipated harvests. In response to uncertainties, markets in agricultural commodities became organized around "forward" contracts to buy or sell a particular crop ahead of the harvest at an agreed upon price.[23] Once the terms are formalized and documented, the forward contract essentially eliminates all price risks.[24] In time, these assets were organized into "futures" markets, where the futures contracts to buy or sell a particular commodity at a certain price at a stated date were traded. In effect, speculators were gambling on the rise or fall of commodity prices and their deviation at the stated date from the price specified in the futures contract.[25]

The process of capitalization continuously commodifies claims on future expected incomes, whether they accrue from surplus value, taxation, or wages.[26] Risks are therefore systemic to the realization of profit. Dick Bryan and colleagues explain: "Financial contingencies of accumulation are incorporated into valuations by the measurement of capital's rate of return relative to risk. . . . When risks and returns are being calculated, decisions are being made on the allocation of assets, with the intention of enhancing (projected) returns relative to (perceived) risk."[27] Within finance capitalism, different strategies have been developed to either minimize or transfer risk. Indeed, with financial derivatives, as Dimitris P. Sotiropoulos and Spyros Lapatsioras note, "concrete risks can be singled out and transferred to another party without giving up the ownership of the underlying commodity."[28]

For Lapavitsas, this constitutes a form of "financial expropriation," an "exploitative relationship representing the direct appropriation of personal money income, or of loanable capital and plain money that belongs to others."[29] He explains that: "Workers and others enter financial transactions in order to obtain use-values, whether immediately in the form of wage goods or in the future through a pension. In contrast, financial institutions approach financial transactions in order to make profits." Lapavitsas concludes that "there are systematic differences in information, organization and social power between the two counterparties, which potentially allow financial institutions to exploit the holders of personal income."[30]

We are therefore necessarily confronted with the way decisions are rendered with respect to capitalist investment. For example, do capitalists invest in labor (in the hiring of more waged workers), or do they invest in labor-saving technologies, such as automation and robotics? Do capitalists invest in safety devices that minimize occupational injury and mortality, or do they invest in nonproductive outlets, including stocks, derivatives, and other components of financial capital? The transformation of production processes from living labor to dead labor, which is the transformation from variable capital to constant capital, is a recurrent feature of the deepening subsumption of society to capital. But as we have seen, these technological transformations are accompanied by biological transformations, as increased reliance on dead labor (in the form of constant capital) intensifies also the vulnerability of living laborers, since their employment conditions are rendered ever more precarious.

In his assessment of working conditions in England's factories, Marx wrote extensively on the deplorable conditions experienced by laboring bodies. He documented how unsafe working conditions exacted a horrendous toll, both physically and mentally, and how the employers of these factories profited immensely from these conditions, squeezing profit from sinew and flesh as one would juice from a tomato. In many places, these same conditions remain, although hidden from view behind locked doors and barred windows of the world's sweatshops. The writings of Engels highlight, therefore, how real subsumption allowed industrial capitalism to encompass the whole of society through the generalization of the wage relation and of exchange value, with profound effects on the habits and mode of life of employees.[31] Now, however, a new form of exploitation has emerged, one that follows from a simple question: Is it possible also to profit from the death of workers? McNally caustically writes: "Entranced by the seeming dematerialization of money and the increasingly esoteric operations of finance-capital, a slew of postmodernist commentators have sealed their complicity with the fetishism of commodities by conjuring away the laboring bodies upon which the circuits of capital rest."[32] This again has a tremendous bearing on our epistemologies of violence, for an ongoing fetishism of commodities conjures away the *perception* of the violence that financial capitalism exerts on those laboring bodies who remain hidden from view. But the reality remains, and Marx opened the factory doors and forced us to see the men, women, and children who died prematurely in the production of surplus value. It is necessary at this point to read between the lines of fictitious capital and gain sight of these same workers being exploited *through their death* by corporate maleficence. Life insurance, as a form of fictitious capital, is a case in point.

Mortal Profits

There is a long-standing relationship between population studies and actuarial services. Indeed, as Zohreh Bayatrizi reveals, the advent of demography, for example, coincided with an effort among Western sciences to "find the proper institutional place for dealing with death."[33] It was at this point that "insurance underwriters became interested in mortality rates as a useful instrument for predicting which segments of the population were at higher risk of death and, therefore, unsuitable for purchasing insurance policies at the standard premium, if at all."[34] However, as Shaun French and James Kneale correctly observe, there has been "surprisingly little explicit consideration of the ways in which the practices of financialization and the politics of life itself . . . intersect: that is, the ways in which financialization operates as a form of biopower."[35] To this end, the recent spate of research directed toward "biofinancialization" is particularly informative.[36]

Life insurance, broadly speaking, was introduced as a means of providing security for families in the event of death. The primary rationale of life insurance policies is to make sure that a family is not left destitute in the case of a family member's death.[37] With individually owned life insurance (IOLI) policies, for example, the insured is the policyholder and his or her dependents are the beneficiaries of the policy. Death benefits in these policies are meant to replace the insured's economic support and, in theory make, the beneficiaries "whole" upon the death of the insured, rather than to profit the beneficiaries by the death of the insured.[38] However, during the late-seventeenth and eighteenth centuries, "insurance-brokering boomed, taking on a money-making, capital-accumulating logic of its own."[39]

Accordingly, it became more important to take account of the differences in mortality rates across social groups and, therefore, to weed out or penalize those who were at a higher risk of dying prematurely.[40] Such is the occasion for the work of demographers John Graunt and Richard Price, among others, who sought to "determine the price of annuities on lives by means of an estimation of the risk of death and, by extension, the chances of survival for each age group."[41] Throughout this period, a demographic approach to death emerged, an event that coincided with the political economic transformation from feudalism to mercantilism, and eventually, to capitalism. Death became something calculable and, by extension, something to be managed. As Bayatrizi explains:

> Physicians, environmental epidemiologists, philanthropists, and statisticians highlighted as problematic deaths caused by accidents, epidemics, malnutrition, and negligence. Although no specific term was used to designate these deaths, what they all had in common was that they were now deemed to be unnatural, that is, ultimately avoidable and therefore, in a sense, "premature." They included any form of death that could be considered preventable, depending on the state of medical knowledge and public health, as well as on the extant cultural expectations of longevity. Unnatural death was implicitly contrasted to the notion of a timely death that happened at the end of a fulfilled life and resulted from "natural" causes, which meant from conditions associated with old age.[42]

Traditionally, therefore, insurers would seek to invest in those individuals not at risk of premature death. When individuals would acquire life insurance policies, the insurers would generate capital, for example, through the payment of premiums on the policy. It was more profitable, therefore, for insurance companies to cover those individuals *not* at risk of immediate death. The longer the insured lived, the more interest-bearing premiums would be collected, and the less pay-outs would have to be made. As a consequence, it became imperative to take account (literally) of differential mortality rates across social groups and to not cover, or to penalize, those who were at a higher risk of premature death.[43] Simply put, it was beneficial for underwriters to insure healthy populations while denying insurance to populations that were at greater risk of premature death.

Early in the history of life insurance, government officials were concerned about the possibility of fraud, corruption, and indeed, the possibility of mortal manipulations. Throughout the eighteenth century, for example, English courts permitted life-wagering contracts in which one citizen would gamble on the death of another by taking out a life insurance policy on that person.[44] In 1774, however, the British Parliament required that the purchaser of a policy must demonstrate an "insurable interest" in the person insured. This was introduced to minimize the likelihood that the purchaser of the policy might be tempted to kill the insured. With individually owned life insurance, for example, there is a presumption that family members have an insurable interest[45] in the person covered, that it is in the dependents best interest that the insured does not die.[46] When the United States adopted English common laws in the eighteenth century, states followed suit, requiring an insurable interest for life insurance policies.[47]

This began to change somewhat in the early twentieth century. In 1911, the U.S. Supreme Court deliberated the case of an ill man who had sold his life insurance policy to a doctor in order to pay for surgery.[48] The man's insurance company protested this transaction on the grounds that the sale violated the insurable interest laws. In a surprising twist, however, the court ruled that insurance interest applies only when the policy is first purchased. Indeed, Chief Justice Oliver Wendell Holmes Jr. argued: "Life insurance has become in our days one of the best recognized forms of investment and self-compelled savings. So far as reasonable safety permits, it is desirable to give to life policies the ordinary characteristic of property."[49] This marked a significant step in the real subsumption of mortality to the dictates and demands of capitalism. Not only had labor been commodified and treated as property, but now the insurance of living labor was increasingly commodified. As Anne Phillips writes, we are well aware under capitalism that "anyone agreeing to work for another—in whatever sphere of employment—makes herself vulnerable to a loss of personal autonomy, and that she experiences this vulnerability through her body."[50] Now, an important step forward was taken that would lead to the capitalization of dead labor. In a perverse twist, the act of living constitutes an impediment to capital accumulation.

Today, it remains commonly understood that the primary rationale of life insurance policies is to make sure that a family is not left destitute in the case of a family member's death.[51] In reality, life insurance has become a significant component of finance capital and the biofinancialization of the global economy. Specifically, life insurance policies have become significant commodities to be bought and sold. Consider the practice of insuring "deathbed" individuals. The transfer of life insurance policies to pay for medical services for treatment of a disease, for example, is called a "viatical settlement." Strictly speaking, viatical settlements are targeted at terminally ill life insurance policyholders, people with a certified life expectancy of fewer than twenty-four months.[52] It is not coincidental that the viatical industry experienced remarkable growth in the United States during the 1980s amidst the growing HIV/AIDS epidemic. During these years, a diagnosis of AIDS was generally a death sentence with a short stay of execution and the costs for medicine for treatment were exorbitant. As Patrick Burns explains, "investors were happy to be on the purchasing end of the policies—AIDS patients had short life expectancies, which allowed investors to profit handsomely—and AIDS victims could take advantage of cash payments on policies that would not otherwise help them after their deaths."[53] But this boon was short-lived. The discovery of anti-HIV drugs extended the lives of tens of thousands of people with AIDS; in short, advances in the health-care sector "scrambled the calculations of the viatical industry.[54] As Neil Doherty and Hal Singer explain, "what had for investors been a safe, rapid return on investment—founded on the certainty of the short life expectances of AIDS patients—was rendered far less attractive by the advent of 'drug cocktails' and other advances in AIDS treatments."[55]

Investors required a more reliable dying population, and accordingly, in the early 1990s, they diversified their business to patients diagnosed with cancer and other terminal illnesses.[56] Life insurance settlement schemes, unlike viaticals, are long-term investments but remain centered on the certainty of death. Here, the investor acquires the life insurance policy of a living person, pays all future policy premiums, and receives the proceeds of the policy after the death of the insured. At this point, the investor receives the full death benefit, and since the buyer provides the previous policyholder with an amount less than the full face value of the insurance policy, typically 30–80 percent, the potential return to the investor can be quite high.[57] Notably, the buyer accrues greater profits if the insured person dies sooner, since he pays fewer premiums. Conversely, the investor's profits decline as the life of the insured is prolonged and the payment of premiums is extended over time.[58]

By the twenty-first century, due mainly to marketplace innovation, the market expanded to include tens of millions of middle-aged and older life insurance policyholders.[59] Financial institutions such as Credit Suisse and Deutsche Bank were spending millions of dollars buying life insurance policies on (usually) wealthy seniors.[60] And to protect their investments, these institutions, along with myriad others, formed the Institutional Life Markets Association in an effort to promote the life-settlement industry and to lobby against efforts to restrict the business. Subsequently, as demand for life insurance policies grew, other strategies were developed. Some brokers, for example, began paying elderly persons who did not carry life insurance to take out policies, and these nascent policies were immediately "flipped" to speculators for resale. By 2006, the so-called "spin-life" policies market was worth approximately US$13 billion.[61]

There are several reasons why an insured person might sell his or her policy. For instance, designated beneficiaries to the life insurance policy (e.g., a spouse or children) may die or the financial independence of beneficiaries may remove the need for such policies. However, other factors may impel a person to sell a policy not by choice, but because of necessity: the onset of a chronic but nonterminal illness or disability and the need for medical care; a sudden, sharp decline in economic condition, such as being unemployed; divorce; or the inability to pay for premiums.[62] It is noteworthy how many of these factors interact with the broader conditions of political economy. For example, congressional attempts to reduce health care translates into more out-of-pocket costs, which may in fact drive the secondary market in life insurance policies. As more and more people are faced with the sudden need for money to pay for unexpected and/or long-term health care, they may seek liquidity (if available) from long-term assets, including life insurance policies.[63]

Since their inception, the existence and promotion of viatical and life insurance settlements has been surrounded with controversy. Supporters maintain that such policies are necessary monetary opportunities for the aging and the ill, offering a means to ease financial burdens and help them die with dignity. Conversely, critics contend that the trade is immoral and exploitative, violating the sanctity of life and creating a perverse interest in premature death, and that it is simply offensive for one person to profit from the death of another in a speculative way, effectively reducing human death to the level of an economic commodity.[64] Thus, critics argue that these policies take advantage of those individuals who require immediate and expensive medical care but, because of poverty or the lack of adequate health care, are unable to obtain necessary treatments. Indeed, it is readily observed that viatical and life insurance settlements constitute forms of fictitious capital, which seem, at first blush, to be apart from the production, circulation, and consumption of commodities. And yet, one must ask why these men and women were unable to obtain adequate health care, or why they may not have been able to afford necessary medicines and treatments. The answer, of course, relates to their exploitation in the labor market and inability to survive on exploitative wages.

Despite often vocal condemnation of viatical and life settlements, the twenty-first century has witnessed a continuing subsumption of mortality to the demands of capital. As Sarah Quinn explains, "in a narrow sense, life insurance has facilitated the belief that the association of death and markets is beneficial, not dangerous."[65] She concludes, "the more people have been exposed to life insurance institutions, and to the experiences and understandings that these institutions organize, the less likely they are to maintain that reselling policies is inherently corrupt."[66] Indeed, as with so many contractual relations within capitalism, viaticals are presented as voluntary, consensual, and mutually beneficial. But this is to fetishize the practice. The underlying profit motive and the attendant dangers of profiting from the speculation of premature death are hidden within the noise of the so-called free market. And so, the profitability of anticipatory death remains high, with some forecasts indicating that the industry will exceed US$160 billion in sales by 2040.[67]

It should come as no surprise that the capitalization of life insurance has progressed beyond the selling of policies in a secondary market to the outright purchase of primary life insurance policies. And other more egregious forms of violent and fictitious capital have emerged, such as corporate-owned life insurance (COLI). In the case of COLI, employers (or corporations) own the life insurance policy on the employee, pay the premiums, and usually become the sole beneficiary under the contract.[68] On the surface, therefore, these would appear to violate the insurable interest clause, in that the beneficiary (the company) is not closely related by blood or affinity. However, these policies differ from STOLI (stranger-owned life insurance) in that (following Supreme Court rulings) companies have been found to exhibit an insurable interest in the well-being of "key personnel." In other words, the Supreme Court determined that corporations have reasonable expectations of pecuniary benefit from the continued life of the insured. On the presumption that *some* workers (key personnel) are so crucial to the success of a company because of, for example, extensive training, firms could "hedge" the risk of premature death by insuring their investment. Thus, if a key employee died, the company could collect, and thus recoup some of its outlay. Similar to IOLI (insurance-owned life insurance), key-person life insurance makes the corporate beneficiary "whole" in the event of the death of the insured; again, it is not in principle designed as a profit-making venture.[69]

Throughout the 1980s and 1990s, as the result of intensive lobbying on behalf of the insurance industry, most American states expanded the concept of insurable interest to include low-level, low-skilled, non-essential employees.[70] These are euphemistically termed "dead-janitor" or "dead-peasant" policies and constitute a fetishized form of violence unique to advanced capitalism. No longer concerned with protecting one's corporeal investment in key employees, dead-peasant policies were (and are) taken out on any and all employees, regardless of the length of employment or the "value" of their services. Moreover, policies often remain in force after employee termination or retirement, and indeed, companies frequently use the database of deaths maintained by the Social Security Administration to track employees by social security number after termination or retirement, and thus are able to receive COLI death benefits upon their death.[71]

COLI policies generate capital through the death of those insured. Investors now bank on the expectation of premature death and call into question the insurable interest extended to workers. There have been demonstrated cases, for example, in which life insurance policies have been taken out on hourly workers. One notable legal case is that of *Mayo v. Hartford Life Insurance.* Here, Camelot, Transworld Entertainment Corporation, and Walmart purchased COLI policies on many employees, often without knowledge of the employees. Walmart, for example, purchased policies on every hourly employee on the expectation that enough workers would die to allow the firm to turn a profit.[72] Walmart's policy, in effect, took advantage of an economy of scale based on the idea of "shared mortality." In other cases, even workers who were fired after working only two months were covered by policies that remained in effect until the employee died. And perhaps most egregious, a Georgia law allowed employers to collect death benefits on the children and spouses of their employees.[73]

The widespread practice of COLI highlights the mystification of fictitious capital and the fetishization of violence. On the one hand, COLI appears to be a form of financial capital whereby money begets money in the form of M-M'. However, it is imperative not to lose sight of those *hourly* waged workers who continue to labor in the production circuit. Now, however, it becomes necessary to reconsider the expanded circuit of simply production (M-C-M') to consider the profitability of premature death. Recall that M-C-M' hides a key relationship: the necessity of labor power (LP) to transform (M) into commodity form (C) to be sold for profit (M'). With COLI policies, however, there arises a hidden incentive for employers to cut costs on working conditions and to deny health insurance. Simply put, COLI policies "create an improper incentive for employers to accelerate the deaths of the employees."[74] Earl Spurgin concurs, noting that "corporations have duties, both legal and ethical, to employees" and yet "the rights of corporations to collect proceeds on the deaths of their rank-in-file employees calls into question their abilities to be committed to safety."[75] Burns elaborates: "The COLI system creates a scenario by which an employer is incentivized for her employee to die quickly. . . . An employer could overwork an employee or become less concerned about dangerous working conditions. A company could place insured workers into more dangerous jobs or spend less money on safety accommodations. Additionally, COLI policies may have contributed to the decisions that several companies have made to refuse to provide employees with health care plans."[76] In other words, corporations stand to profit in two ways: first through the lack of providing health care or safe working conditions, and second through the premature death of those workers.[77] In this respect, workers are exposed to a double exploitation. It is for this reason that, in the context of COLI and other forms of fictitious capital, we must rewrite Marx's formula as M-C . . . (DL) . . . M', with "DL" denoting the literal dead laborer.

Given the precariousness of human beings (all people will at some point die), the insuring of a large percentage of its employees guarantees a company a sizeable payout. Moreover, there are other lucrative advantages of betting on the premature death of employees. When COLI was first introduced, there was widespread fraud and corruption. Employees often did not know that their employer had taken out life insurance and yet would possibly pay the premiums as part of their so-called benefits plans. And, while some of the most outlandish fraudulent practices have been curtailed by the Internal Revenue Service, other practices continue to afford financial advantages. Currently, in the United States: "Any money received on the payout of a life insurance policy is excluded from gross income and not subject to federal income taxation. Therefore, the beneficiary of a policy collects any money received tax-free when an insured dies."[78] This translates into immense profits for corporations that widely insure their employees.

Conclusions

Geographers, demographers, epidemiologists, and other social scientists have long documented the strong correlation between income and life expectancy.[79] Moreover, substantial empirical evidence indicates correlation between low income and "minority" populations. Together, this indicates a deeply disturbing scenario in which selected populations (e.g., African Americans and single mothers) not only experience more deplorable working conditions, poorer health, and ultimately, lowered life expectancies, but now also provide an added profit motive to corporations. In their study of income inequalities in Britain, for example, Mary Shaw and her colleagues conclude that, given appropriate political will, a reduction in inequalities—and hence an improvement in the health of hundreds of thousands of people—could be achieved.[80] Sadly, it is perhaps less a lack of political will than it is economic motive that hinders this. With the existence of corporate-owned life insurance policies, it has become more profitable for corporations to let their employees die than to require them to continue to work. As Spurgin concludes, "whereas corporations typically are better off if particular rank-in-file employees continue to live and work, corporations that own COLI are better off if those employees die."[81] Here we see clearly the deadly confluence of contemporary processes of financialization and biopolitics.

Under finance capitalism, new global patterns of class exploitation, elite insularity, immiseration, and social exclusion have taken place.[82] "The logic guiding the current phase of advanced capitalism does not value people as workers or as (mass) consumers."[83] Indeed, according to Saskia Sassen, "there has been a strengthening of dynamics that expel people from the economy and from society, and these dynamics are now hardwired into the normal functioning of these spheres."[84] Increasingly, "people as consumers and workers play a diminished role in the profits of a range of economic sectors."[85] Under conditions of finance capital, people become truly disposable. Liam Pleven and Rachel Silverman write: "Life settlements appeal to investors' appetite for 'uncorrelated' investments—ones that generate steady returns largely independent of the forces swaying stocks and bonds. People die with relative consistency, whether markets are rising or falling."[86] And herein lies the tragic irony, for the return on investments is far from being an uncorrelated investment: the correlation is directly associated with the overall morality of society, with the political and economic decisions regarding health care and social welfare.

Within a mode of industrial production, people have two subjectivities: as labor power, people are understood as having exchange value; and as consumers, people have use value. Within an epoch of finance capital, however, those populations deemed redundant or disposable are no longer needed as producers or consumers. Those people are increasingly positioned within capitalism as having neither exchange value or use value. *Productive* life itself is devalued: those rendered precarious are left to die, neglected by a mode of production that no longer requires their labor. Yet, capitalism is infinitely malleable. In a variety of settings, we see how capital has been able to profit from waste by transforming previously redundant subjects (e.g., living laborers) into valued commodities (e.g., precisely dead laborers).

Whether it is understood as biocapitalism or biofinancialization, we are presently witness to a new form of violence, a *derivative* violence that results from the profitability of becoming dead. Viaticals, life settlements, and corporate-owned life insurance schemes are founded on a notion of anticipatory death. As an investment opportunity, risks are minimized simply by the biologic fact that all humans will ultimately die. The uncertainty is occasioned by the timing of death, but this variable can be partly mitigated by targeting those persons of advanced age or those diagnosed with terminal illnesses. Michael Sandel writes: "Beyond the systemic risk and economic damage that reckless, rampant speculation can bring, it also carries a moral cost: heaping rewards on speculative pursuits that are untethered from socially useful purposes is corrosive of character. It is corrosive not only of individual character but also of the virtues and attitudes that make for a just society."[87] What incentive is there to promote societal health care if it is becoming more profitable for people to die? As an investment strategy, the vulnerability but ultimate inevitability of death minimizes financial risk; and premature death results in even greater returns on one's investment. Simply put, the biopolitics of finance capital has created a market in which death is becoming more lucrative and more cost-effective than life itself.

5. DISASSEMBLED BODIES

In 1983, H. Barry Jacobs, a physician from Virginia, founded the International Kidney Exchange with the goal of brokering the sale of kidneys from live donors to patients in need of transplants.[1] More precisely, Jacobs proposed the sale of kidneys from persons in the global south to affluent Americans for whatever price was needed to induce the former to sell. According to Jacobs, the commercial enterprise would be a "very lucrative business."[2]

Advances in medical technologies have made possible the transplantation of a range of body parts (bone, cartilage, cornea, fascia, heart, joints, kidney, liver, lung, lymph nodes, nerves, pancreas, skin, spleen, and tendons) from a donor body into the living body of a recipient.[3] Such transplants have become a part of everyday society, but not without their social effects, for as Cecil Helman observes, the image of the coherent body has become fragmented.[4] More broadly, however, the ability to swap organs and other bodily parts from one person to another has profoundly altered social relationships and, in the process, fundamentally transformed the universality of life and death.

In the early 1980s, when Jacobs announced his biocapitalist venture, public and governmental outcry was immediate. Prompted in part by Jacobs's proposal, the U.S. Congress passed the 1984 National Organ Transplantation Act (NOTA), thus beginning the process of developing a comprehensive framework for considering organ transplantation policy.[5] Overall, the NOTA was nonregulatory, rather providing for the funding of the Organ Procurement and Transplantation Network and grants for the planning, establishment, initial operation, and expansion of other qualified organ-procurement organizations. These efforts arose in part from the recognition that organ-transplantation procedures provided new hope to thousands of patients whose end-stage organ failure would lead inevitably to total disability and death.[6] Indeed, Congress discovered that upward of twenty thousand people died prematurely each year because of a shortage of suitable transplantable organs.

However, Congress expressed alarm over the prospect of endorsing the marketization of human body parts. Then-Representative Al Gore explained: "Putting organs on a market basis is abhorrent to our system of values. . . . It seems to be something inconsistent with our view of humanity."[7] Consequently, the one explicitly mandatory provision of the act was its ban on the purchase or sale of human organs. The Senate's report specifically stated that "it is the sense of the Committee that individuals or organizations should not profit by the sale of human organs for transplantation."[8] According to Robert Veatch, part of the motivation to prohibit a market in body parts stemmed directly from the testimony presented by Jacobs. "The impression he left was one of the worst imaginable. Even those who came into the sessions open to the possibility of some kind of financially-based incentive system to encourage organ procurement left appalled at the possibility that organs might be marketed to the highest bidder like deodorant or potato chips."[9]

By prohibiting the commercialization of human organs, Congress effectively restricted the development of any type of direct financial inducement for the procurement of organs.[10] In the intervening years, however, repeated efforts have called for the marketization of body parts. That the human body has been increasingly subject to commercialization in recent years, Suzanne Holland writes, can be correlated with a rise in biotechnology as a multibillion-dollar industry; indeed, she quips that we are witnessing nothing less than a new kind of gold rush, and the territory is the body.[11] This has far-reaching implications for our understanding of premature death, for ultimately, "the effects of new technologies are not determined by the technologies themselves but by how they mesh with a view of the person living in the world, a way of life."[12] Here, we begin to witness not only the profitability of surplus or disposable labor but also the profitability of disassembled laborers. Here, it is not the *whole* laborer that is required, nor even his or her ability to labor, but rather just a few spare parts. Simply put, the body (of the other) is becoming a collection of parts or pieces, with spares available when they finally wear out.[13]

In the previous chapter, I introduced biofinancialization: profiting through the death of laborers, a situation whereby premature death is economically incentivized. Here, I consider the possibility of premature death resultant from the sale of bodily organs. In so doing, I challenge the presumption of a shared mortality, for the extension of one person's life may quite literally come at the potential cost of another's life. More specifically, I consider the ethics of organ markets and the sale of so-called "spare" or "surplus" organs from people very much alive. As Gina Gatarin explains, the emergence of a market for organs creates a locus that reinforces inequalities in the right to life.[14]

Lesley Sharp finds that: "The human body is a tremendously profitable source of reusable parts. . . . Together with the major organs (heart, liver, lungs, kidneys, pancreas, and small intestine), a range of others, categorized as tissues, include approximately fifty regularly salvaged body parts."[15] Surgical procedures offer the prospect for the extension of life, notably by protection from premature death from certain diseases. Advances in kidney transplantation, for example, promise longer lives of higher quality for people suffering from kidney diseases.[16] However, the underlying political economy is highly unequal, engendering fear among critics that a market will arise in which the most vulnerable of society are further marginalized and subjected to premature death. For, the compulsion to sell one's body parts, just as is the case with the compulsion to sell one's labor capacity, emerges from the continued existence of structural inequalities. In effect, the commodification of body parts calls attention to the increased vulnerability to premature death among those living laborers made precarious or rendered surplus through displacement and dispossession.

Reworking the Meaning of Life and Death

In this section, I provide a historical overview of organ transplantation. I do so with the aim of detailing how advances in medicine contributed, however inadvertently, to those conditions that currently make possible the commodification of the disassembled body. In so doing, I highlight the asymmetric social and spatial relationships between so-called donors and recipients and how the extension of life for some comes at the expense, both financial and biological, of others.

Throughout the seventeenth and eighteenth centuries, a new demographic approach to the concepts of life and death emerged, a transformation that coincided with the political economic transition from feudalism to mercantilism and, eventually, to capitalism. For our present purposes, the most salient aspect is necessarily the practices and the calculations by which governments rule and regulate, discipline and control, the populations within their territorial domains. As Jeremy Crampton and Stuart Elden write, "forms of organizing, conceptualizing and managing the population can be seen in technologies such as the census and representational discourses, statistics, planning and cartography, as well as political expressions such as geopolitics, government and colonial ordering."[17] However, these calculations may also be seen as the state's right to intervene in matters of life and death.

The elaboration of a concept of "population" was a gradual process, one that was both technical and theoretical, relying on the development of statistics and census taking and the techniques of epidemiology, demography, and political philosophy. This has significant implications for our understanding of matters of life and death, in that the political meaning of "population" was fundamentally transformed. With the emergence of the territorial state, populations were no longer conceived as the simple sum of individuals inhabiting a territory. Instead, populations were conceived as a technical-political object of management and governance. The relationship between the sovereign and the population is therefore not simply one of obedience or the refusal of obedience. Rather, populations become productive through state interventions, meaning through a series of techniques, practices, and calculations.[18] From this moment onward, according to Michel Foucault, government "has as its purpose not the act of government itself, but the welfare of the population, the improvement of its condition, the increase of its wealth, longevity, health, etc.; and the means that the governments uses to attain these ends are themselves all in some sense immanent to the population; it is the population itself on which government will act either directly . . . or indirectly."[19]

Conceptually, the idea of populations as a collective of bodies constituting some kind of definable unit to which measurements pertain emerged beginning in the sixteenth century.[20] This is seen, for example, in the writings of John Graunt, William Petty, William Farr, Johann Peter Süssmilch, and Thomas Malthus, among others. Graunt, for example, identified certain regularities within populations, such as that child mortality is always higher than adult mortality and that populations exhibit a slightly higher proportion of male births compared to female births, but that male mortality is higher, thus leading to a more equal proportion of boys and girls. Süssmilch likewise demonstrated the existence of certain statistical regularities in population data. While searching for a divine order or evidence of God's planning (he was a clergyman and published a book titled *The Divine Ordinance Manifested in the Human Race through Birth, Death, and Propagation*), he examined masses of demographic data, and in his quest for regularities, Süssmilch discerned the balance of births and deaths and subsequently produced a life table, knowledge that was in fact used for actuarial purposes well into the nineteenth century.[21]

The idea that "life" could be studied, Sharon Kaufman and Lynn Morgan assert, owes its emergence (in part) to the rise of theories of evolution and its expansion to concepts formed through the sciences of physiology and, more recently, molecular biology and genetics.[22] More broadly, we recognize that (Western) societies (especially the United States) have inherited a legacy of viewing the human body from a biomedical perspective. In other words, the knowable body that we have inherited is one that was "visualized by such a clinical gaze, as it appeared in the hospital, on the dissection table, and was inscribed in the anatomical atlas," to quote Nicholas Rose: "The body was a vital living system, or a system of systems—it was an organically unified whole. The skin enclosed a 'natural' volume of functionally interconnected organs, tissues, functions, controls, feedbacks, reflexes, rhythms, circulations, and so forth."[23]

The "knowing" of bodies is intimately associated with changing biomedical and bioeconomic practices because knowledge of the body-as-object is produced toward the goal of predicting and preventing premature death. From the Renaissance onward, Sharp explains, "dissection offered new ways of seeing, understanding, and . . . fragmenting the body, generating, in turn, new forms of knowledge and, ultimately, sociopolitical power."[24] Marie-Francois Xavier Bichat would write in *Anatomie Générale* (1803): "For twenty years, from morning to night, you have taken notes at patients' bedsides on affections of the heart, the lungs, and the gastric viscera, and all is confusion for you in the symptoms of which, refusing to yield up their meaning, offer you a succession of incoherent phenomena. Open up a few corpses: you will dissipate at once the darkness that observation alone could not dissipate."[25] Accordingly, a new investment of the body was made, as "illness and disease became not a matter of the whole body, but were located in body parts and their pathologies."[26]

The opening of bodies created its own political economy of death. As the learning of anatomy by dissection emerged from the seventeenth century onward as a crucial element in medical education, there emerged a corresponding need for dead bodies. Initially, the demand was satisfied through the use of executed prisoners. However, with the growth of the medical sciences and associated centers of learning, demand rapidly exceeded "natural" supplies. Within this context emerged the growth of a new laborer, the body snatcher.[27] As Ruth Richardson details: "Corpses were priced up, haggled over, negotiated for, discussed in terms of supply and demand, delivered, imported, exported, and transported. Human bodies were compressed into boxes, packed in sawdust, packed in hay, trussed up in sacks, roped up like hams, sewn in canvas, packed in cases, casks, barrels, crates, and hampers, salted, pickled, and injected with preservative. They were carried in carts and wagons, in steamboats and barrows, manhandled, damaged in transit, hidden under loads of vegetables. They were stored in cellars and on quays. Human bodies were dismembered and sold in pieces, or measured and sold by the inch."[28] Not surprisingly, efforts were soon promoted to provide a legitimate supply of corpses to the medical community and to end the gruesome practices of grave-robbing. The solution, however, speaks volumes about existent social attitudes toward death. In England, for example, an Act of Parliament in 1828 provided that those who died in poverty, men and women without money enough for a funeral, would be liable to be taken away for dissection. This suited the dominant politics of the day, which was strongly in favor of cutting public expenditure by penalizing poverty.[29] Indeed, the Anatomy Act effectively decreed that the destitute were to be dissected in the name of scientific progress.[30]

In parallel with the growing practices of dissecting the dead body, medical practitioners searched for particular signs that would account for death and, if possible, identify ways to prevent death. A wide assortment of physical signs and tests of death were developed and utilized between the eighteenth and nineteenth centuries. In part, the necessity for improved techniques arose out of the growing knowledge of biophysical conditions that mimicked death, such as alcoholic and opiate stupors, extreme cold, hemorrhage, apoplexy, suffocation, fever, head injury, injuries from lightning strikes, diabetic ketoacidosis, epilepsy, drowning, and fainting.[31] More broadly, a suite of practices was forwarded to assess better the "fact" of death, accurate confirmation of signs that death has in fact occurred: the cessation of heart action and respiration; the onset of rigor mortis; the lack of muscle movement from electrical stimulation; and the relaxation and open state of the anus. Many tests bordered on the macabre and would certainly cause death if the unfortunate patient was not already dead. One physician, F. E. Foderé, proposed drawing an incision in the left chest to feel manually whether the heart was still beating, while other methods included: applying acid, electricity, or warm water to the soles of the feet; placing tissue paper over the nose and mouth; pumping scotch up the nose; funneling ammonia down the throat; severing the jugulars; separating the carotid arteries; cutting the medulla in half; and piercing the heart.[32] Frequently, however, medical practitioners simply followed the time-honored practice of waiting for the onset of the putrefaction of the body.[33] Indeed, it was this latter test that led to the widespread use of mortuaries: a site in which corpses could be left to putrefy in hygienic isolation.[34] In the process, death underwent a gradual disappearance from everyday lived experiences in the public sphere and a subsequent reappearance as a proliferating subject of scientific, statistical, medical, sociological, and actuarial discourses.[35]

It was during this period that the concept of "premature" death became firmly entrenched in the bio-logics of governance, that death as preventable risk became established.[36] Prior to this time, the length of human life was premised to follow immutable divine and or natural laws: natural death would happen when all dangers of life were avoided and the individual reached seventy to eighty years of age. The demographic work of Graunt, Petty, and other early modern statisticians, however, transformed the scientific *and political-economic* understanding of death and occasioned the concept of premature death. In the process, death went from being determined by fate as a predestinted moment to being a statistically calculable contingency. In effect, death was increasingly understood as a risk, as something preventable or avoidable.[37] As Zohreh Bayatrizi explains:

> Physicians, environmental epidemiologists, philanthropists, and statisticians highlighted as problematic deaths caused by accidents, epidemics, malnutrition, and negligence. Although no specific term was used to designate these deaths, what they all had in common was that they were now deemed to be unnatural, that is, ultimately avoidable and therefore, in a sense, "premature." They included any form of death that could be considered preventable, depending on the state of medical knowledge and public health, as well as on the extant cultural expectations of longevity. Unnatural death was implicitly contrasted to the notion of a timely death that happened at the end of a fulfilled life and resulted from "natural" causes, which meant from conditions associated with old age.[38]

Bayatrizi writes elsewhere: "Death, previously treated as a tragedy of personal and social history, became a public issue of political and economic geography. The personal embodied space-time of mortality was translated into the impersonal, abstract and aggregate space-time of demographic tables, and packaged into the numerous average of life expectancy for private, political and economic consumption."[39] Consequently, by the eighteenth century, birth, death, divorce, and accidents were no longer seen as personal fates but were explained, instead, in terms of quantifiable, impersonal, and socially relative risk factors.[40] As demographers sought to establish statistical correlations between premature death and a host of individual and societal variables, the mathematical reconstruction of death as a contingent risk assumed a normative function. The improvement of population health and prevention of so-called "unnecessary" deaths called for the systematic monitoring of specific groups of the population that were found to be prone to illness and premature death due to biological (e.g., age or sex) or socioeconomic factors (e.g., lifestyle, living conditions, and economic class).[41] Increasingly, the morbid classification of social groups along moral lines became associated with a new capitalist work ethic: a life of hard work translated into a long life.[42]

Mortality as a process amenable to risk calculation and management assumed a strong class dimension that belied any semblance of a shared mortality.[43] Progressively, it became accepted not only that those who were virtuous could avoid premature death but also that, if necessary, the more affluent could take active measures to repair failing bodies. It was not simply the ability to *see* inside the human body, but rather the opportunity to *perfect* the body, for as Sharp concludes, it was not merely dissection per se (the opening up and peering into the body) but also the art of surgery in which associated technologies rendered possible permanent transformations of the body.[44]

Humans have long sought to transplant organs from one body to another.[45] This includes the transplantation of organs and other body parts not only from both living and deceased humans but also from nonhuman organisms.[46] Initial attempts were hindered by a failure of surgeons to understand the deleterious, indeed fatal, effects of warm ischemia, the amount of time that an organ remains at body temperature after its blood supply has been stopped or reduced.[47] The first use of a human kidney, for example, occurred in 1936 when Yurii Voronoy, a Ukrainian surgeon working in Kiev, performed the first in a series of six transplants to treat dying patients, all of which failed, however, because of the length of time between organ removal and organ implantation in the recipient (in one instance, upward of six hours after the donor died).[48]

Repeated efforts to successfully transplant organs met with failure also because of the problem of the immune response. When a person receives an organ from someone else during transplant surgery, that person's immune system may recognize that it is foreign and, hence, reject the transplanted organ.[49] Initial efforts conducted during and after the Second World War sought to control the immune response through the use of irradiation. However, these proved either ineffectual or lethal.[50] It was not until the introduction of chemical immunosuppression that organ transplantation was revolutionized. Indeed, following the development of azathioprine and, more notably, the discovery of the immunosuppressant effects of ciclosporin in the mid-1970s, the outcome of kidney transplants dramatically improved.[51]

A series of remarkable breakthroughs in the history of solid organ transplantation occurred from the 1960s onward. Throughout the 1960s, basic research on animals explored the possibilities of transplanting a myriad of body parts, including vital organs, whole limbs, digits, breasts, teeth, uteruses, and even brains. Prospects for human clinical trials included transplantation of the liver, heart, brain parts, lungs, bone marrow, intestines, connective tissue (including skin), hair, and even the gonads.[52] In short, the medical profession was prolonging life in an attempt to prevent death.[53] Initially, the provision of organs was satisfied primarily through the use of cadavers. Procedures were notably rare, and consequently, a system for procuring large numbers of cadaveric donor organs was not a concern during the early years of clinical transplantation.[54] However, as procedures became more commonplace, there emerged a shortfall in the number of suitable donor organs available.[55] Equally problematic was that many organ recipients who received transplants from cadavers died soon after surgery. Most members of the medical community believed that live donors would improve the odds of success, although surgeons were understandably uneasy and reluctant to remove organs from live patients, even if they had catastrophic brain injuries.[56]

Arguably, the most salient transformation from a purely bio-logic conception of death to a bio-politically informed understanding of death occurred in 1968 when criteria for a condition that would become known as "brain death" were established. In that year, an ad hoc committee of the Harvard Medical School declared the nonfunctioning brain to be the fundamental medical criteria of death. As Kaufman and Morgan attest, this single administrative action "moved, blurred, and troubled the traditional boundary between life and death, a boundary which had never before been publically questioned or clinically debated."[57] Indeed, this administrative fiat would transform a whole class of bodies under intensive care from "patients" into "corpses."[58]

On one hand, the 1968 decision can be viewed as a reflection of decades of medical advances designed to delay death. On the other hand, the decision introduced a new form of "death," one with far-reaching implications. Prior to the nineteenth century, for example, when a person's heart stopped beating and/or his or her breathing stopped, death was all but inevitable. However, during the mid-twentieth century, techniques for artificial respiration were developed, coupled with advents in resuscitation techniques. For Sharp, "not only could this new technology sustain brain-damaged patients, but, when paired with cardiopulmonary resuscitation, the ventilator permitted health professionals to revive the dead, assess their subsequent status, and then, through an unusual form of triage, ultimately determine whether subsequent care should focus on healing or . . . preparation for organ procurement as yet another form of death."[59] Death was no longer a momentary event. As Sharp elaborates: "Some patients might well be described as the 'thrice dead' because they die, first, from a head injury, accompanied by cardiac and/or pulmonary crisis, only to be resuscitated by emergency medical technicians through CPR and then placed on a ventilator. These patients' second deaths, so to speak, occur when they are pronounced brain dead while still sustained by machines. The third (and final cardiac) death, or death of the body, occurs during procurement surgery."[60]

However, biomedical advances in the realm of organ transplantation had the perverse effect of lengthening the life of one body at the expense of another. This point cannot be overemphasized: death became relational, in that one person's death (i.e., the taking of life or, more euphemistically, "letting die") could mean another person's life (i.e., the making of life). Whereas CPR is a practice conducted on one body with the intent of saving that body's life, the practice of organ transplantation is dependent on two bodies: the organ donor and the organ recipient. This relational component of death (and life) would have wide-ranging effects, introducing a calculus into our understanding of death, a trade-off between bodies in which the disallowance of life for one body (the "brain-dead" patient) could give life to another body (the donor recipient).

This co-relational approach to death created (or, arguably, responded to) a demand for organs, but also for a class of bodies that would occupy a threshold space between death and life. Simply put, biomedical advances and the biotechnological improvement in life-support devices made open heart surgery and heart transplants possible, while the artificial kidney increased the longevity of end-stage renal disease patients, thereby increasing the demand for kidney transplants.[61] However, a major cause of failure in kidney transplants (among others) at the time was the use of cadaver organs that had deteriorated during or after the conventional death of the donor. In other words, successful transplants were predicated on the ability to shorten the time (and sometimes space) between death and organ removal. Waiting too long for dying to take place would risk damaging viable, transplantable organs. The argument was that, if a patient was irreversibly "dead," although still somewhat living, it should be possible (permissible?) to retrieve those organs that might save the life of another patient. Thus, adopting a strong utilitarian position, it was determined that one patient would be disallowed life so that another may live. As Mita Giacomini writes, "the brain-dead could not be allowed to become 'too dead' for the purpose of organ donation."[62]

Since 1968, we have witnessed the confluence of biopolitical and bio-economic understandings of life, death, and the body-object, and each new technique that has been developed to establish brain death has been accompanied by concerns to facilitate organ transplants and/or financial concerns surrounding health-care spending.[63] As Sharp observes, today, "the human body is a treasure trove of reusable parts, including the major organs (lungs, heart, liver, kidneys, pancreas, intestine, and bowel); tissue (a category that includes bone, bone marrow, ligaments, corneas, and skin); reproductive fragments (sperm, ova, placenta, and fetal tissue); as well as blood, plasma, hair, and even the whole body."[64] Consequently, with over 150 "reusable parts," the cadaveric human body is worth more than US\$230,000 on the open market, and these parts, moreover, circulate within a biomedical market that is worth billions.[65] This begs the obvious question: How much are fresh organs from living bodies worth?

Disassembled Bodies

The human body, Sharp writes, "may be fragmented both metaphorically and literally through language, visual imaging, or the actual surgical reconstruction, removal, or replacement of specific parts."[66] Accordingly, Sharp asks what such (de)constructions say about body boundaries, the integrity of the self, and the shifting social worth of human beings.[67] Here, I take seriously the problematic of *valuing* the human body and its constituent parts within the dictates of capital. In contemporary (and especially Western) society, a bio-logics predominates our conceptual understanding of life and, increasingly, death. At this point, references to the commodification of the human body are as much material as they are metaphorical. Indeed, as Lori Andrews and Dorothy Nelkin write: "The language of science is increasingly permeated with the commercial language of supply and demand, contracts, exchange, and compensation. Body parts are *extracted* like a mineral, *harvested* like a crop, or *mined* like a resource."[68] Commodities, we understand, comprise both use values and exchange values. A commodity must be useful to some potential buyer, but it also has an exchange value: it can be exchanged for other commodities. Advances in medical practices have ensured that "body parts and tissues now have unprecedented use value."[69]

Organ shortage globally is one of the challenges facing those who require transplant surgery. In recent decades, in part because of the lobbying efforts of transplantation organizations, professionals, and patients' rights group, more and more people are eligible for and in need of organ transplants.[70] Unfortunately, long waiting lists preclude many patients from life-savings procedures. In the United States, for example, an estimated 110,000 patients are awaiting organ transplants, and yet fewer than 15,000 donors become available each year.[71] The gap between organ demand and organ supply has established a peculiar political economy of body parts. As Behrooz Broumand and Reza Saidi explain, the demand for organ transplants in relatively more prosperous countries is rising much more quickly than the supply of organs donated through traditional means, and in response, a small but growing number of the world's poor people are selling their body parts for transplantation.[72] Such is the context for the phenomenal growth of transplant or medical "tourism."[73]

Broadly conceived, organ tourism occurs when individuals in countries with existing organ transplant procedures are unable to procure an organ by using those transplant procedures in enough time to save their lives. In such situations, individuals with sufficient resources solicit organ brokers in foreign countries and have an organ procured for them.[74] In practice, myriad forms exist, including both formal and informal, both legal and illegal means. For example, as governments attempt to regulate the global market in organ vending, it is becoming more common for both organ sellers and organ buyers to travel to third countries in order to bypass legal barriers.[75] The reasons are multiple. As Dominique Martin explains, "although many medical travels are motivated by access to cheaper or better health care, others seek access to services that are subject to regulatory restrictions or prohibitions in their countries of origins due to ethical concerns rather than economic constraints."[76] Accordingly, myriad niche markets, some formal but many informal, have developed in which access to a unique class of medical resources underpins patient motivation to travel, including the procurement of organs, cells, and tissues used in transplantation.[77] It is vitally important to recognize also that, in the market for organs, the medical tourist is "not autonomous but interdependent" with myriad other so-called "stakeholders," including but not limited to organ recruiters, brokers, surgeons, and perhaps most salient, the providers.[78]

How are we to interpret this biomarket, and how does it relate to our overall concern with the political economy of premature death? The answer relates directly to the commodification of living laborers and the incessant subsumption of death to the market logics of capital. Throughout *Capital,* Marx sought to demonstrate how the appearance of "equal exchange" of commodities in the market camouflages systemic inequality and exploitation.[79] In his chapter on "The Sale and Purchase of Labor-Power" in *Capital,* Marx identifies two conditions for the sale of labor power. To begin, "labor-power can appear on the market only as a commodity [and] only if, and in so far as, its possessor, the individual whose labor-power it is, offers it for sale or sells it as a commodity."[80] For this to occur, however, the seller must "be the free proprietor of his own labor-capacity, hence of his person."[81] Secondly, "the possessor of labor-power, instead of being able to sell commodities in which his labor has been objectified, must rather be compelled to offer for sale as a commodity that very labor-power which exists *only in his living body.*"[82] In other words, in order for the transaction between body and value to be commercially viable, the worker must be nominally free, disposed of the means of subsistence, and alive; slavery and death become the limits of the commodification of labor.[83]

The conflation of medical advances and neoliberal practices has radically transformed the commodification of living labor. Writing in the nineteenth century, Marx premised that "the worker must be free in a double sense that as a free individual he can dispose of his labor-power as his own commodity, and that, on the other hand, *he has no other commodity for sale.*"[84] In the context of biocapitalism, dispossessed workers now have a vital commodity to be sold: their bodily organs. Consequently, when the sale of one's labor power is no longer sufficient, when one must consent to sell one's body parts, those populations rendered surplus are further subjugated to the brutality of the market. The extraction of value is derived from the vital extraction of kidneys and corneas, or lobes of lungs and liver.

Modern medical technologies, Sharp writes, have an overwhelming capacity to challenge the boundaries between life and death, but they also privilege some bodies while excluding others.[85] Well into the twenty-first century, the medical procedure of organ transplant is becoming even more subsumed to the dictates of capital. Organ procurement increasingly goes beyond the harvesting of living dead bodies to that of bodies quite alive. In part, this trend is bio-logical in nature: the need to obtain ever fresher organs. However, the growing acceptance of reaping kidneys and other so-called surplus body parts is driven by global inequalities whereby some are able to extend their lives at the risk of shortening the lives of others. Anne Phillips asks: "In a world of social, economic, and gender equality, why would some of us choose, out of all possible activities, to specializes in kidney vending?"[86] For Phillips, it is hard to conceive what would propel anyone to sell one's body parts, though it is correspondingly easy to imagine that many people would offer to donate. Indeed, when grieving parents agree to the use of their child's organs, Phillips explains, it is often with a sense that they do not want other parents to suffer the same kind of loss.[87] The altruistic donation of one's own body parts or the body parts of a loved one, however, differs fundamentally from the *necessity* of selling one's body parts on the market. When the sale of one's labor power is inadequate, what does the destitute possess beyond his or her own disassembled self?

Since the initial outcry over the marketing of body parts, the continued demand for live organs, coupled with the existence of robust informal economy of organ exchange, has intensified calls for the formation of a legal market of body parts procured from living laborers.[88] In the 1980s and early 1990s, for example, there appeared a proliferation of articles, usually appearing in law reviews and economics journals, advocating the commercialization of body organs.[89] Thus, we now find "a growing number of economists and bioethicists who believe that the sale of body parts has become 'morally imperative.'"[90] Indeed, as Julian Koplin writes, "the near-universal condemnation of financial incentives in the early days of [live] organ transplantation is increasingly under challenge as waiting lists continue to grow."[91]

Most proponents of the commercialization of body organs adopt a libertarian view of the individual's right to enter into contracts that treat the body and its parts as disposable property, and the cultural priorities invoked by these writers include individual autonomy, rational self-interest, and freedom from onerous governmental interference.[92] More to the point, Nancy Scheper-Hughes maintains that "the 'right' to buy or sell human organs is increasingly defended . . . so as to bring it into alignment with neoliberal conceptions of the human, the body, labor, value, rights and economics."[93] In short, we are witness to the further subsumption of living labor to the market logics of biocapital, not merely as surplus populations, but as living assemblages of marketable parts.

The anxiety about commodification is that the buying and selling of human organs will lead to an increasing objectification of the human body and that, by extension, commerce in organs would encourage people to view individual human beings as saleable commodities.[94] In this way, most ethical deliberations about one's body in terms of possession boil down to the question of self-determination and autonomy.[95] For commercialization advocates, selling an organ is no different in kind from selling one's labor; consequently, the physical risk and potential exploitation is arguably a matter of degree, rather than of kind.[96] Recall that an important feature of capitalist market exchange is that all forms of property, labor, goods, and services are exchangeable commodities.[97] Further, body parts should be considered one's own property and, accordingly, available to be exchanged on the market. Advocates call attention to the fact that many other body parts and substances are bought and sold on the market. Indeed, there currently exist myriad legal markets for the exchange of body parts or bodily substances: blood, sperm, eggs, hair, and so on. When discussing the production and exchange of body parts, however, it is necessary to pay attention to differences in the material in question.[98] Thus, when considering the sale of body parts such as kidneys or lobes of lungs or livers, all is not equal. The sale of kidneys on the market, for example, raises more serious ethical concerns than selling blood, sperm, or milk because it involves a part or substance that is not regenerable and the removal of which is invasive and carries long-term health risks.[99] Thus, while live-organ transplant procedures are becoming more and more common, the removal of a kidney is still not like a tooth extraction or the drawing of blood.[100] To put it bluntly: the sale of sperm is not life-threatening; the sale of a kidney is. Accordingly, the argument that selling one's kidney or other body part is no less exploitative and risky than any other exchange on the market is categorically flawed and, thus, yields invalid ethics.

Through the marketing of body parts, we may chart the interconnections of global poverty, circuits of capital, and processes of racialization. By way of example, Donald Joralemon and Phil Cox write: "Working as a diamond miner in South Africa is demonstrably dangerous to life and limb; selling the right lobe of one's liver, or a lung, is also demonstrably dangerous. Both force a devil's bargain on the economically desperate of trading life and limb for sustenance. Yet admitting the exploitative and hence ethically objectionable nature of highly dangerous working conditions is not an argument for expanding the range of dangerous occupations or risky labor-body exchanges."[101] They conclude that "objecting to such kinds of exploitation or to the selling of one's labor or physical well-being should be taken as a reason for working to reduce the kinds of work or exchange that are so risky."[102] Here, it becomes clear that workers rendered superfluous or disposable are subject to ever-greater forms of exploitation and oppression; economic salvation comes not in better working conditions, but through the granular commodification of laboring bodies.

Proponents emphasize also the concept of autonomy, the right of persons to sell their body parts.[103] To this end, advocates for the marketization of body parts "argue that compensated donation will not only help patients languishing on the waiting list, but also substantially improve the well-being of those who sell a 'spare' kidney."[104] The so-called opportunity to obtain revenue through the sale of a kidney or other body part is heralded as progressive. When these parts are portrayed (erroneously) as spare, however, it becomes easier to convince the destitute that *not selling* a second kidney is loss of a source revenue. As Richard Demme writes, "kidneys, corneas, and lungs may be anatomically redundant, but they are not superfluous."[105] He goes on to explain that being born with two kidneys does not mean that a second kidney is an extra one; after all, the reason for kidney transplantation is that, despite having two kidneys, many people die from kidney failure.[106]

The marketing of organs and other body parts also occasions a situation ripe for abuse. As Debra Satz explains, in India and elsewhere, kidneys are viewed as potential collateral and moneylenders acquire incentives to seek out additional borrowers, as well as to change the terms of loans and place pressure on those who owe money. If kidney selling, for example, becomes widespread, a poor person who does not want to sell her kidney may find it harder to obtain loans. Increasingly, as kidneys and other parts become not only resources but also forms of collateral, one's ability to secure a loan may be dependent on one's agreement to put up his or her kidney as collateral.[107] The disassembling of one's body becomes the price of obtaining a loan. Such practices, moreover, must be considered within the colonial present, within the ongoing processes of displacement and dispossession. As Nancy Scheper-Hughes explains, "for those living in parts of the world that have been subjected to centuries of colonialization, forced labor and peonage . . . the idea of selling a spare body part seems as natural and ordinary as any other form of indentured labor."[108]

The possibility of coercive practices of treating body parts as collateral is not limited to the global south. Demme asks: "In this era of underemployment, and home foreclosures, why couldn't a bank request that you sell your kidney and the kidneys from your spouse and children if you wanted to keep your home? Or, why couldn't you be made to sell a kidney before you would be eligible for Medicaid or food stamps?"[109] If these scenarios seem far-fetched, one would be well-informed to consider the litany of invasive and unjust practices currently in place for the poor to receive welfare. The path from mandatory drug testing to the sale of body parts is not so very far. The point, Demme stresses, is that: "If everyone accepts that organs are commodities like anything else that could be bought or sold, then organs could be treated like other things of value. . . . In such a system, it would be logical that creditors might have a say about what happens to your assets."[110]

The assumption that individuals experience economic benefits from selling a kidney also does not map onto what is known about the consequences of allowing poor individuals to exchange kidneys for cash.[111] Numerous studies indicate that sellers of kidneys did not see a marked financial improvement in their lives. Indeed, most sellers experienced a more precarious quality of life. On the one hand, many so-called vendors experienced physical deterioration and long-term health problems. A major study in India, for example, found that 87 percent of kidney sellers reported a deterioration of health status. Moreover, one third experienced a decrease in family income. Of 292 persons who sold a kidney to pay off debts, 74 percent remained in debt six years later, and the number of those living in poverty increased from 54 percent prior to the sale to 71 percent afterward.[112] Similar findings have been reached elsewhere. In a survey of 239 impoverished persons in Pakistan, nearly 90 percent reported no economic improvement after surgery and 98 percent indicated a deterioration in health status, and in Iran, out of 300 kidney sellers, 79 percent reported that they were unable to attend follow-up visits because of their impoverished condition.[113]

A deterioration in health and physical ability is augmented, and vulnerability to premature death is intensified, when one considers that the vast majority of organ sellers are manual laborers, often living in exceptionally impoverished conditions. With minimal access to clean water and adequate nutrition, organ sellers become more vulnerable to premature death. As Scheper-Hughes writes, in the global south, "poor people cannot really 'do without' their 'extra' organ." She notes that "living kidney donors from shantytowns, inner cities, or prisons face extraordinary threats to their health and personal security through violence, accidents, and infectious disease that can all too readily compromise their remaining kidney."[114]

Proponents of a free market for body parts insist that such findings exist only in informal markets. Defenders of the commodification of body parts maintain that increased regulations would eliminate most, if not all, of the questionable practices associated with the informal trade of body parts. Setting aside the observation that advocates of the free market frequently champion deregulation, it simply does not hold that any market in body parts, however regulated, would constitute an exchange between two equal partners. As Nancy Jecker explains, a central ethical concern must include the question of how we regard the would-be seller in any market exchange.[115] Within capitalist markets, there remains a mistaken belief that participants freely enter transactions on an equal footing. As Samuel Gorovitz explains: "A free-market model is based on the values of competition, individual initiative, and the elasticity of supply and demand in response to market forces. But medical need is no respector of success in the world of commerce. The poor are more likely, not less likely, to be seriously ill, and their ability to obtain medical care is seriously compromised by their poverty."[116] This raises two interrelated problems. The first is the observation that, just as Jacobs's endeavor encouraged, only the affluent would be able to purchase life-extending body parts. The second is that only the most destitute would sell their organs. Simply put, as Phillips notes, the desperate need in the kidney (or other solid-organ) trade is twofold: the desperate need of those suffering kidney failure and facing a reduced life on dialysis or early death and the desperate need of those who decide to sell.[117] Consequently, it is highly dubious that existent inequalities would not manifest in the market exchange of body parts.

The commodification and commercialization of body parts bring donors and "targets" (persons and laboratories, people and markets, agencies and consumers) into different kinds of relations, but as Sallie Yea cautions, the power and vulnerability in the relationship between the provider and the recruiter or broker should immediately dispel any notion of a free and equal exchange: "Vulnerability on the part of the provider is easily established with economic marginality as the key site of vulnerability for all providers."[118] For the vast majority of people who are denied access to the means of production, there is no option other than to enter the labor market to obtain the money with which to pay rent, buy groceries, and feed and clothe the family.[119] When this option is curtailed, whether because of automation or redundancy, the disassembly of one's corporal body becomes the last viable option. As Satz concludes, "a market exchange based in desperation, humiliation, or begging or whose terms of remediation involve bondage or servitude is not an exchange between equals."[120] Indeed, at present, the very poor in the more destitute parts of the world find that their second kidney is an economic bonanza if they can sell it to a rich person.[121] Subsequently, throughout the global south, organ brokers encounter little difficulty in finding impoverished men and women willing to exchange kidneys for cash.[122]

The underemployed and the unemployed are those lacking health insurance and are effectively priced out of the market, thereby ensuring that the wealthy have access to life-extending medical procedures while the poor succumb to premature death. But here's the rub: those who are impoverished, those who, as a class, are too poor to obtain needed medical treatment, will become the source of organs for the wealthier. As Scheper-Hughes argues: "There is little consciousness of the vulnerability of some social classes and ethnic groups who can be described as the

'designated donor' populations. In the United States, this group is disproportionately poor—including whites, Latinos, and African Americans."[123]
Denied access to adequate wages and health care, those positioned as
surplus or redundant within the global economy are compelled to sell
their body parts. In the process, we are witness to the disassembly of living labor on a planetary scale.

By way of summary, it is worthwhile to consider the argument put forward by Veatch, who is professor emeritus of medical ethics and, throughout his long career, had been steadfastly opposed to the marketization of
body parts. In recent years, however, he has shifted his position and now
views the marketization of body parts as a necessary form of welfare,
given that "society continues to refuse to provide a decent minimum of
health and welfare services for its most needy citizens."[124] Initially, and
in testimony before the U.S. Congress, Veatch condemned the immoral
attitudes of lawmakers. He explains: "What was unethical was that the
ones contemplating the authorization of economic incentives to procure
organs—i.e., the United States Congress—had at their disposal the means
to address the desperate situations of the very poor in the United States.
They could rather easily have raised the minimum wage, offered a guaranteed annual income, provided a minimally decent standard of living
for all in the United States, or undertaken some other plan to address
the desperation of the poorest of the poor. It was the fact that the decision makers, in effect, would be forcing the poor to sell their organs by
withholding alternative means of addressing their problems that made
an American policy of legalizing a market in organs unethical."[125] Consequently, Congress's indifference and refusal to respond to the desperate
plight of those most vulnerable in American society impelled Veatch to
modify his position. For Veatch, the sale of body parts now constitutes
a viable, if imperfect, option for responding to those most precarious.
Given that "people are still homeless, chronically unemployed, and without basic medical care," Veatch concedes that "the kidney in their body
may be their most valuable and marketable possession."[126]

Veatch forwards a particularly troubling position: society has demonstrated a moral weakness of the will to address those in need; accordingly,
it falls upon those most destitute to capitalize their own bodies simply to
survive. He laments: "If we are a society that deliberately and systematically turns its back on the poor, we must confess our indifference to the

poor and lift the prohibition on the one means they have to address the problems themselves."[127] For Veatch, this is a very pragmatic position. It is also a defeatist position that will not markedly, if at all, improve the lives of the vast majority of impoverished men and women compelled to risk death in order to live and may even hasten their premature death. The continued inability to guarantee minimum wages and health services within a system that has proven to be unequal and unjust opens the door for the possibility of even more exploitative and oppressive practices. In short, Veatch understands, rightly so, that governments in both the global north and global south continue to cut back on much-needed social services, but for that reason, he argues that it is better to impel poor people to undergo unnecessary and life-threatening medical procedures in order to live: "The time has come to admit defeat, join with the conservatives who have always accepted monetizing of the body, and legalize financial incentives to encourage consent to procure organs from both cadaveric and living sources. They will no longer be donors, they will be vendors selling their bodies because the alternatives are all foreclosed to them."[128]

Veatch forwards an exceptionally depressing argument. He is certainly correct to identify the failures of society—but mostly those in power—to redress problems of inequality, inequities, and injustices. But it does not follow to further subject the impoverished to the market logics of capital and, in so doing, exacerbate their vulnerability to premature death. Biocapitalist market exchanges within a context of vital asymmetries is not the solution. As Scheper-Hughes argues, "perhaps we should look for better ways of helping the destitute than dismantling them."[129]

Conclusions

More and more, our bodies are being experienced as objects to be honed and worked on, as personal projects to prevent premature death. It is hardly a coincidence that neoliberal medicine has arisen at the same time that an ever-growing number of people regard their bodies as do-it-yourself projects.[130] What is distinctive, Rose writes, is that, now, "recipients of [medical] interventions are consumers, making access choices on the basis of desires that can appear trivial, narcissistic, or irrational, shaped not by medical necessity but by the market and consumer culture."[131] We can augment our limbs and penises. We can augment our breasts, butts, cheeks, and lips. We can whiten our skin simply by swallowing a pill (e.g., glutathione), despite the risk of liver damage or death. As Arthur Frank concludes, the "possibility of fixing renders inescapable the question of whether or not to fix."[132] Such a fixation with the "promise" and "potential" of embodied projects should not lose sight of the inequalities associated with producible, consumable bodies. To this end, for example, we are "well aware of the ease with which rich people can alter their bodies to make them look younger or thinning."[133]

We are witnessing also the ability of the affluent to extend their lives through the poor's unequal vulnerability to death. As Catherine Waldby states: "Our experiences of our bodies increasingly involves their potential for biotechnical fragmentation. New surgical and clinical practices enable the donation of new kinds of biological fragments to others and the reciprocal incorporation of others' fragments."[134] She continues that "our health and fertility are more likely to be owed to the therapeutic effects of another's fragments—organs, blood, ova, semen, embryos or stem cells."[135] In many instances, the extension of one life is predicated on the immediate cessation of another's; at other times, life extensions come at the potential premature death of another. Not all populations have access to the "choices" offered on Rose's medical buffet; there are, in fact, multiple and unequal geographies to object bodies. The class-based implications of biomedical interventions, as well as the vulnerability to premature death, should also not be overlooked. The growing patient-as-consumer model, in fact, establishes a situation that empowers those with sufficient resources and disenfranchises others who lack these resources. As Kaufman and Morgan write, "choice is at best an illusion for most of the world's peoples."[136]

From harvesting body parts from cadavers to the reaping of organs from brain-dead patients to the purchasing of so-called spare parts from living laborers, a brave new form of necrocapitalism has emerged. History reveals a steady experimentation with organ transplantation as a means of staving off death. The effectiveness of contemporary procedures has arisen at a particular moment of the capitalist mode of production. Advances in medical treatments and surgical procedures after the Second World War coincided with a sweeping restricting of the global economy and the concomitant retrenchment of the welfare state. Consequently, as

Scheper-Hughes surmises, "the spread of transplant capabilities created a global scarcity of transplantable organs at the same time that economic globalization released an exodus of displaced persons and a voracious appetite for foreign bodies to do the shadow work of production and to provide 'fresh' organs for medical consumption."[137] In turn, this has produced, again in the words of Scheper-Hughes, "a grotesque niche market for solid organs, tissues, and other body parts."

The time has come, John Lizza writes, "to come clean on the fact that defining death is more than a biological matter."[138] For, "just as technological advances enable persons to live in ways that previously were impossible, they enable us to die in ways that were previously impossible."[139] By extension, the real subsumption of living labor to the dictates of a marketized bio-logics enables profits to be derived from the mortality of people in ways not previously imagined. The disassembly of surplus, redundant, and disposable bodies thus constitutes a different form of commodified labor that typifies our present era of necrocapitalism.

POSTSCRIPT

From Premature Death to Truncated Life

Death figures prominently in the writings of Karl Marx, for Marx was deeply concerned about the injustices inherent to the capitalist mode of production. As an economic system predicated on the commodification of labor power and the fetishization of the market, capitalism, for Marx, constitutes an exploitative system whereby surplus value accumulates at the expense of living labor. Denied access to the means of production, workers are compelled to sell their labor capacity in order to live. For, as Marx writes, "the worker has the misfortune to be a living capital, and therefore a capital with needs."[1] And yet, as Joseph Choonara explains, "for many in capitalist society the one thing worse than being exploited is *not* being exploited."[2] Indeed, the poverty faced by those who are no longer useful to the capitalist—those rendered surplus or those whose health (physical, mental, or both)—makes them less useful to the capitalists is an indictment of a system built around the extraction of surplus value.[3]

In *Dead Labor,* I situate the concept of premature death within a context of Marxist political economy, for I find in the writings of Marx a fruitful path of inquiry, a route that promises greater synergy between geography and the "valuation" of life and death. Indeed, as Michael Dillon and Luis Lobo-Guerrero observe, we are witnessing two momentous trends that hold tremendous potential for geography and allied fields in the twenty-first century: "the transformation of what it is to be a living thing . . . [and] the transformation of life into value, in the form of commodity and capital."[4] For, in the case of dead-peasant's insurance and the growing market for human organs, we see the ongoing subsumption of death into capital, with capital increasingly extracted from dead or dying laborers. Consequently, throughout this book, I reflect on the "survivability" of populations and address a layered demographic question: within any given place, who lives, who dies, and who increasingly profits from the death of the other?

In the first volume of *Capital,* Marx postulates, "labor-power exists only as a capacity of the *living* individual."[5] He continues: "Given the existence of the individual, the production of labor-power consists in his reproduction of himself or his maintenance."[6] In other words, a certain amount of subsistence is required to ensure the daily reproduction of the self, the mere ability to live from day to day. Capital, of course, is largely indifferent to many forms of labor. It matters little who works on the assembly line or performs stoop labor on farms; all that is required is the continued access to labor in the abstract.

Historically, mortality has posed a peculiar problem for the perpetuation of capital. As Marx writes, "the owner of labor-power is mortal."[7] Consequently: "Labor-power withdrawn from the market by wear and tear, and by death, must be continually replaced by, at the very least, an equal amount of fresh labor-power. Hence, the sum of means of subsistence necessary for the production of labor-power must include the means necessary for the worker's replacements, i.e., his children, in order that this race of peculiar commodity-owners may perpetuate its presence on the market."[8] Well into the twenty-first century, we need to recalculate and recalibrate Marx's premises on the political economy of premature death, for necropolitical logics enact a politics of death in the name of vitality that defines which lives are worth living and which are deemed surplus, redundant, or disposable.[9]

Premature death is a bio-economic concept, one that is intimately bound to the modernist ordering of life that dominates our contemporary understanding of both bodies and populations. Simply put, premature death as preventable risk originated as a bio-logical concept in the mid-seventeenth century. According to Zohreh Bayatrizi, this depended on the development of new scientific techniques for measuring longevity and mortality rates and for identifying the most common causes of death.[10] Life-tables and mortality rates, for example, provided crucial knowledge whereby death became ordered and managed. Over time, however, the concept of premature death transformed according to bio-economic logics in which mortality as something calculable and predictable became something manageable, governable, and even profitable. In short, premature death as a concept was (and remains) bound to the spatial and temporal regularities of mortality.

It is within this context that I propose a shift in terminology: we should return the concept of "premature death" to the eighteenth century and replace it with "trunctated life." Mortality, upon which premature death originates, is death in the abstract. John Graunt writes that "premature death constituted the preferred semantic field for the scientific, objective, and instrumental studies of mortality" and, thereby, "made death an object of instrumental calculations."[11] Premature death, understood as such, is not the application of violence, but instead the abstract application of instrumental calculations that stand to profit from life and death. Conversely, the concept of truncated life directs attention to the scale of the body. Here, there is no statistical expectation of life and a person's death is not measured against an abstract, artificial norm. Where premature death is abstract, truncated life is concrete. Truncated life is vitality sundered. Truncated life is that which ends abruptly, socially murdered by material inequalities born of bio-political and bio-economic regimes driven by market logics and the pursuit of capital accumulation. As Emma Laurie and Ian Shaw conclude, "truncated life names the injustice of premature death."[12]

For Marx, "the determination of the value of labor-power contains a historical and moral element."[13] This is simply another way of expressing the idea that societies are defined by their treatment of those most vulnerable. We are presently witness to the ongoing dehumanization of neoliberalism, but there is so much more to the story. On the one hand, we are witnessing the unfolding of a crisis of *indifference*, in which the plight of dehumanized "Others" is neglected or ignored. On the other hand, we have entered a period of *necrocapitalism*, an era in which not only has living labor become superfluous, but dead laborers have become profitable.

At a societal level, we are aware of the gross inequalities that lead to stark differences in life expectancies. Corporations and governments are all too often aware of the deplorable conditions confronting those who are harmed or killed because of inadequate wages, safety regulations, or lack of health care. And increasingly, neither corporations nor the state take responsibility for the plight of any particular individual if, as totally free agents, he or she is assumed to be fully responsible for his or her condition.[14] As Katharyne Mitchell and colleagues argue, the "devolution of more and more 'choice' to a seemingly ever more autonomous individual who must rationally calculate the benefits and costs of all aspects of life . . . is part of a much broader set of practices that tend to increase productivity and profits for the employer while reducing the responsibility of both the employer and the state in managing and sustaining the reproduction of labor-power."[15]

And yet, as the example of "dead-peasant" insurance illustrates, these same corporations are eager to profit from laborers who die from unsafe work conditions, minimal health care, and the imposition of so-called living wages. In short, within neoliberal capitalism, as long as capitalists and the state are presumed to refrain from direct harm (i.e., direct violence), they are under no obligation to promote or undertake positive duties that appear discordant with a market-based ideology of rationality, efficiency, and justice. As such, those individuals that become "the precariat" are abandoned—subjected to a truncated life—by a pervasive indifference that is systemic to capitalism itself. And, in an ironic twist, life and death are further subsumed into the dictates of necrocapitalism, for as Laurie and Shaw write, truncated life is also "life that is robbed of its potential."[16] Financial capitalism, however, demonstrates that death is no longer outside capital, but rather constitutes a source of potential profits. The death of living laborers may entail a loss of potential labor capacity, but such losses may be compensated by monies received upon death through insurance schemes.

An engagement with social justice entails more than a simple recognition that some people are better off than others; it calls for a conscious effort to promote change. As Laurie and Shaw write, "we must challenge those autopsies that return 'natural' causes of deaths," for "social murder hangs across the truncated lives of capitalism."[17] A promotion of social justice requires a transformation both individually and collectively, a change in those conditions, both structural and institutional, that produce inequalities and injustices.[18] But how are we to proceed? The bio-ethicist and geographer Tom Koch argues that it is time to "put off 'death talk' and think about 'care talk,' about what the fragile of our society need and how better to provide it."[19] Koch's appeal resonates well with the ongoing "moral turn" evident in geography and allied fields.[20]

As we move through the twenty-first century, Linda McDowell writes, "it seems evident that global economic and political processes are now more brutal, both transforming and exacerbating class, gender and racialized inequalities."[21] These transformations, she explains, "have profound implications for local communities and for individual women, men and children across the globe, adding urgency to geographers' responsibilities to theorize the global construction of the local, to the task of connecting material transformations and new structures of inequality to the recognition of cultures of difference."[22] Accordingly, McDowell "considers the implications of replacing the current dominance of the ideal citizen as an independent individual fully participating in the labor market . . . by a more socialist ideal of solidarity and mutuality between networks of individuals in relationships of different forms of interdependence."[23] Such a reconsideration aligns well with the replacement of the liberal subject with the vulnerable subject, and of premature death with truncated life. We all share the fact of mortality; but how this is experienced is far from equal under the current market logics of capitalism.

Death and life are relational. Accordingly, for Clare Madge, it is vitally necessary to address forthrightly "the relationship between organic life and an embodied geopolitics, one which acknowledges that many of us also benefit from the violences/mortality of others, owing to inherited privileges of race, class, place and species, among other things."[24] Indeed, as Paul Cloke states, "we exist amid historical harm and wrongdoing, and among inherited and institutionalized advantage and disadvantage."[25] This is seen in the rampant and rapidly expanding inequalities throughout the world, wrought by dispossession and displacement, but it is also readily seen in the subsumption of these inequalities to the dictates of capital and the logic of the market. Victoria Lawson explains: "We live in times defined by the relentless extension of market relations into almost everything. This deepening of market relations is reaching into arenas where the social good should (but often does not) take precedent over profitability and the efficient operation of markets."[26]

By way of illustration, Cloke claims homelessness as a form of ordinary evil "by which individuals, families, landlords, public-sector departments, charities and governments are bound together in social relations which produce and reproduce the harmful effects which we construct as homelessness." He concludes that "it is usual for no one but the victims themselves to be held responsible for homelessness."[27] In similar fashion, the commodification, dispossession, and displacement of populations, the production and reproduction of surplus and redundant populations, and the literal disassembly of society's most vulnerable, the precariat, all constitute various forms of ordinary evil that are systemic to an incipient necrocapitalism.

ACKNOWLEDGMENTS

This project has been many years in the making, and many individuals played important roles in its development. First, Don Mitchell provided the inspiration. Some time ago, Don gave a colloquium at Kent State University in which he spoke on "dead labor" and of the need to think beyond this concept in metaphorical turns. This idea has long stayed with me, unformed but always present. It was not until 2012 that Chris Philo, then editor at *Progress in Human Geography,* asked me to write a trio of reports on the status of population geography. In no small part, these papers served as the core of my present project. I am sincerely grateful for the advice, insight, and criticism provided by both Don and Chris over the intervening years on this and related projects. Of course, this book would not have been possible without the support of the staff at the University of Minnesota Press, including Jason Weidemann and Gabe Levin. Jason has been remarkably supportive of this project and has provided exceptional feedback and insight throughout the entire process. I extend thanks also to the editorial board at the University of Minnesota Press and the external reviewers.

Citations and references embedded in the manuscript fail to articulate fully the development of my thoughts. My reflections on the political economy of premature death have greatly benefited from numerous conversations, both formal and informal, at conferences, colloquiums, and other academic gatherings: a statement made over a glass of wine at a reception in Florence; a comment made while walking to a presentation in Stockholm; a remark made during a field trip in Reykjavik. In effect, this project is the culmination of myriad conversations with friends, colleagues, and scholars, including but not limited to Alec Brownlow, Noel Castree, Thom Davies, Lorraine Dowler, Salvatore Engel-DiMauro, Kathryn Gillespie, Jim Glassman, Josh Inwood, Patricia Lopez, Geoff Mann, Michael McIntyre, Don Mitchell, Heidi Nast, Dick Peet, Chris Philo, Laura Pulido, Ian Shaw, Simon Springer, and Melissa Wright. I have been fortunate over the years to work also with several remarkable graduate students, and each, in their own way, has helped shaped the ideas reflected in this manuscript. I especially want to thank Gabriela Brindis Alvarez, Steve Butcher, Sutapa Chattopadhyay, Chhunly Chhay, Jaerin Chung, Alex Colucci, Gordon Cromley, Christabel Devadoss, Sam Henkin, Donna Houston, Josh Inwood, Sokvisal Kimsroy, Rob Kruse, Olaf Kuhlke, Mark Rhodes, Stian Rice, Andy Shears, Dave Stasiuk, and Rachel Will.

As noted earlier, the core of this project appeared as a series of reports for *Progress in Human Geography*. I am grateful to SAGE Publications for the permission to reproduce portions of these reports. Additionally, I have been fortunate to give presentations at the following venues: The International Conference on Hong Kong in China / Cosmopolitan Journeys, Hong Kong; James Blaut Memorial Lecture at the annual meetings of the American Association of Geographers, Washington, D.C.; the Seventh Nordic Geographers Conference, Stockholm, Sweden; and the Fifth Nordic Geographers Conference, Reykjavik, Iceland.

Closer to home I thank my parents, Dr. Gerald Tyner and Dr. Judith Tyner, for their continued support and inspiration. I thank my now-eighteen-year-old puppy, Bond; reading at home while he naps (and snores) makes it all worthwhile. My daughters, Jessica and Anica, have progressed from princess dolls and stuffed animals to school dances and sporting events, but they remain my little girls. I hope that this project and all that it represents will help contribute in some small way to a better, more socially just future. Last, I dedicate this book to my life-partner, Belinda. Words cannot express my feelings toward Belinda, nor can words express my admiration and respect for all she does. And so I will simply write *mahal na mahal kita.*

NOTES

Preface

1. Twelve of the deaths were first responders (Kristi Metzger, Hammad Akram, Bonnie Feldt, Kahler Stone, Stephanie Alvey, Sandi Henley, Alicia Hernandez, Sharon Melville, Tracy Haywood, and David Zane, "Epidemiologic Investigation of Injuries Associated with the 2013 Fertilizer Plant Explosion in West, Texas," *Disaster Medicine and Public Health Preparedness* 10, no. 4 [2016]: 583–90).

2. Investigators later found that the cause of the fire was deliberate (David Sirota, Alex Kotch, Jay Cassano, and Josh Keefe, "Texas Republicans Helped Chemical Plant that Exploded Lobby Against Safety Rules," *International Business Times,* August 31, 2017, ibtimes.com/political-capital/texas-republicans -helped-chemical-plant-exploded-lobby-against-safety-rules, accessed September 5, 2017). See also Carrie Arnold, "A Strong Case for Prudent School Siting: The West Fertilizer Company Explosion," *Environmental Health Perspectives* 124, no. 10 (2016): A187.

3. Arnold, "A Strong Case," A187.

4. Arnold, "A Strong Case," A187.

5. Arnold, "A Strong Case," A187.

6. Rebecca Harrington, Lydia Ramsey, and Dana Varinsky, "Texas, Louisiana

Begin Long Recovery from Catastrophic Flooding as the Remnants of Hurricane Harvey Move Northeast," *Business Insider,* August 31, 2017, finance.yahoo.com/news/catastrophic-flooding-continues-harvey-moves-135700978.html, accessed September 5, 2017.

7. Karen Graham, "Arkema Chemical Plant Had Help in Blocking EPA Safety Regulations," *Digital Journal,* August 31, 2017, digitaljournal.com/tech-and-science/technology/arkema-chemical-plant-had-help-in-blocking-epa-safety-regulations/article/501331, accessed September 5, 2017.

8. Fifteen first responders were hospitalized (Graham, "Arkema Chemical Plant").

9. Sirota et al., "Texas Republicans Helped."

10. Graham, "Arkema Chemical Plant."

11. Sirota et al., "Texas Republicans Helped."

12. Johnnie Banks, "Dangerously Close: The CSB's Investigation into the Fatal Fire and Explosion in West, Texas," *Process Safety Progress* 35, no. 4 (2016): 312–16, at 313.

13. Banks, "Dangerously Close," 312.

14. Roddy Scheer and Doug Moss, "The West Texas Fertilizer Plant Explosion Was Not a Freak Event," EarthTalk, *Scientific American,* July 6, 2013, scientificamerican.com/article/west-texas-could-happen-anywhere/, accessed September 5, 2017.

15. Scheer and Moss, "The West Texas Fertilizer Plant Explosion."

16. Joseph Choonara, *Unravelling Capitalism: A Guide to Marxist Political Economy* (London: Bookmark, 2017), 25.

17. Karl Marx, *Capital: A Critique of Political Economy,* vol. 1, trans. Ben Fowkes (New York: Penguin 1990), 165.

18. See, for example, Laurent Baronian, *Marx and Living Labor* (London: Routledge, 2013).

19. Baronian, *Marx and Living Labor,* 12.

20. Marx, *Capital,* 1:346.

21. Karl Marx, *Economic and Philosophic Manuscripts of 1844* (New York: Prometheus, 1988), 71.

22. Don Mitchell, "Dead Labor: The Geography of Work-Place Violence in America and Beyond," *Environment and Planning A* 32, no. 5 (2000): 761–68.

23. See Jacque Lynn Foltyn, "The Corpse in Contemporary Culture: Identifying, Transacting, and Recoding the Dead Body in the Twenty-first Century," *Mortality* 13, no. 2 (2008): 99–104; Sheila Harper, "The Social Agency of Dead Bodies," *Mortality* 15, no. 4 (2010): 308–22; Ingrid Fernandez, "The Lives of Corpses: Narratives of the Image in American Memorial Photography," *Mortality* 16, no. 4 (2011): 343–64; and Craig Young and Duncan Light, "Corpses, Dead

Body Politics and Agency in Human Geography: Following the Corpse of Dr Petru Groza," *Transactions of the Institute of British Geographers* 38, no. 1 (2013): 135–48.

24. See, for example, Katherine Verdery, *The Political Lives of Dead Bodies: Reburial and Postsocialist Insecurity* (New York: Columbia University Press, 2013); and Margaret Schwartz, *Dead Matter: The Meaning of Iconic Corpses* (Minneapolis: University of Minnesota Press, 2015).

25. Friedrich Engels, *The Condition of the Working Class in England,* trans. Florence Wischnewetzky, ed. Victor Kiernan (New York: Penguin, 2005), 127–28.

26. Terry Eagleton, *Why Marx was Right* (New Haven, Conn.: Yale University Press, 2011), 2.

27. Julie Matthaei, "Why Feminist, Marxist, and Anti-Racist Economists Should Be Feminist-Marxist-Anti-Racist Economists," *Feminist Economics* 2 (1996): 22–42, at 36.

28. Emma W. Laurie and Ian G. R. Shaw, "Violent Conditions: The Injustices of Being," *Political Geography* 65 (2018): 8–16, at 8 (emphasis original).

29. For such treatments, see Verdery, *The Political Lives of Dead Bodies*; *Governing the Dead: Sovereignty and the Politics of Dead Bodies,* ed. Finn Stepputat (Oxford: Oxford University Press, 2014); and *Human Remains in Society: Curation and Exhibition in the Aftermath of Genocide and Mass-Violence,* ed. Élisabeth Anstett and Jean-Marc Dreyfus (Oxford: Oxford University Press, 2016).

30. J. D. Taylor, *Negative Capitalism: Cynicism in the Neoliberal Era* (Winchester, UK: Zero Books, 2013), 9.

31. For an alternative use of the term "necrocapitalism," see Subhabrata Bobby Banerjee, "Necrocapitalism," *Organization Studies* 29, no. 12 (2008): 1541–63. For discussions on necro-economics, see Warran Montag, "Necro-Economics: Adam Smith and Death in the Life of the Universal," *Radical Philosophy* 134 (2005): 7–17; Anna M. Agathangelou, "Bodies to the Slaughter: Global Racial Reconstructions, Fanon's Combat Breath, and Wrestling for Life," *Somatechnics* 1, no. 1 (2011): 209–48; and Chaka Uzondu, "Theorizing Necro-Ontology, Resisting Necro-Economics," *Atlantic Studies* 10, no. 3 (2013): 323–49.

32. James A. Tyner, *Violence in Capitalism: Devaluing Life in an Age of Responsibility* (Lincoln: University of Nebraska Press, 2016).

33. Uzondu, "Theorizing Necro-Ontology," 324.

34. Rosemarie Garland-Thomson, "Misfits: A Feminist Materialist Disability Concept," *Hypatia* 26, no. 3 (2011): 591–609.

35. Jesse Roman, "Hurricane Maria: A Preventable Humanitarian and Heath Care Crisis Unveiling the Puerto Rican Dilemma," *Annals of the American Thoracic Society* 15, no. 3 (2018): 293–95, at 293.

36. Jeremy Konyndyk, "President Trump has No Idea What's Happening in

Puerto Rico," *The Washington Post,* October 6, 2017, washingtonpost.com/news/
posteverything/wp/2017/10/06/president-trump-has-no-idea-whats-happening
-in-puerto-rico, accessed April 18, 2018.

37. Konyndyk, "President Trump has No Idea."

38. Roman, "Hurricane Maria," 293.

39. Roman, "Hurricane Maria," 293.

40. Ted Alcorn, "Puerto Rico's Health System after Hurricane Maria," *The Lancet* 390, no. 10103 (2017): e24.

41. Roman, "Hurricane Maria," 293.

42. Quoted in Alcorn, "Puerto Rico's Health System," e24.

43. Carmen D. Zorrilla, "The View from Puerto Rico—Hurricane Maria and its Aftermath," *The New England Journal of Medicine* 377, no. 19 (2017): 1801–3, at 1803.

44. Alexis R. Santos-Lozada, "Why Puerto Rico's Death Toll from Hurricane Maria is So Much Higher than Officials Thought," *The Conversation,* January 3, 2018, theconversation.com/why-puerto-ricos-death-toll-from-hurricane-maria -is-so-much-higher-than-officials-thought-89349, accessed April 18, 2018.

45. Roman, "Hurricane Maria," 294.

46. Ruth W. Gilmore, *Golden Gulag: Prisons, Surplus, Crisis, and Opposition in Globalizing California* (Berkeley: University of California Press, 2007), 28; see also Gilmore, "Fatal Couplings of Power and Difference: Notes on Racism and Geography," *The Professional Geographer* 54, no. 1 (2002): 15–24.

1. Living Labor

1. Sébastien Rioux, "Embodied Contradictions: Capitalism, Social Repro-duction and Body Formation," *Women's Studies International Forum* 48 (2015): 194–202, at 195. See also Reecia Orzeck, "What Does Not Kill You: Historical Materialism and the Body," *Environment and Planning D: Society and Space* 25 (2007): 496–514; Joseph Fracchia, "The Capitalist Labour-Process and the Body in Pain: The Corporal Depths of Marx's Concept of Immiseration," *Historical Materialism* 16 (2008): 35–66; and Rioux, "International Historical Sociology: Recovering Sociohistorical Causality," *Rethinking Marxism* 21, no. 4 (2009): 585–604.

2. Rioux, "Embodied Contradictions," 194–95.

3. Linda McDowell, *Gender, Identity and Place: Understanding Feminist Ge-ographies* (Minneapolis: University of Minnesota Press, 1999), 36.

4. Orzeck, "What Does Not Kill You," 497.

5. Karl Marx, *The Eighteenth Brumaire of Louis Bonaparte,* in *Karl Marx:*

Selected Writings, ed. David McLellan, 2nd ed. (Oxford: Oxford University Press, 2000), 329–55, at 329.

6. Karl Marx and Friedrich Engels, *The German Ideology* (Amherst, N.Y.: Prometheus, 1998), 37.

7. Joseph Fracchia, "Beyond the Human-Nature Debate: Human Corporeal Organization as the 'First Fact' of Historical Materialism," *Historical Materialism* 13, no. 1 (2005): 33–61, at 40.

8. Karl Marx, "Theses on Feuerbach," in Marx and Engels, *German Ideology*, 570.

9. Marx and Engels, *German Ideology*, 37. Fracchia explains that their phrase is most frequently translated as "the physical organization of human beings" ("Beyond the Human-Nature Debate," 39). However, the original German version is "körperliche Organisation deer Menschen," clearly in reference to "corporeality" rather than merely "physicality."

10. Fracchia, "Beyond the Human-Nature Debate," 40. See also Allen W. Wood, *Karl Marx*, 2nd ed. (New York: Routledge, 2004), 63.

11. Orzeck, "What Does Not Kill You," 497.

12. Fracchia, "Beyond the Human-Nature Debate," 41.

13. Marx and Engels, *German Ideology*, 37.

14. Karl Marx, *Economic and Philosophic Manuscripts of 1844*, trans. Martin Milligan (Amherst, N.Y.: Prometheus, 1988), 86.

15. Marx and Engels, *German Ideology*, 37.

16. Rioux, "Embodied Contradictions," 195.

17. Karl Marx, *A Contribution to the Critique of Political Economy*, in *Knowledge: Critical Concepts*, ed. Nico Stehr and Reiner Grundman, vol. 1, *The Foundations of Knowledge* (New York: Routledge, 2005), 180.

18. Fracchia, "Beyond the Human-Nature Debate," 51.

19. Orzeck, "What Does Not Kill You," 500.

20. Rioux, "Embodied Contradictions," 195.

21. Rioux, "Embodied Contradictions," 195.

22. Rioux, "Embodied Contradictions," 196.

23. Marx, *Contribution to the Critique*, 180.

24. See, for example, Jairus Banaji, *Theory as History: Essays on Modes of Production and Exploitation* (Chicago: Haymarket, 2011). The "mode of production," in other words, is an expansive concept, one that is not reducible to a genealogy of self-contained epochs (e.g., feudalism, mercantilism, capitalism, and communism), as is generally thought. It is just such an erroneous and simplistic reading that has caused much confusion over the years.

25. Marx and Engels, *German Ideology*, 38.

26. Françoise Dastur, *How Are We to Confront Death? An Introduction to Philosophy*, trans. Robert Vallier (New York: Fordham University Press, 2012), 3.

27. David McNally, *Bodies of Meaning: Studies on Language, Labor, and Liberation* (Albany: State University of New York, 2001), 7.

28. Orzeck, "What Does Not Kill You," 500.

29. Orzeck, "What Does Not Kill You," 500.

30. Gillian Rose, "A Body of Questions," *Using Social Theory: Thinking through Research*, edited by M. Pryke, G. Rose, and S. Whatmore (London: Sage, 2003), pp. 47–64; at 48.

31. Linda Blackman, *The Body: The Key Concepts* (New York: Berg, 2008), 4.

32. Gillian Rose, *Feminism and Geography: The Limits of Geographical Knowledge* (Minneapolis: University of Minnesota Press, 1993).

33. Elizabeth Grosz, "Bodies-Cities," in *Places Through the Body*, ed. H. J. Nast and S. Pile (New York: Routledge, 1998), 42–51, at 43.

34. Emma W. Laurie and Ian G. R. Shaw, "Violent Conditions: The Injustices of Being," *Political Geography* 65 (2018): 8–16, at 8.

35. See discussions in Jeffrey R. Botkin and Stephen G. Post, "Confusion in the Determination of Death: Distinguishing Philosophy from Physiology," *Perspectives in Biology and Medicine* 36, no. 1 (1992): 129–38; Edward T. Bartlett, "Differences Between Death and Dying," *Journal of Medical Ethics* 21, no. 5 (1995): 270–76; John P. Lizza, *Persons, Humanity, and the Definition of Death* (Baltimore, Md.: Johns Hopkins University Press, 2006); Steven Luper, *The Philosophy of Death* (Cambridge: Cambridge University Press, 2009); and Bernard M. Schumacher, *Death and Mortality in Contemporary Philosophy*, trans. Michael J. Miller (Cambridge: Cambridge University Press, 2011).

36. Luper, *Philosophy of Death*, 14.

37. James L. Bernat, "The Biophilosophical Basis of Whole-Brain Death," *Social Philosophy and Policy* 19, no. 2 (2002): 324–42, at 333.

38. Bernat, "The Biophilosophical Basis," 334–35.

39. Botkin and Post, "Confusion in the Determination," 129.

40. Schumacher, *Death and Mortality*, 13.

41. Luper, *Philosophy of Death*, 39.

42. Luper, *Philosophy of Death*, 42.

43. Luper, *Philosophy of Death*, 40–41.

44. Luper, *Philosophy of Death*, 43.

45. Bernat, "The Biophilosophical Basis," 331.

46. Luper, *Philosophy of Death*, 42.

47. Botkin and Post, "Confusion in the Determination," 130.

48. Botkin and Post, "Confusion in the Determination," 130.

49. Lizza, *Persons*, 4.

50. Zygmunt Bauman, *Mortality, Immortality & Other Life Strategies* (Stanford, Calif.: Stanford University Press, 1992), 9.

51. Orzeck, "What Does Not Kill You," 508.

52. Luper, *Philosophy of Death*, 58.

53. For more in-depth discussion of these terms, see Nancy Ettlinger, "Precarity Unbound," *Alternatives* 32 (2007): 319–40; Brett Neilson and Ned Rossiter, "Precarity as a Political Concept, or, Fordism as Exception," *Theory, Culture & Society* 27, no. 7–8 (2008): 51–72; Louise Waite, "A Place and Space for a Critical Geography of Precarity?" *Geography Compass* 3, no. 1 (2009): 412–33; Nancy Worth, "Feeling Precarious: Millennial Women and Work," *Environment and Planning D: Society and Space* 34, no. 4 (2016): 601–16; and Kendra Strauss, "Labour Geography I: Towards a Geography of Precarity?" *Progress in Human Geography,* July 7, 2017), doi: 10.1177/0309132517717786.

54. Judith Butler, *Frames of War: When is Life Grievable?* (New York: Verso, 2009), 25. See also Butler, *Precarious Life: The Powers of Mourning and Violence* (London: Verso, 2004).

55. Butler, *Frames of War,* 25.

56. Christopher Harker, "Precariousness, Precarity, and Family: Notes from Palestine," *Environment and Planning A* 44 (2012): 849–65, at 859.

57. Butler, *Frames of War,* 25.

58. Orzeck, "What Does Not Kill You," 503.

59. Orzeck, "What Does Not Kill You," 503.

60. Kathryn A. Gillespie and Patricia J. Lopez, "Introducing Economies of Death," in *Economies of Death: Economic Logics of Killable Life and Grievable Death,* ed. Patricia J. Lopez and Kathryn A. Gillespie (New York: Routledge, 2015), 1–13, at 8.

61. Jason Read, *The Micro-Politics of Capital: Marx and the Prehistory of the Present* (Albany: State University of New York Press, 2003), 10 and 55.

62. Martha A. Fineman, "The Vulnerable Subject: Anchoring Equality in the Human Condition," *Yale Journal of Law and Feminism* 20, no. 1 (2008): article 2 (23 pp.), at 10.

63. Fineman, "The Vulnerable Subject," 2.

64. Fineman, "The Vulnerable Subject," 2–3.

65. Fineman, "The Vulnerable Subject," 3. Fineman notes also that the equal protection doctrine does not provide protection against subject positions not identified by the legal system.

66. Berta Hernández-Truyol, "Glocalizing Women's Health and Safety: Migration, Work, and Labor," *Santa Clara Journal of International Law* 48 (2017): 48–76, at 53.

67. Hernández-Truyol, "Glocalizing Women's Health," 53.

68. Fineman, "The Vulnerable Subject," 3.

69. Fineman, "The Vulnerable Subject," 4.

70. Fineman, "The Vulnerable Subject," 10.

71. Linda McDowell, "Work, Workfare, Work/Life Balance and an Ethic of Care," *Progress in Human Geography* 28, no. 2 (2004): 145–63, at 156. See also Worth, "Feeling Precarious," 604.

72. Giorgio Agamben, *Homo Sacer: Sovereign Power and Bare Life* (Stanford, Calif.: Stanford University Press, 1998), 1.

73. Agamben, *Homo Sacer,* 144.

74. Hosna J. Shewly, "Abandoned Spaces and Bare Life in the Enclaves of the India–Bangladesh Border," *Political Geography* 32 (2013): 23–31, at 26.

75. Fineman, "The Vulnerable Subject," 10.

76. Fineman, "The Vulnerable Subject," 11.

77. Fineman, "The Vulnerable Subject," 12.

78. Rosemarie Garland-Thomson, "Misfits: A Feminist Materialist Disability Concept," *Hypatia* 26, no. 3 (2011): 591–609, at 592.

79. Garland-Thomson, "Misfits," 592.

80. Garland-Thomson, "Misfits," 594.

81. Nancy Duncan, "(Re)placings," in *Bodyspace: Destabilizing Geographies of Gender and Sexuality,* ed. Nancy Duncan (New York: Routledge, 1996), 1–10, at 2.

82. Garland-Thomson, "Misfits," 600.

83. Waite, "A Place and Space," 427.

84. Laura Pulido, "Flint, Environmental Racism, and Racial Capitalism," *Capitalism Nature Socialism* 27, no. 3 (2016): 1–16, at 1.

85. Gillespie and Lopez, "Introducing Economies of Death," 9.

86. Butler, *Precarious Life,* xiv–xv.

87. Rioux, "Embodied Contradictions," 195.

88. Karl Marx, *Capital: A Critique of Political Economy,* vol. 1, trans. Ben Fowkes (New York: Penguin 1990), 381.

89. Marx, *Capital,* 1:381.

2. Commodified Labor

1. See Steve Shaviro, "Capitalist Monsters," *Historical Materialism* 10, no. 4 (2002): 281–90; Mark Neocleous, "Let the Dead Bury Their Dead," *Radical Philosophy* 128 (2004): 23–32; Neocleous, "The Political Economy of the Dead: Marx's Vampires," *History of Political Thought* 24, no. 4 (2003): 668–84; Richard Godfrey, Gavin Jack, and Campell Jones, "Sucking, Bleeding, Breaking: On the Dialectics of Vampirism, Capital, and Time," *Culture and Organization* 10, no. 1 (2004):

25–36; David McNally, *Monsters of the Market: Zombies, Vampires and Global Capitalism* (Chicago: Haymarket, 2012); Jason J. Morrissette, "Marxferatu: The Vampire Metaphor as a Tool for Teaching Marx's Critique of Capitalism," *PS: Political Science and Politics* 46, no. 3 (2013): 637–42.

2. McNally, *Monsters of the Market*, 13.

3. Karl Marx, *Capital: A Critique of Political Economy*, vol. 1, trans. Ben Fowkes (New York: Penguin, 1990), 346.

4. Marx, *Economic and Philosophic Manuscripts of 1844* (New York: Prometheus, 1988), 19.

5. Ellen Meiksins Wood, *Empire of Capital* (London: Verso, 2003), 9. There is of course no monolithic "capitalist" mode of production. As Geoff Mann succinctly writes, "capitalism does not look the same everywhere you go" (*Disassembly Required: A Field Guide to Actually Existing Capitalism* [Baltimore, Md.: AK Press, 2013], 12).

6. Michael Heinrich, *An Introduction to the Three Volumes of Karl Marx's* Capital (New York: Monthly Review Press, 2012), 181.

7. Warren Montag, "Necro-Economics: Adam Smith and Death in the Life of the Universal," *Radical Philosophy* 134 (2005): 7–17, at 16.

8. Montag, "Necro-Economics," 16.

9. Stephen A. Resnick and Richard D. Wolff, *Class Theory and History: Capitalism and Communism in the USSR* (New York: Routledge, 2002), 8.

10. Resnick and Wolff, *Class Theory*, 8.

11. Resnick and Wolff, *Class Theory*, 9.

12. Resnick and Wolff, *Class Theory*, 9.

13. Frantz Fanon, *The Wretched of the Earth*, trans. Richard Philcox (New York: Grove Press, 2004), 5.

14. See Leslie McCall, "The Complexity of Intersectionality," *Signs: Journal of Women in Culture and Society* 30, no. 3 (2005): 1771–1800; Kimberlé Crenshaw, "Demarginalizing the Intersection of Race and Sex: A Black Feminist Critique of Antidiscrimination Doctrine, Feminist Theory and Antiracist Politics," *University of Chicago Legal Forum*, 1989, 139–67; and Jennifer C. Nash, "Re-Thinking Intersectionality," *Feminist Review* 89 (2008): 1–15.

15. Ha-Joon Chang, "Breaking the Mould: An Institutionalist Political Economy Alternative to the Neo-Liberal Theory of the Market and the State," *Cambridge Journal of Economics* 26 (2002): 539–59, esp. 540–42.

16. Mark A. Martinez, *The Myth of the Free Market: The Role of the State in a Capitalist Economy* (Sterling, Va.: Kumarian, 2009), 37.

17. Martinez, *The Myth of the Free Market*, 207.

18. Chang, "Breaking the Mould," 543.

19. Martinez, *The Myth of the Free Market*, 207.

20. Bernard E. Harcourt, *The Illusion of Free Markets: Punishment and the* *Myth of Natural Order* (Cambridge, Mass.: Harvard University Press, 2011), 33.

21. Harcourt, *The Illusion of Free Markets,* 17.

22. Harcourt, *The Illusion of Free Markets,* 40–41.

23. Harcourt, *The Illusion of Free Markets,* 41.

24. David J. Roberts and Minelle Mahtani, "Neoliberalizing Race, Racing Neoliberalism: Placing 'Race' in Neoliberal Discourses," *Antipode* 42, no. 2 (2010): 248–57, at 253.

25. See, for example, D. J. Silton, "U.S. Prisons and Racial Profiling: A Covertly Racist Nation Rides a Vicious Cycle," *Law & Inequality: A Journal of Theory and Practice* 20, no. 1 (2002): 53–90.

26. William Y. Chin, "Racial Cumulative Disadvantage: The Cumulative Effects of Racial Bias at Multiple Decision Points in the Criminal Justice System," *Wake Forest Journal of Law & Policy* 6, no. 2 (2016): 441–58.

27. Harcourt, *The Illusion of Free Markets,* 48.

28. Karl Marx, *Capital,* 1:163.

29. Heinrich, *An Introduction,* 72.

30. Marx, *Capital,* 1:164–65.

31. Don Mitchell, "Dead Labor and the Political Economy of Landscape— California Living, California Dying," in *Handbook of Cultural Geography,* ed. Kay Anderson, Mona Domosh, Steve Pile, and Nigel Thrift (Thousand Oaks, Calif.: Sage, 2003), 233–48.

32. Heinrich, *An Introduction,* 73.

33. Marx, *Capital,* 1:271.

34. Marx, *Capital,* 1:272.

35. Jamie Peck, *Work Place: The Social Regulation of Labor Markets* (New York: Guilford, 1996), 27.

36. Robert Albritton, *Economics Transformed: Discovering the Brilliance of Marx* (Ann Arbor, Mich.: Pluto, 2007), 26.

37. Marx, *Capital,* 1:138.

38. Karl Marx, *Capital: A Critique of Political Economy,* vol. 2, trans. David Fernbach (New York: Penguin, 1992), 156.

39. Joseph Fracchia, "The Capitalist Labor-Process and the Body in Pain: The Corporeal Depths of Marx's Concept of Imiseration," *Historical Materialism* 16 (2008): 35–66, at 45.

40. Fracchia, "The Capitalist Labour-Process," 43.

41. Fracchia, "The Capitalist Labour-Process," 43.

42. Marx, *Capital,* 1:300.

43. Paul D'Amato, *The Meaning of Marxism* (Chicago: Haymarket, 2006), 56.

44. Fracchia, "The Capitalist Labour-Process," 43.

45. Karl Marx and Friedrich Engels, *The Communist Manifesto* (London: Verso, 2012), 42.

46. Jason Read, *The Micro-Politics of Capital: Marx and the Prehistory of the Present* (Albany: State University of New York Press, 2003), 10.

47. Marx, *Capital,* 1:645.

48. Marx, *Capital,* 1:376.

49. Fracchia, "The Capitalist Labour-Process," 44.

50. Fracchia, "The Capitalist Labour-Process," 44.

51. Marx, *Capital,* 1:716.

52. Marx, *Capital,* 1:342.

53. Fracchia, "The Capitalist Labor-Process," 45.

54. Marx, *Capital,* 1:341.

55. Marx, *Capital,* 1:376.

56. Dermont O'Reilly and Michael Rosato, "Worked to Death? A Census-Based Longitudinal Study of the Relationship between the Numbers of Hours Spent Working and Mortality Risk," *International Journal of Epidemiology* 42, no. 6 (2013): 1820–30, at 1826–27.

57. See Allard E. Dembe, J. Bianca Erickson, Rachel G. Delbos, and Steven M. Banks, "The Impact of Overtime and Long Work Hours on Occupational Injuries and Illnesses: New Evidence fom the United States," *Occupational and Environmental Medicine* 62, no. 9 (2005): 588–97; and Erik Gonzalez-Mulé and Bethany Cockburn, "Worked to Death: The Relationships of Job Demands and Job Control with Mortality," *Personnel Psychology* 70 (2017): 73–112.

58. Huong Dinh, Lyndall Strazdins, and Jennifer Welsh, "Hour-Glass Ceilings: Work-Hour Thresholds, Gendered Health Inequities," *Social Science & Medicine* 176 (2017): 42–51, at 42.

59. Marx, *Capital,* 1:377.

60. Marx, *Capital,* 1:129.

61. Alex Callinicos, *The Revolutionary Ideas of Karl Marx* (Chicago: Haymarket, 2011), 137.

62. Marx, *Capital,* 1:436–37.

63. Ben Fine and Alfredo Saad-Filho, *Marx's "Capital,"* 5th ed. (New York: Pluto, 2004), 32.

64. David Harvey, *The Limits to Capital,* updated ed. (New York: Verso, 2006)29.

65. Harvey, *Limits to Capital,* 29.

66. Harvey, *Limits to Capital,* 31.

67. David Bisell and Vincent J. Del Casino, "Whiter Labor Geography and the Rise of the Robots?" *Social & Cultural Geography* 18, no. 3 (2017): 435–42, at 436.

68. Fine and Saad-Filho, *Marx's "Capital,"* 38.

69. See ch. 13 of Marx, *Capital,* vol. 1.

70. Marx, *Capital,* 1:439 and 441.

71. Fracchia, "The Capitalist Labour-Process," 48–49.

72. Marx, *Capital,* 1:1024.

73. Marx, *Capital,* 1:1034–35.

74. Marx, *Capital,* 1:1035.

75. Marx, *Capital,* 1:1040.

76. Marx, *Capital,* 1:486.

77. Marx, *Capital,* 1:481–82.

78. Marx, *Capital,* 1:280.

79. Marx, *Capital,* 1:280.

80. Friedrich Engels, *The Condition of the Working Class in England* (New York: Penguin, 2005), 115.

81. Joshua Barkan, "Use Beyond Value: Giorgio Agamben and a Critique of Capitalism," *Rethinking Marxism* 21, no. 2 (2009): 243–59, at 256.

82. See Arthur Schatzkin, "Health and Labor-Power: A Theoretical Investigation," *International Journal of Health Services* 8, no. 2 (1978): 213–34, at 214.

83. Martha A. Fineman, "The Vulnerable Subject: Anchoring Equality in the Human Condition," *Yale Journal of Law and Feminism* 20, no. 1 (2008): article 2 (23 pp.), at 10.

84. M. Fineman, "The Vulnerable Subject," 10.

85. Jairus Banaji, "The Fictions of Free Labor: Contract, Coercion, and So-Called Unfree Labour," *Historical Materialism* 11, no. 3 (2003): 69–95, at 82.

86. M. Fineman, "The Vulnerable Subject," 2.

87. Banaji, "The Fictions of Free Labor," 70.

88. M. Fineman, "The Vulnerable Subject," 10.

89. Marx, *Capital,* 1:271.

90. Marx, *Capital,* 1:272.

91. Marx, *Capital,* 1:874–75.

92. Harcourt, *Illusion of Free Markets,* 34.

93. Schatzkin, "Health and Labor-Power," 214.

94. Jonathan Fineman, "The Vulnerable Subject at Work: A New Perspective on the Employment At-will Debate," *Southwestern Law Review* 43 (2013): 275–317, at 277–78.

95. J. Fineman, "The Vulnerable Subject at Work," 280.

96. J. Fineman, "The Vulnerable Subject at Work," 298.

97. J. Fineman, "The Vulnerable Subject at Work," 304.

98. J. Fineman, "The Vulnerable Subject at Work," 305.

99. J. Fineman, "The Vulnerable Subject at Work," 306.

100. Fred Magdoff and Harry Magdoff, "Disposable Workers: Today's Reserve Army of Labor," *Monthly Review* 55, no. 11 (2004): 18–35, at 21.

101. Hans A. Baer, "On the Political Economy of Health," *Medical Anthropology Newsletter* 14, no. 1 (1982): 1–2 and 13–17, at 14.

102. Kathi Weeks, *The Problem with Work: Feminism, Marxism, Antiwork Politics, and Postwork Imaginaries*, (Durham, N.C.: Duke University Press), 6.

103. Weeks, *The Problem with Work*, 8.

104. Weeks, *The Problem with Work*, 10.

105. Michael J. Piore, "Notes for a Theory of Labor Market Stratification," *Working Paper Department of Economics Number 95*, Massachusetts Institute of Technology, 1972, 2.

106. See, for example, Heidi Hartmann, "The Unhappy Marriage of Marxism and Feminism: Towards a More Progressive Union," *Capital & Class* 3 (1979): 1–33; Evelyn Nakano Glenn, "Racial Ethnic Women's Labor: The Intersection of Race, Gender and Class Oppression," *Review of Radical Political Economics* 17 (1985): 86–108; and Julie Mattaei, "Why Feminist, Marxist, and Anti-Racist Economists Should be Feminist-Marxist-Anti-Racist Economists," *Feminist Economics* 2 (1996): 22–42.

107. Jane Wills and Brian Linneker, "In-Work Poverty and the Living Wage in the United Kingdom: A Geographical Perspective," *Transactions of the Institute of British Geographers* 39, no. 2 (2014): 182–94, at 182.

108. Fran Bennett, "The 'Living Wage,' Low Pay and in Work Poverty: Rethinking the Relationships," *Critical Social Policy* 34, no. 1 (2014): 46–65, at 55–56.

109. Marx, *Capital*, 1:376.

110. Schatzkin, "Health and Labor-Power," 215.

111. Marx, *Capital*, 1:711.

112. Marx, *Capital*, 1:375.

113. Karl Marx, *Grundrisse: Foundations of the Critique of Political Economy* (New York: Penguin, 1973), 90.

114. See, for example, Oren M. Levin-Waldman, "Exploring the Politics of the Minimum Wage," *Journal of Economic Issues* 32, no. 3 (1998): 773–802; and David H. Plowman and Chris Perryer. "Moral Sentiments and the Minimum Wage," *The Economic and Labour Relations Review* 21, no. 2 (2010): 1–21.

115. Marx and Engels, *The Communist Manifesto*, 43.

116. Maria Mies, *Patriarchy and Capital Accumulation on a World Scale: Women in the International Division of Labor* (New York: Palgrave Macmillan, 1998), 31.

117. Marx, *Capital*, 1:275.

118. Marx, *Capital*, 1:271–72.

119. Read, *Micro-Politics of Capital*, 135.

120. Stuart C. Aitken, *Family Fantasies and Community Space* (New Brunswick, N.J.: Rutgers University Press, 1998), 27.

121. Silvia Federici, *Caliban and the Witch: Women, the Body and Primitive Accumulation* (Brooklyn, N.Y.: Autonomedia, 2004), 75.

122. Federici, *Caliban and the Witch*, 75. See also Leopoldina Fortunati, *The Arcane of Reproduction: Housework, Prostitution, Labor and Capital* (Brooklyn, N.Y.: Autonomedia, 1995).

123. See, for example, Nakano Glenn, "Racial Ethnic Women's Labor"; Patricia Hill Collins, "Intersections of Race, Class, Gender, and Nation: Some Implications for Black Family Studies," *Journal of Comparative Family Studies* 29, no. 1 (1998): 27–36; Linda Peake, "Toward an Understanding of the Interconnectedness of Women's Lives: The 'Racial' Reproduction of Labor in Low-Income Urban Areas," *Urban Geography* 16, no. 5 (1995): 414–39; and Migno Duffy, "Reproducing Labor Inequalities: Challenges for Feminists Conceptualizing Care at the Intersections of Gender, Race, and Class," *Gender & Society* 19, no. 1 (2005): 66–82.

124. Nakano Glenn, "Racial Ethnic Women's Labor," 102.

125. Nakano Glenn, "Racial Ethnic Women's Labor," 102–4.

126. See Sander Kelman, "Toward the Political Economy of Medical Care," *Inquiry* 8, no. 3 (1971): 30–38; Vicente Navarro, "From Public Health to Health of the Public: The Redefinition of Our Task," *American Journal of Public Health* 64, no. 6 (1974): 538–42; Navarro, "The Labor Process and Health: A Historical Materialist Interpretation," *International Journal of Health Services* 12, no. 1 (1982): 5–29; Navarro, "U.S. Marxist Scholarship in the Analysis of Health and Medicine," *International Journal of Health Services* 15, no. 4 (1985): 525–45; Schatzkin, "Health and Labor-Power"; Howard Waitzkin, "A Marxist View of Medical Care," *Annals of Internal Medicine* 89 (1978): 264–78; Baer, "On the Political Economy of Health"; and Michael L. Schwalbe and Clifford L. Staples, "Class Position, Work Experience, and Health," *International Journal of Health Services* 16, no. 4 (1986): 583–602.

127. Baer, "On the Political Economy," 14.

128. Magdoff and Magdoff, "Disposable Workers," 21.

129. Schatzkin, "Health and Labor-Power," 215.

130. Schatzkin, "Health and Labor-Power," 218.

131. Quoted in Schatzkin, "Health and Labor-Power," 218.

132. E. Richard Brown, "Public Health in Imperialism: Early Rockefeller Programs at Home and Abroad," *American Journal of Public Health* 66, no. 9 (1976): 897–903.

133. Brown, "Public Health," 897.

134. Brown, "Public Health," 898.

135. Schatzkin, "Health and Labor-Power," 220.

136. Chris Harman, *Zombie Capitalism: Global Crisis and the Relevance of Marx* (Chicago: Haymarket, 2010), 165.

137. Giuliano Bonoli, "Time Matters: Postindustrialization, New Social Risks, and Welfare State Adaptation in Advanced Industrial Democracies," *Comparative Political Studies* 40, no. 5 (2007): 495–520, at 496.

138. Robert Crawford, "You Are Dangerous to Your Health: The Ideology and Politics of Victim Blaming," *International Journal of Health Services* 7, no. 4 (1977): 663–80, at 664.

139. Crawford, "You Are Dangerous," 664.

140. See, for example, Fiona Williams, "Racism and the Discipline of Social Policy: A Critique of Welfare Theory," *Critical Social Policy* 20, no. 2 (1987): 4–29; and Wendy M. Limbert and Heather E. Bullock, "'Playing the Fool': US Welfare Policy from a Critical Race Perspective," *Feminism & Psychology* 15, no. 3 (2005): 253–74.

141. Adam D. Dixon, *The New Geography of Capitalism: Firms, Finance, and Society* (Oxford: Oxford University Press, 2014), 109.

142. Garry Leech, *Capitalism: A Structural Genocide* (New York: Zed, 2012), 33.

143. Alfredo Saad-Filho, "Marxian and Keynesian Critiques of Neoliberalism," *Socialist Register* 44 (2008): 337–45, at 342.

144. Michael Roberts, *The Long Depression: How It Happened, Why It Happened, and What Happens Next* (Chicago: Haymarket, 2016), 60–61.

145. Peck, *Work Place*, 2.

146. Crawford, "You Are Dangerous," 666.

147. See Lawrence W. Green and Marshall W. Kreuter, "Health Promotion as a Public Health Strategy for the 1990s," *Annual Review of Public Health* 11 (1990): 319–34; Meredith Minkler, "Personal Responsibility for Health? A Review of the Arguments and the Evidence at Century's End," *Health Education & Behavior* 26, no. 1 (1999): 121–40; Nurit Guttman and William Harris Ressler, "On Being Responsible: Ethical Issues in Appeals to Personal Responsibility in Health Campaigns," *Journal of Health Communication* 6, no. 2 (2001): 117–36; Gavin Brookes and Kevin Harvey, "Peddling a Semiotics of Fear: A Critical Examination of Scare Tactics and Commercial Strategies in Public Health Promotion," *Social Semiotics* 25, no. 1 (2015): 57–80; and Allison M. Baker and Linda M. Hunt, "Counterproductive Consequences of a Conservative Ideology: Medicaid Expansion and Personal Responsibility Requirements," *American Journal of Public Health* 106, no. 7 (2016): 1181–87.

148. Victor Fuchs, "Health Care and the United States Economic System," *Milbank Memorial Fund Quarterly* 50, no. 2 (1972): 211–39.

149. Guttman and Ressler, "On Being Responsible," 118.

150. Guttman and Ressler, "On Being Responsible," 119.

151. Brookes and Harvey, "Peddling a Semiotics of Fear," 59.

152. See Brooks and Harvey, "Peddling a Semiotics of Fear," 59; and Minkler, "Personal Responsibility."

153. Minkler, "Personal Responsibility," 124.

154. Magdoff and Magdoff, "Disposable Workers," 32.

155. World Hunger Education Service, "Hunger in America: 2011 United States Hunger and Poverty Facts," worldhunger.org/articles/Learn/old/us_hunger_facts.htm.

156. Center for Family Policy & Research, "The State of Children and Families, 2009," core.ac.uk/download/pdf/62757059.pdf.

157. National Center for Children in Poverty, "Demographics of Poor Children," nccp.org/profiles/state_profile.php?state=US&id=7.

158. World Hunger Education Service, "Hunger in America: 2011."

159. Rakesh Kochhar, Richard Fry, and Paul Taylor, "Twenty-to-One: Wealth Gaps Rise to Record Highs Between Whites, Blacks and Hispanics," *Pew Research Center,* July 26, 2011, pewsocialtrends.org/2011/07/26/wealth-gaps-rise-to-record-highs-between-whites-blacks-hispanics/, accessed August 18, 2011.

160. K. D. Kochanek, J. Q. Xu, S. L. Murphy, et al. "Deaths: Preliminary Data for 2009," *National Vital Statistics Reports* 59, no. 4 (2011): Table 6.

161. Deborah Hardoon, Wealth: Having it All and Wanting More," *Oxfam International,* January 19, 2015, oxfam.org/en/research/wealth-having-it-all-and-wanting-more.

162. Hardoon, "Wealth."

163. Hardoon, "Wealth."

164. Richard Florida, Charlotta Mellander, and Isabel Ritchie, *The Geography of the Global Super Rich,* University of Toronto, Martin Prosperity Institute Working Paper Series, July 26, 2016, martinprosperity.org/content/insight-the-geography-of-the-super-rich/.

165. Gholam Khiabany, "Refugee Crisis, Imperialism and Pitiless Wars on the Poor," *Media, Culture and Society* 38, no. 5 (2016): 755–62, at 761.

166. Saez and Zucman, "Wealth Inequality," 573.

167. David B. Grusky and Alair MacLean, "The Social Fallout of a High-Inequality Regime," *Annals of the American Academy of Political and Social Sciences* 663 (2016): 33–52, at 44.

168. Raj Chetty, Michael Stepner, Sarah Abraham, Shelby Lin, Benjamin Scuderi, Nicholas Turner, Augustin Bergeron, and David Cutler, "The Association Between Income and Life Expectancy in the United States, 2001–2014," *Journal of the American Medical Association* 315, no. 16 (2016): 1750–66, at 1753.

169. C. Matthew Snipp and Sin Yi Cheung, "Changes in Racial and Gender

Inequality since 1970," *Annals of the American Academy of Political and Social Sciences* 663 (2016): 80–98.

170. David R. Williams and Chiquita Collins, "US Socioeconomic and Racial Differences in Health: Patterns and Explanations," *Annual Review of Sociology* 21 (1995): 349–86, at 360.

171. Jo C. Phelan and Bruce G. Link, "Is Racism a Fundamental Cause of Inequalities in Health?" *Annual Review of Sociology* 41 (2015): 311–30, at 314.

172. Maeve Wallace, Joia Crear-Perry, Lisa Richardson, Meshawn Tarver, and Katherine Theall, "Separate and Unequal: Structural Racism and Infant Mortality in the US," *Health and Place* 45 (2017): 140–44, at 140. See also Joe Feagin and Zinobia Bennefield, "Systemic Racism and US Health Care," *Social Science and Medicine* 103 (2014): 7–14; Alicia Lukachko, Mark L. Hatzenbuehler, and Katherine M. Keyes, "Structural Racism and Myocardial Infarction in the United States," *Social Science and Medicine* 103 (2014): 42–50; and Jennifer Jee-Lyn García and Mienah Zulfacar Sharif, "Black Lives Matter: A Commentary on Racism and Public Health," *American Journal of Public Health* 105, no. 8 (2015): e27–e30.

173. Robert Albritton, *Let Them Eat Junk: How Capitalism Creates Hunger and Obesity* (New York: Pluto, 2009), 27.

174. Marx, *Capital*, 1:382.

175. See, for example, Allen E. Buchanan, "Marx, Morality, and History: An Assessment of Recent Analytical Work on Marx," *Ethics* 98, no. 1 (1987): 104–36.

176. Marx, *Economic and Philosophic Manuscripts,* 20.

177. Engels, *The Condition of the Working Class,* 127.

3. Surplus Labor

1. Holly Yan and Jason Morris, "San Antonio Driver Says He Didn't Know Immigrants Were in Truck," *CNN,* July 25, 2017, amp.cnn.com/cnn/2017/07/24/us/san-antonio-trailer-migrants/index.html, accessed July 26, 2017; Joel Rose and Shaheen Ainpour, "Death at the Southern Border: An Increasing Risk for Migrants," *NPR Now,* July 25, 2017, npr.org/2017/07/25/539263390, accessed July 26, 2017.

2. Alexandra Délano Alonso and Benjamin Nienass, "Deaths, Visibility, and Responsibility: The Politics of Mourning at the US-Mexico Border," *Social Research* 83, no. 2 (2016): 421–51, at 423.

3. IOM Global Immigration Data Analysis Centre, "Migrant Fatalities Worldwide: Latest Global Figures (2017)," *Missing Migrants Project,* missingmigrants.iom.int/latest-global-figures.

4. Délano Alonso and Nienass, "Deaths," 423–24. See also Wayne A.

Cornelius, "Death at the Border: Efficacy and Unintended Consequences of US Immigration Control Policy," *Population and Development Review* 27, no. 4 (2001): 661–85.

5. Jason De León, *The Land of Open Graves: Living and Dying on the Migrant Trail* (Oakland: University of California Press, 2015), 4.

6. Susan Ferguson and David McNally, "Precarious Migrants: Gender, Race and the Social Reproduction of a Global Working Class," *Socialist Register* 51 (2014): 1–23, at 3 (http://davidmcnally.org/wp-content/uploads/2011/01/Ferguson_McNally.pdf).

7. Ferguson and McNally, "Precarious Migrants," 7.

8. Raúl Delgado Wise, "The Migration and Labor Question Today: Imperialism, Unequal Development, and Forced Migration," *Monthly Review,* February 2013, 25–38, at 25.

9. Nicholas De Genova, "Migrant 'Illegality' and Deportability in Everyday Life," *Annual Review of Anthropology* 31 (2002): 419–47, at 423. See also Nicole Trujillo-Pagán, "Emphasizing the 'Complex' in the 'Immigration Industrial Complex,'" *Critical Sociology* 40, no. 1 (2014): 29–46; De Genova, "Detention, Deportation, and Waiting: Toward a Theory of Migrant Detainability," *Global Detention Project Working Paper No. 18,* November 2016, 1–10.

10. Gholam Khiabany, "Refugee Crisis, Imperialism and Pitiless Wars on the Poor," *Media, Culture and Society* 38, no. 5 (2016): 755–62, at 760.

11. Prabhat Patnaik, "Contemporary Imperialism and the World's Labor Reserves," *Social Scientist* 35, no. 5–6 (2007): 3–18, at 3.

12. Michael McIntyre, "Race, Surplus Population and the Marxist Theory of Imperialism," *Antipode* 43, no. 5 (2011): 1489–515.

13. See Fred Magdoff and Harry Magdoff, "Disposable Workers: Today's Reserve Army of Labor," *Monthly Review* 55, no. 11 (2004): 18–35; John Bellamy Foster, Robert W. McChesney, and R. Jamil Jonna, "The Global Reserve Army of Labor and the New Imperialism," *Monthly Review* 63, no. 6 (2011): 1–31; Ferguson and McNally, "Precarious Migrants"; and Khiabany, "Refugee Crisis."

14. Montserrat Gea-Sánchez, Álvaro Alconada-Romero, Erica Briones-Vozmediano, Roland Pastells, Denise Gastaldo, and Fidel Molina, "Undocumented Immigrant Women in Spain: A Scoping Review on Access to and Utilization of Health and Social Services," *Journal of Immigrant and Minority Health* 19, no. 1 (2017): 194–204, at 195.

15. Karl Marx, *Capital: A Critique of Political Economy,* vol. 1, trans. Ben Fowkes (New York: Penguin, 1990), 782.

16. See Michael McIntyre and Heidi Nast, "Bio(necro)polis: Marx, Surplus Populations, and the Spatial Dialectics of Reproduction and 'Race,'" *Antipode* 43, no. 5 (2011): 1465–88; Heidi Nast, "'Race' and the Bio(necro)polis," *Antipode*

43, no. 5 (2011): 1457–64; and Antonis Balasopoulos, "Dark Light: *Utopia* and the Question of Relative Surplus Population," *Utopian Studies* 27, no. 3 (2016): 615–29.

17. McIntyre and Nast, "Bio(necro)polis," 1465.

18. Marx, *Capital,* 1:794.

19. Foster et al., "Global Reserve Army," 9.

20. Marx, *Capital,* 1:795.

21. Marx, *Capital,* 1:796.

22. Foster et al., "Global Reserve Army," 10.

23. As Michael Denning writes, Marx was no sympathizer of the *Lumpenproletariat* ("Wageless Life," *New Left Review* 66, no. November–December (2010): 79–97, 87). Indeed, in his support of the proletariat, the "legitimate" *moral* working class, Marx viewed the *Lumpenproletariat* as an unproductive, parasitic layer of society.

24. Marx, *Capital,* 1:797.

25. Marx, *Capital,* 1:797.

26. Tony C. Brown, "The Time of Globalization: Rethinking Primitive Accumulation," *Rethinking Marxism* 21, no. 4 (2009): 571–84, at 574.

27. Marx, *Capital,* 1:784.

28. Werner Bonefeld, "History and Social Constitution: Primitive Accumulation is Not Primitive," *The Commoner,* March 2002, 1–8, at 2–3.

29. Bonefeld, "History and Social Constitution," 5.

30. Bonefeld, "History and Social Constitution," 4.

31. Karl Marx, *Capital,* vol. 3, trans. David Fernbach (New York: Penguin, 1991), 354–55.

32. David Harvey, *The New Imperialism* (Oxford: Oxford University Press, 2003), 145.

33. Harry Cleaver, *Reading* Capital *Politically* (San Francisco: AK Press, 2000), 85.

34. Jim Glassman, "Primitive Accumulation," *Progress in Human Geography* 30, no. 5 (2006): 608–25, at 616.

35. Glassman, "Primitive Accumulation," 616.

36. Cleaver, *Reading* Capital *Politically,* 86.

37. Cleaver, *Reading* Capital *Politically,* 85.

38. Karl Marx, *Grundrisse: Foundations of the Critique of Political Economy,* trans. Martin Nicolaus (New York: Penguin, 1993), 736.

39. Marx, *Capital,* 1:896.

40. Marx, *Capital,* 1:896.

41. Marx, *Capital,* 1:897.

42. Marx, *Capital,* 1:897–98.

43. Cleaver, *Reading* Capital *Politically,* 85.

44. Marx, *Capital,* 1:875.

45. Marx, *Capital,* 1:915.

46. Jason Read, *The Micro-Politics of Capital: Marx and the Prehistory of the Present* (Albany: State University of New York Press, 2003), 17.

47. Read, *The Micro-Politics of Capital,* 98.

48. Andrea Fumagalli, "The Concept of Subsumption of Labor to Capital: Towards Life Subsumption in Bio-Cognitive Capitalism," in *Reconsidering Value and Labor in the Digital Age,* ed. Eran Fisher and Christian Fuchs (London: Palgrave Macmillan, 2015), 224–45, at 229.

49. Read, *The Micro-Politics of Capital,* 113. Importantly, these social relationships include not only those between capital and labor but also those between other subject positions distinguished by race, gender, sex, citizenship, and so forth.

50. Marx, *Capital,* 1:899.

51. Marx, *Capital,* 1:899.

52. This transformation should not be underemphasized. It has become somewhat de rigueur among historians of violence to argue that capitalism has *led* to a reduction of violence. This argument, however, can be made only if one neglects the deepening of structures of violence, including, for example, the lack of access to health care, negligence in occupational safety requirements, food products loaded with toxins, and polluted environments that result in premature death.

53. Marx, *Capital,* 3:344. See also Foster et al., "Global Reserve Army," 13.

54. Foster et al., "Global Reserve Army," 13.

55. Foster et al., "Global Reserve Army," 3.

56. Delgado Wise, "The Migration and Labor Question," 28.

57. Ferguson and McNally, "Precarious Migrants," 9.

58. Richard Freeman, "China, India and the Doubling of the Global Labor Force: Who Pays the Price of Globalization?" *The Asia-Pacific Journal* 3, no. 8 (2005): apjjf.org/-Richard-Freeman/1849/article.html.

59. Magdoff and Magdoff, "Disposable Workers," 20.

60. Delgado Wise, "The Migration and Labor Question," 26.

61. Raúl Delgado Wise and David Martin, "The Political Economy of Global Labour Arbitrage," in *The International Political Economy of Production,* ed. Kees van der Pijl (Cheltenham: Edward Elgar, 2015), 59–75, at 2.

62. Foster et al., "Global Reserve Army," 13–14.

63. Foster et al., "Global Reserve Army," 14.

64. Raúl Delgado Wise, "Forced Migration and US Imperialism: The Dialectic of Migration and Development," *Critical Sociology* 35, no. 6 (2009): 767–84, at 769.

65. Delgado Wise, "The Migration and Labor Question," 30.

66. Delgado Wise, "The Migration and Labor Question," 30.

67. Raúl Delgado Wise, Humberto Márquez Covarrubias, and Ruben Puentes, "Reframing the Debate on Migration, Development and Human Rights," *Population, Space and Place* 19 (2013): 430–43, at 432.

68. Iosif Kovras and Simon Robins, "Death at the Border: Managing Missing Migrants and Unidentified Bodies at the EU's Mediterranean Frontier," *Political Geography* 55 (2106): 40–49, at 43.

69. Saskia Sassen, *Expulsions: Brutality and Complexity in the Global Economy* (Cambridge, Mass.: Belknap, 2014), 4.

70. Marie-Andrée Jacob, "Form-Made Persons: Consent Forms as Consent's Blind Spot," *PoLAR: Political and Legal Anthropology Review* 30, no. 2 (2007): 249–68.

71. James A. Tyner, *Space, Place, and Violence: Violence and the Embodied Geographies of Race, Sex, and Gender* (New York: Routledge, 2012), 156.

72. Jacob, "Form-Made Persons," 251.

73. Jacob, "Form-Made Persons," 251.

74. De Genova, "Migrant 'Illegality,'" 429.

75. Saskia Sassen, "Economic Internationalization: The New Migration in Japan and the United States," *International Migration* 31, no. 1 (1993): 73–99, at 73.

76. Raúl Delgado Wise and Humberto Márquez Covarrubias, "Strategic Dimensions of Neoliberal Globalization: The Exporting of Labor Force and Unequal Exchange," Advances in Applied Sociology 2, no. 2 (2012): 127–34, at 128.

77. Delgado Wise, "The Migration and Labor Question," 31.

78. See, for example, Peter Andreas, *Border Games: Policing the U.S.-Mexico Divide* (Ithaca, N.Y.: Cornell University Press, 2000); De Genova, "Migrant 'Illegality'"; Joseph Nevins, *Dying to Live: A Story of U.S. Immigration in an Age of Global Apartheid* (San Francisco, Calif.: City Lights, 2008); Nevins, *Operation Gatekeeper and Beyond: The War on 'Illegals' and the Remaking of the U.S.-Mexico Boundary* (New York: Routledge, 2010); Jill Lindsey Harrison and Sarah E. Lloyd, "Illegality at Work: Deportability and the Productive New Era of Immigration Enforcement," *Antipode* 44, no. 2 (2012): 365–85; and Marcel Paret, "Legality and Exploitation: Immigration Enforcement and the US Migrant Labor System," *Latino Studies* 12, 4 (2014): 503–26.

79. Delgado Wise, "The Migration and Labor Question," 31–32.

80. Douglas S. Massey, "The Mexico-U.S. Border in the American Imagination," *Proceedings of the American Philosophical Society* 160, no. 2 (2016): 160–77, at 160.

81. Massey, "The Mexico-U.S. Border," 160.

82. Justin Akers Chacón and Mike Davis, *No One Is Illegal: Fighting Racism*

and State Violence on the U.S.-Mexico Border (Chicago: Haymarket, 2006), 99–100.

83. Nicholas De Genova, "The Legal Production of Mexican/Migrant 'Illegality,'" *Latino Studies* 2, no. 2 (2004): 160–85, at 162.

84. De Genova, "The Legal Production," 162.

85. Andreas, *Border Games,* 86.

86. Pia Oberoi and Eleanor Taylor-Nicholson, "The Enemy at the Gates: International Borders, Migration and Human Rights," *Laws* 2, no. 3 (2013): 169–86, at 171.

87. Chacón and Davis, *No One Is Illegal,* 104.

88. Pierrette Hondagneu-Sotelo, *Gendered Transitions: Mexican Experiences of Immigration* (Berkeley: University of California Press, 1994), 20–21.

89. Chacón and Davis, *No One Is Illegal,* 110.

90. De Genova, "The Legal Production," 162.

91. Chacón and Davis, *No One Is Illegal,* 110.

92. De Genova, "The Legal Production," 163.

93. Andreas, *Border Games,* 33.

94. De Genova, "The Legal Production," 162.

95. Marta Tienda, "Looking to the 1990s: Mexican Immigration in Sociological Perspective," in *Mexican Migration to the United States: Origins, Consequences, and Policy Options,* ed. Wayne Cornelius and J. A. Bustamante (San Diego: Center for U.S.-Mexican Studies; University of California San Diego, 1989), 109–50, at 115.

96. De Genova, "The Legal Production," 163.

97. De Genova, "The Legal Production," 163.

98. Patricia Zamudio, "Mexico: Mexican International Migration," in *Migration and Immigration: A Global View,* ed. Marua I. Toro-Morn and Marixsa Alicea (Westport, Conn.: Greenwood, 2004), 129–45, at 133.

99. Hondagneu-Sotelo, *Gendered Transitions,* 22.

100. De Genova, "The Legal Production," 164.

101. De Genova, "The Legal Production," 164.

102. De Genova, "The Legal Production," 164.

103. Ronald L. Mize Jr., "Mexican Contract Workers and the U.S. Capitalist Agricultural Labor Process: The Formative Era, 1942–1964," *Rural Sociology* 71, no. 1 (2006): 85–108, at 100.

104. De Genova, "The Legal Production," 164.

105. Hondagneu-Sotelo, *Gendered Transitions,* 22.

106. De Genova, "The Legal Production," 165.

107. Zamudio, "Mexico," 133.

108. Hondagneu-Sotelo, *Gendered Transitions,* 23.

109. De Genova, "The Legal Production," 165.

110. Trujillo-Pagán, "Emphasizing the 'Complex,'" 34.

111. Zamudio, "Mexico," 134.

112. Andreas, *Border Games*, 35.

113. Susan Tiano, "Maquiladora Women: A New Category of Workers?" in *Women Workers and Global Restructuring*, ed. Kathryn Ward (Ithaca, N.Y.: ILR Press, 1990), 193–223, at 196.

114. Raúl Delgado Wise and Humberto Márquez Covarrubias, "The Reshaping of Mexican Labor Exports under NAFTA: Paradoxes and Challenges," *International Migration Review* 41, no. 3 (2007): 656–79, at 663.

115. Altha J. Cravey, *Women and Work in Mexico's Maquiladoras* (Lanham, Md.: Rowman and Littlefield, 1998), 15. See also Tiano, "Maquiladora Women."

116. Raúl Delgado Wise and James M. Cypher, "The Strategic Role of Mexican Labor under NAFTA: Critical Perspectives on Current Economic Integration," *The Annals of the American Academy of Political and Social Science* 610, no. 1 (2007): 119–42, at 134.

117. Raúl Delgado Wise and Humberto Márquez Covarrubias, "Capitalist Restructuring, Development and Labour Migration: the Mexico–US Case," *Third World Quarterly* 29, no. 7 (2008): 1359–74, at 1364.

118. Tiano, "Women and Work," 197.

119. Delgado Wise and Márquez Covarrubias, "Capitalist Restructuring," 1362.

120. Nevins, *Operation Gatekeeper*, 167.

121. Delgado Wise and Cypher, "The Strategic Role," 131.

122. Raúl Delgado Wise, "Critical Dimensions of Mexico–US Migration under the Aegis of Neoliberalism and NAFTA," *Canadian Journal of Development Studies/Revue canadienne d'études du développement* 25, no. 4 (2004): 591–605, at 597.

123. Chacón and Davis, *No One Is Illegal*, 120.

124. Trujillo-Pagán, "Emphasizing the 'Complex,'" 36.

125. Chacón and Davis, *No One Is Illegal*, 120.

126. Chacón and Davis, *No One Is Illegal*, 120–21.

127. Ferguson and McNally, "Precarious Migrants," 10.

128. Elaine Levine, "Mexican Migrants and Other Latinos in the US Labor Market since NAFTA," *Journal of Latino/Latin American Studies* 2, no. 1 (2006): 103–33, at 119.

129. Delgado Wise and Cypher, "The Strategic Role," 131.

130. Agustín Escobar Latapí and Mercedes González de la Rocha, "Crisis, Restructuring and Urban Poverty in Mexico," *Environment and Urbanization* 7, no. 1 (1995): 57–75, at 60.

131. Escobar Latapí and González de la Rocha, "Crisis, Restructuring," 65.

132. Ferguson and McNally, "Precarious Migrants," 9.

133. Delgado Wise and Márquez Covarrubias, "Capitalist Restructuring," 1361.

134. Delgado Wise and Cypher, "The Strategic Role," 122.

135. Levine, "Mexican Migrants," 119.

136. Delgado Wise and Márquez Covarrubias, "Capitalist Restructuring," 1361.

137. Barry Bluestone and Bennett Harrison, *The Deindustrialization of America: Plant Closings, Community Abandonment, and the Dismantling of Basic Industry* (New York: Basic Books, 1982), 9.

138. Delgado Wise and Márquez Covarrubias, "Capitalist Restructuring," 1367.

139. Delgado Wise and Márquez Covarrubias, "Capitalist Restructuring," 1367.

140. Nicola Phillips, "Migration as Development Strategy? The New Political Economy of Dispossession and Inequality in the Americas," *Review of International Political Economy* 16, no. 2 (2009): 231–59, at 238.

141. Delgado Wise and Cypher, "The Strategic Role," 134.

142. Delgado Wise, "Critical Dimensions," 598.

143. Mathew Coleman, "U.S. Statecraft and the U.S.-Mexico Border as Security/Economy Nexus," *Political Geography* 24 (2005): 185–209, at 190.

144. Harrison and Lloyd, "Illegality at Work," 366.

145. See Harrison and Lloyd, "Illegality at Work."

146. De Genova, "Migrant 'Illegality,'" 436.

147. Douglas S. Massey and Karen Pren, "Unintended Consequences of US Immigration Policy: Explaining the Post-1965 Surge from Latin America," *Population and Development Review* 38, no. 1 (2012): 1–29, at 5.

148. See Douglas S. Massey, "The Counterproductive Consequences of Border Enforcement," *CATO Journal* 37, no. 3 (Fall 2017): 539–54 (object.cato.org/sites/cato.org/files/serials/files/cato-journal/2017/9/cato-journal-v37n3-11-updated.pdf, accessed October 9, 2017).

149. Massey and Pren, "Unintended Consequences," 5.

150. Bluestone and Harrison, *The Deindustrialization of America*, 9.

151. See Leo R. Chavez, *Covering Immigration: Population Images and the Politics of the Nation* (Berkeley: University of California Press, 2001); Chavez, *The Latino Threat: Constructing Immigrants, Citizens, and the Nation* (Stanford, Calif.: Stanford University Press, 2008); Eric A. Stewart, Ramiro Martinez Jr., Eric P. Baumer, and Marc Gertz, "The Social Context of Latino Threat and Punitive Latino Sentiment," *Social Problems* 62, no. 1 (2015): 68–92; and Justin T. Pickett,

"On the Social Foundations for Crimmigration: Latino Threat and Support for Expanded Police Powers," *Journal of Quantitative Criminology* 32, no. 1 (2016): 103–32.

152. Susan T. Fiske, *Envy Up, Scorn Down: How Status Divides Us* (New York: Sage, 2011), 89.

153. Susan T. Fiske, "What We Know Now about Bias and Intergroup Conflict, the Problem of the Century," *Current Directions in Psychological Science* 11, no. 4 (2002): 123–28, at 127.

154. Fiske, "What We Know," 127.

155. See Massey, "Counterproductive Consequences."

156. Coleman, "U.S. Statecraft," 191.

157. Coleman, "U.S. Statecraft," 191.

158. Gilberto Rosas, "The Border Thickens: In-Securing Communities after IRCA," *International Migration* 54, no. 2 (2016): 119–30, at 120.

159. Massey and Pren, "Unintended Consequences," 9.

160. Maria Jimenez, *Humanitarian Crisis: Migrant Deaths at the U.S.-Mexico Border* (San Diego, Calif.: American Civil Liberties Union and Mexico's National Commission of Human Rights, 2009), 21.

161. Andreas, *Border Games,* 95; see also his discussion on 96–100.

162. Vicki Squire, "Desert 'Trash': Posthumanism, Border Struggles, and Humanitarian Politics," *Political Geography* 39 (2014): 11–21, at 12. See also Jeremy Slack, Daniel E. Martínez, Alison E. Lee, and Scott Whiteford, "The Geography of Border Militarization: Violence, Death and Health in Mexico and the United States," *Journal of Latin American Geography* 15, no. 1 (2016): 7–32.

163. Slack et al., "The Geography of Border Militarization," 8.

164. Jimenez, *Humanitarian Crisis,* 21.

165. See Roxanne Lynn Doty, "Bare Life: Border-Crossing Deaths and Spaces of Moral Alibi," *Environment and Planning D: Society and Space* 29 (2011): 599–612.

166. Délano Alonso and Nienass, "Deaths," 423.

167. Jimenez, *Humanitarian Crisis,* 21.

168. Nevins, *Dying to Live,* 21; see also Jimenez, *Humanitarian Crisis,* 17.

169. Harrison and Lloyd, "Illegality at Work," 370.

170. Douglas S. Massey, Jorge Durand, and Karen A. Pren, "Why Border Enforcement Backfired," *American Journal of Sociology* 121, no. 5 (2016): 1557–600, at 1559.

171. Massey and Pren, "Unintended Consequences," 17.

172. Ferguson and McNally, "Precarious Migrants," 6.

173. Ferguson and McNally, "Precarious Migrants," 6. See also Trujillo-Pagán, "Emphasizing the 'Complex'"; Yolanda Vázquez, "Constructing Crimmigration:

Latino Subordination in a 'Post-Racial' World," *Ohio State Law Journal* 76, no. 3 (2015): 599–657; and Felicia Arriaga, "Understanding Crimmigration: Implications for Racial and Ethnic Minorities within the United States," *Sociology Compass* 10, no. 9 (2016): 805–12.

174. Vázquez, "Constructing Crimmigration," 627.

175. Vázquez, "Constructing Crimmigration," 628.

176. Vázquez, "Constructing Crimmigration," 633.

177. De Genova, "Detention," 4.

178. Robert F. Castro, "Busting the Bandito Boyz: Militarism, Masculinity, and the Hunting of Undocumented Persons in the U.S.-Mexico Borderlands," *Journal of Hate Studies* 6 (2007–2008): 7–30. See also Tyner, *Space, Place, and Violence,* 156–57.

179. Trujillo-Pagán, "Emphasizing the 'Complex,'" 43.

180. Vázquez, "Constructing Crimmigration," 635.

181. Bridget Hayden, "Impeach the Traitors: Citizenship, Sovereignty and Nation in Immigration Control Activism in the United States," *Social Semiotics* 20 (2010): 155–74, at 160.

182. Castro, "Busting the Bandito Boyz," 12.

183. De Genova, "The Legal Production," 161.

184. Ruth M. Campbell, A. G. Klei, Brian D. Hodges, David Fisman, and Simon Kitto, "A Comparison of Health Access Between Permanent Residents, Undocumented Immigrants and Refugee Claimants in Toronto, Canada," *Journal of Immigrant and Minority Health* 16, no. 1 (2014): 165–76, at 166.

185. Gea-Sánchez et al., "Undocumented Immigrant Women," 195.

186. Ferguson and McNally, "Precarious Migrants," 6.

187. Paret, "Legality and Exploitation," 516.

188. Ferguson and McNally, "Precarious Migrants," 6 (emphasis original).

189. Ruth Gomberg-Muñoz, "Criminalized Workers: Introduction to Special Issue on Migrant Labor and Mass Deportation," *Anthropology of Work Review* 37, no. 1 (2016): 3–10, at 3.

190. Melissa Cook, "Banished for Minor Crimes: The Aggravated Felony Provision of the Immigration and Nationality Act as a Human Rights Violation," *Boston College Third World Law Journal* 23, no. 2 (2003): 293–329, at 296.

191. Gomberg-Muñoz, "Criminalized Workers," 3.

192. Alissa R. Ackerman and Rich Furman, "The Criminalization of Immigration and the Privatization of the Immigration Detention: Implications for Justice," *Contemporary Justice Review* 16, no. 2 (2013): 251–63, at 253.

193. Gomberg-Muñoz, "Criminalized Workers," 3.

194. Mathew Coleman, "Immigration Geopolitics Beyond the Mexico-U.S. Border," *Antipode* 39, no. 1 (2007): 54–76, at 58.

195. Coleman, "Immigration Geopolitics," 59.

196. Cook, "Banished for Minor Crimes," 298.

197. Luis Gomez Romero, "Just Who Are the Millions of 'Bad Hombres' Slated for US Deportation?" *The Conversation*, November (2016): 1–5.

198. Gomberg-Muñoz, "Criminalized Workers," 6.

199. Ackerman and Furman, "The Criminalization of Immigration," 254–55.

200. Gomberg-Muñoz, "Criminalized Workers," 6.

201. Ackerman and Furman, "The Criminalization of Immigration," 255.

202. Gomberg-Muñoz, "Criminalized Workers," 6.

203. Gomberg-Muñoz, "Criminalized Workers," 6.

204. Josiah Heyman, "Unequal Relationships between Unauthorized Migrants and the Wider Society: Production, Reproduction, Mobility, and Risk," *Anthropology of Work Review* 37, no. 1 (2016): 44–48, at 44.

205. Trujillo-Pagán, "Emphasizing the 'Complex,'" 30.

206. Delgado Wise and Márquez Covarrubias, "Capitalist Restructuring," 1369.

207. Ferguson and McNally, "Precarious Migrants," 6. See also Lisa Marie Cacho, *Social Death: Racialized Rightlessness and the Criminalization of the Unprotected* (New York: New York University Press, 2012).

208. Marx, *Capital*, 1:784.

209. Foster et al., "Global Reserve Army," 6.

210. Foster et al., "Global Reserve Army," 6.

211. Magdoff and Magdoff, "Disposable Workers," 32.

212. Robert Albritton, *Let Them Eat Junk: How Capitalism Creates Hunger and Obesity* (Ann Arbor, Mich.: Pluto, 2009), 38.

213. Magdoff and Magdoff, "Disposable Workers," 32.

214. Albritton, *Let Them Eat Junk*, 39.

4. Redundant Labor

1. Zygmunt Bauman, *Wasted Lives: Modernity and its Outcasts* (Malden, Mass.: Polity, 2004), 11–12.

2. Ranjana Khanna, "Disposability," *differences: A Journal of Feminist Cultural Studies* 20, no. 1 (2009): 181–98, at 184.

3. See, for example, Annalisa Colombino and Paolo Giaccaria, "Dead Liveness/Living Deadness: Thresholds of Non-Human Life and Death in Biocapitalism," *Environment and Planning D: Society and Space* 34, no. 6 (2016): 1044–62.

4. David McNally, *Monsters of the Market: Zombies, Vampires and Global Capitalism* (Chicago: Haymarket, 2011), 151.

5. McNally, *Monsters of the Market*, 152.

6. Ian Fraser and Lawrence Wilde, *The Marx Dictionary* (New York: Continuum, 2011), 98.

7. Karl Marx, *Capital: A Critique of Political Economy,* vol. 3, trans. David Fernbach (New York: Penguin, 1991), 318–19.

8. Marx, *Capital,* 3:319. The "law" of the tendential fall in the rate of profit is not without its problems, but this is not the moment to rehash the long-standing debates. Interested readers are directed to the following: Andrew Kliman, *Reclaiming Marx's 'Capital': A Refutation of the Myth of Inconsistency* (New York: Lexington Books, 2007); Chris Harman, *Zombie Capitalism: Global Crisis and the Relevance of Marx* (New York: Verso, 2009); Vladimiro Giacché, "Marx, the Falling Rate of Profit, Financialization, and the Current Crisis," *International Journal of Political Economy* 40, no. 3 (2011): 18–32; Michael Heinrich, "Crisis Theory, the Law of the Tendency of the Profit Rate to Fall, and Marx's Studies in the 1870s," *Monthly Review* 64, no. 11 (2013): 15–31; Alex Callinicos and Joseph Choonara, "How Not to Write About the Rate of Profit: A Response to David Harvey," *Science and Society* 80, no. 4 (2016): 481–94; and Michael Roberts, *The Long Depression: How It Happened, Why It Happened, and What Happens Next* (Chicago: Haymarket, 2016).

9. Karl Marx, *Grundrisse: Foundations of the Critique of Political Economy,* trans. Martin Nicolaus (New York: Penguin, 1973), 748–49.

10. Marx, *Grundrisse,* 750.

11. Alex Callinicos, *The Revolutionary Ideas of Karl Marx* (Chicago: Haymarket, 2012), 143.

12. Geoff Mann, *Disassembly Required: A Field Guide to Actually Existing Capitalism* (Edinburgh: AK Press, 2013), 155.

13. Mann, *Disassembly Required,* 155.

14. Mazen Labban, "Against Value: Accumulation in the Oil Industry and the Biopolitics of Labor under Finance," *Antipode* 46, no. 2 (2014): 477–96, at 477.

15. Costas Lapavitsas, *Profiting without Producing: How Finance Exploits Us All* (New York: Verso, 2013), 4.

16. Michael J. Sandel, "The Moral Economy of Speculation: Gambling, Finance, and the Common Good," *The Tanner Lectures on Human Values* 27 (2013): 335–59, at 339.

17. Lapavitsas, *Profiting without Producing,* 4.

18. Sandel, "The Moral Economy," 340.

19. McNally, *Monsters of the Market,* 153.

20. Lapavitsas, *Profiting without Producing,* 4.

21. McNally, *Monsters of the Market,* 153.

22. Labban, "Against Value," 478.

23. Geoffrey Ingham, *Capitalism* (Malden, Mass.: Polity, 2008), 163.

24. See Obiyathulla I. Bacha, "Derivative Instruments and Islamic Finance:

Some Thoughts for a Reconsideration," *International Journal of Islamic Financial Services* 1, no. 1 (1999): 1–33.

25. Ingham, *Capitalism,* 163.

26. Dimitris P. Sotiropoulos and Spyros Lapatsioras, "Financialization and Marx: Some Reflections on Bryan's, Martin's and Rafferty's Argumentation," *Review of Radical Political Economics* 46, no. 1 (2014): 87–101, at 93.

27. Dick Bryan, Michael Rafferty, and Chris Jefferis, "Risk and Value: Finance, Labor, and Production," *South Atlantic Quarterly* 114, no. 2 (2015): 307–29, at 310.

28. Sotiropoulos and Lapatsioras, "Financialization and Marx," 97.

29. Lapavitsas, *Profiting Without Producing,* 146.

30. Lapavitsas, *Profiting Without Producing,* 146.

31. Andrea Fumagalli, "The Concept of Subsumption of Labor to Capital: Towards Life Subsumption in Bio-Cognitive Capitalism," in *Reconsidering Value and Labor in the Digital Age,* ed. Eran Fisher and Christian Fuchs (London: Palgrave Macmillan, 2015), 224–45, at 229.

32. McNally, *Monsters of the Market,* 155.

33. Zohreh Bayatrizi, *Life Sentences: The Modern Ordering of Mortality* (Toronto: University of Toronto Press, 2008), 5.

34. Bayatrizi, *Life Sentences,* 6.

35. Shaun French and James Kneale, "Excessive Financialisation: Insuring Lifestyles, Enlivening Subjects, and Everyday Spaces of Biosocial Excess," *Environment and Planning D: Society and Space* 27, no. 6 (2009): 1030–53, at 1031.

36. See Kean Birch and David Tyfield, "Theorizing the Bioeconomy: Biovalue, Biocapital, Bioeconomics or . . . What?" *Science, Technology, and Human Values* 38, no. 3 (2012): 299–327; Mark Kear, "Governing *Homo Subprimicus*: Beyond Financial Citizenship, Exclusion, and Rights," *Antipode* 45, no. 4 (2013): 926–46; and Simon Lilley and Dimitris Papadopoulos, "Material Returns: Cultures of Valuation, Biofinancialisation and the Autonomy of Politics," *Sociology* 48, no. 5 (2014): 972–88.

37. Patrick Burns, "Peasants' Revolt: Why Congress Should Eliminate the Tax Benefits on Dead Peasant Insurance," *Hastings Law Journal* 65 (2014): 551–80, at 565.

38. Hugo Nurnberg and Douglas P. Lackey, "Ethical Reflections on Company-Owned Life Insurance," *Journal of Business Ethics* 80, no. 4 (2008): 845–54, at 846.

39. Anita Rupprecht, "Excessive Memories: Slavery, Insurance and Resistance," *History Workshop Journal* 64, no. 1 (2007): 6–28, at 13.

40. Bayatrizi, *Life Sentences,* 77.

41. Bayatrizi, *Life Sentences,* 78.

42. Bayatrizi, *Life Sentences,* 52–53.

43. Bayatrizi, *Life Sentences,* 77.

44. Burns, "Peasants' Revolt," 554.

45. In the United States, the concept of "insurable interest" was codified in the late nineteenth and early twentieth centuries. In general, a beneficiary has an insurable interest if he or she is so closely related by blood or affinity that she/he wants the insured to continue to live, if the beneficiary is a creditor of the insured, or if the beneficiary has a reasonable expectation of pecuniary benefit or advantage from the continued life of the insured (Nurnberg and Lackey, "Ethical Reflections," 846).

46. In reality, of course, many men and women do murder family members for insurance gain.

47. Burns, "Peasants' Revolt," 554.

48. Sarah Quinn, "The Transformation of Morals in Markets: Death, Benefits, and the Exchange of Life Insurance Policies," *American Journal of Sociology* 114, no. 3 (2008): 738–80, at 738.

49. Quoted in Quinn, "The Transformation of Morals," 739.

50. Anne Phillips, *Our Bodies, Whose Property?* (Princeton, N.J.: Princeton University Press, 2013), 10.

51. Burns, "Peasants' Revolt," 565.

52. Terrance G. Gabel and Clifford D. Scott, "An Unsettled Matter of Life and Death: A Public Policy and Marketing Commentary on Life Insurance Settlement," *Journal of Public Policy and Marketing* 28, no. 2 (2009): 162–74, at 162.

53. Burns, "Peasants' Revolt," 557.

54. Sandel, "The Moral Economy," 346.

55. Neil A. Doherty and Hal J. Singer, "Regulating the Secondary Market for Life Insurance Policies," *Journal of Insurance Regulation* 21, no. 4 (2003): 63–99, at 63.

56. Gabel and Scott, "An Unsettled Matter"; Sandel, "The Moral Economy."

57. Katherina Glac, Jason D. Skirry, and David Vang, "What Is So Morbid about Viaticals? An Examination of the Ethics of Economic Ideas and Economic Reality," *Business and Professional Ethics Journal* 31, no. 3–4 (2012): 453–73, at 458. See also John Trinkaus and Joseph A. Giacalone, "Entrepreneurial 'Mining' of the Dying: Viatical Transactions, Tax Strategies and Mind Games," *Journal of Business Ethics* 36, no. 1 (2002): 187–94.

58. Quinn, "The Transformation of Morals," 739.

59. Doherty and Singer, "Regulating the Secondary Market," 163.

60. Sandel, "The Moral Economy," 353.

61. Sandel, "The Moral Economy," 353.

62. Gabel and Scott, "An Unsettled Matter," 163.

63. Doherty and Singer, "Regulating the Secondary Market," 67.

64. Quinn, "The Transformation of Morals," 740–41. See also Doherty and Singer, "Regulating the Secondary Market,"170.

65. Quinn, "The Transformation of Morals," 742.

66. Quinn, "The Transformation of Morals," 742.

67. Gabel and Scott, "An Unsettled Matter," 162.

68. Burns, "Peasants' Revolt," 559.

69. Nurnberg and Lackey, "Ethical Reflections," 846.

70. Nurnberg and Lackey, "Ethical Reflections," 847.

71. Nurnberg and Lackey, "Ethical Reflections," 847.

72. Burns, "Peasants' Revolt," 562, 567.

73. Earl W. Spurgin, "The Problem with 'Dead Peasants' Insurance," *Business and Professional Ethics Journal* 22, no. 1 (2003): 19–36, at 20.

74. Burns, "Peasants' Revolt," 563.

75. Spurgin, "The Problem with 'Dead Peasants,'" 27.

76. Burns, "Peasants' Revolt," 565.

77. In 2005, for example, only 44 percent of Walmart's 1.3 million workers in the United States were provided with health insurance (Burns, "Peasants' Revolt," 566).

78. Burns, "Peasants' Revolt," 567.

79. See, fore example, Jason Beckfield, "Does Income Inequality Harm Health? New Cross-National Evidence," *Journal of Health and Social Behavior* 45, no. 3 (2004): 231–48; Laura M. Woods, Bernard Rachet, Michael Riga, No-ell Stone, Anjali Shah, and Michel P. Coleman, "Geographical Variation in Life Expectancy at Birth in England and Wales Is Largely Explained by Deprivation," *Journal of Epidemiology and Community Health* 59, no. 2 (2005): 115–20; Richard G. Wilkinson and Kate E. Pickett, "Income Inequality and Population Health: A Review and Explanation of the Evidence," *Social Science and Medicine* 62, no. 7 (2006): 1768–84; Salvatore J. Babones, "Income Inequality and Population Health: Correlation and Causality," *Social Science and Medicine* 66, no. 7 (2008): 1614–26; and Jane Wills and Brian Linneker, "In-Work Poverty and the Living Wage in the United Kingdom: A Geographical Perspective," *Transactions of the Institute of British Geographers* 39, no. 2 (2014): 182–94.

80. Mary Shaw, George Davey Smith, and Danny Dorling, "Health Inequalities and New Labour: How the Promises Compare with Real Progress," *BMJ: British Medical Journal* 330, no. 7498 (2005): 1016–21.

81. Spurgin, "The Problem with 'Dead Peasants,'" 30.

82. Wayne Hope, *Time, Communication and Global Capitalism* (London: Palgrave Macmillan, 2016), 89.

83. Saskia Sassen, "Expelled: Humans in Capitalism's Deepening Crisis," *Journal of World Systems Research* 19, no. 2 (2013): 198–201, at 198.

84. Saskia Sassen, *Expulsions: Brutality and Complexity in the Global Economy* (Cambridge, Mass.: Harvard University Press, 2014), 76.

85. Sassen, *Expulsions*, 10.

86. Liam Pleven and Rachel Emma Silverman, "An Insurance Man Builds a Lively Business in Death," *Wall Street Journal*, November 26, 2007), A1, wsj.com/articles/SB119604142916903531.

87. Sandel, "The Moral Economy," 336.

5. Disassembled Bodies

1. Donald Joralemon, "Organ Wars: The Battle for Body Parts," *Medical Anthropology Quarterly* 9, no. 3 (1995): 335–56, at 339. See also Walter Sullivan, "Buying of Kidneys of Poor Attacked," *The New York Times*, September 24, 1983, nytimes.com/1983/09/24/us/buying-of-kidneys-of-poor-attacked.html; and Margaret Engel, "Va. Doctor Plans Company to Arrange Sale of Human Kidneys," *The Washington Post*, September 19, 1983, washingtonpost.com/archive/politics/1983/09/19/va-doctor-plans-company-to-arrange-sale-of-human-kidneys/afdfac69-62ed-4066-b296-fcf892eab758/?utm_term=.7f976fff4214.

2. Samuel Gorovitz, "Against Selling Bodily Parts," *Philosophy and Public Policy* 4, no. 2 (1984): 9–12, at 10.

3. Cecil Helman, "Dr. Frankenstein and the Industrial Body: Reflections on 'Spare Part' Surgery," *Anthropology Today* 4, no. 3 (1988): 14–16, at 15.

4. Helman, "Dr. Frankenstein," 15.

5. Joralemon, "Organ Wars," 339.

6. James F. Blumstein, "Government's Role in Organ Transplantation Policy," *Journal of Health Politics, Policy and Law* 14, no. 1 (1989): 5–39, at 12–14.

7. Quoted in Engel, "Va. Doctor."

8. Blumstein, "Government's Role," 14.

9. Robert M. Veatch, "Why Liberals Should Accept Financial Incentives for Organ Procurement," *Kennedy Institute of Ethics Journal* 13, no. 1 (2003): 19–36, at 30.

10. Blumstein, "Government's Role," 15.

11. Suzanne Holland, "Contested Commodities at Both Ends of Life: Buying and Selling Gametes, Embryos, and Body Tissues," *Kennedy Institute of Ethics Journal* 11, no. 3 (2001): 263–84, at 265–66.

12. Ian Hacking, "Our Neo-Cartesian Bodies in Parts," *Critical Inquiry* 34 (2007): 78–105; at 81.

13. Helman, "Dr. Frankenstein," 15.

14. Gina R. Gatarin, "Masculine Bodies in the Biocapitalist Era: Compromising Human Rights of Commercial Kidney Donors in the Philippines," *Gender, Technology and Development* 18, no. 1 (2014): 107–29, at 122.

15. Leslie Sharp, *Strange Harvest: Organ Transplants, Denatured Bodies, and the Transformed Self* (Berkeley: University of California Press, 2006), 51.

16. Gatarin, "Masculine Bodies," 108.

17. Jeremy W. Crampton and Stuart Elden, "Space, Politics, Calculation: An Introduction," *Social and Cultural Geography* 7, no. 5 (2006): 681–85, at 681–82.

18. Michel Foucault, *Security, Territory, Population: Lectures at the Collège de France, 1977–1978,* trans. Graham Burchell (New York: Picador, 2007), 70–71.

19. Michel Foucault, "Governmentality," in *The Foucault Effect: Studies in Governmentality,* trans. and ed. Graham Burchell, C. Gordon, and P. Miller (Chicago: University of Chicago Press, 1991), 87–104, at 101.

20. John Caldwell, "Demographers and the Study of Mortality: Scope, Perspectives, and Theory," *Annals of the New York Academy of Sciences* 954 (2001): 19–34, at 20.

21. Caldwell, "Demographers," 22.

22. Sharon R. Kaufman and Lynn M. Morgan, "The Anthropology of the Beginnings and Ends of Life," *Annual Review of Anthropology* 34 (2005): 317–41, at 328.

23. Nicholas Rose, *The Politics of Life Itself: Biomedicine, Power, and Subjectivity in the Twenty-First Century* (Princeton, N.J.: Princeton University Press, 2007), 43–44.

24. Lesley A. Sharp, "The Commodification of the Body and Its Parts," *Annual Review of Anthropology* 29 (2000): 287–328, at 296.

25. Quoted in Jeremy Tambling, "*Middlemarch,* Realism, and the Birth of the Clinic," ELH 57, no. 4 (1990): 936–60, at 942.

26. Ian Hacking, "The Cartesian Vision Fulfilled: Analogue Bodies and Digital Minds," *Interdisciplinary Science Reviews* 30, no. 2 (2005): 153–66, at 159.

27. Ruth Richardson, "Human Dissection and Organ Donation: A Historical and Social Background," *Mortality* 11, no. 2 (2006): 151–65, at 154–55.

28. Richardson, "Human Dissection," 156.

29. Richardson, "Human Dissection," 161.

30. Richardson, "Human Dissection," 161.

31. Leslie M. Whetstine, "The History of the Definition(s) of Death: From the Eighteenth Century to the Twentieth Century," in *End-of-Life Communication in the ICU—A Global Perspective,* ed. D. W. Crippen (New York: Springer, 2008), 65–78, at 72.

32. Whetstine, "The History of the Definition(s) of Death," 72.

33. David J. Powner, Brucer M. Ackerman, and Ake Grenvik, "Medical Diagnosis of Death in Adults: Historical Contributions to Current Controversies," *The Lancet* 348, no. 9036 (1996): 1219–23, at 1220.

34. Marc Alexander, "'The Rigid Embrace of the Narrow House': Premature

Burial and the Signs of Death," *Hastings Center Report* 10, no. 3 (1980): 25–31, at 29.

35. Zohreh Bayatrizi, *Life Sentences: The Modern Ordering of Mortality* (Toronto: University of Toronto Press, 2008), 6.

36. Zohreh Bayatrizi, "From Fate to Risk: The Quantification of Mortality in Early Modern Statistics," *Theory, Culture and Society* 25, no. 1 (2008): 121–43, at 121.

37. Bayatrizi, "From Fate to Risk," 124–25.

38. Bayatrizi, *Life Sentences*, 52–53.

39. Bayatrizi, "From Fate to Risk," 130.

40. Zohreh Bayatrizi, "Counting the Dead and Regulating the Living: Early Modern Statistics and the Formation of the Sociological Imagination (1662–1897)," *The British Journal of Sociology* 60, no. 3 (2009): 603–21, at 607.

41. Bayatrizi, "From Fate to Risk," 137.

42. Bayatrizi, "From Fate to Risk," 138.

43. Bayatrizi, "Counting the Dead," 613.

44. Sharp, "The Commodification," 296.

45. See Peter K. Linden, "History of Solid Organ Transplantation and Organ Donation," *Critical Care Clinics* 25, no. 1 (2009): 165–84; C. J. E. Watson and J. H. Dark, "Organ Transplantation: Historical Perspective and Current Practice," *British Journal of Anaesthesia* 108, no. S1 (2012): i29–i42; and Abbas Rana et al., "Survival Benefit of Solid-Organ Transplant in the United States," *Journal of the American Medical Association* 150, no. 3 (2015): 252–59.

46. Watson and Dark, "Organ Transplantation," i29.

47. Nebraska Organ Recovery, "Acceptable Ischemic Times," nedonation.org/donation-guide/organ/acceptable-ischemic-times.

48. Watson and Dark, "Organ Transplantation," i29.

49. U.S. National Library of Medicine, "Transplant Rejection," *MedlinePlus*, medlineplus.gov/ency/article/000815.htm.

50. Watson and Dark, "Organ Transplantation," i29.

51. Watson and Dark, "Organ Transplantation," i30.

52. Mita Giacomini, "A Change of Heart and a Change of Mind? Technology and the Redefinition of Death in 1968," *Social Science and Medicine* 44, no. 10 (1997): 1465–82, at 1468.

53. Rana et al., "Survival Benefit," 252.

54. Linden, "History," 1720.

55. Watson and Dark, "Organ Transplantation," i32.

56. Michael A. De Georgia, "History of Brain Death as Death: 1968 to the Present," *Journal of Critical Care* 29 (2014): 673–78, at 674.

57. Kaufman and Morgan, "The Anthropology," 329.

58. Giacomini, "A Change of Heart," 1465.

59. Sharp, *Strange Harvest*, 48.

60. Sharp, *Strange Harvest*, 48.

61. Giacomini, "A Change of Heart," 1469.

62. Giacomini, "A Change of Heart," 1470.

63. Giacomini, "A Change of Heart," 1465.

64. Sharp, *Strange Harvest*, 11.

65. Sharp, *Strange Harvest*, 11.

66. Sharp, "The Commodification," 289.

67. Sharp, "The Commodification," 289.

68. Lori Andrews and Dorothy Nelkin, *Body Bazaar: The Market for Human Tissue in the Biotechnogy Age* (New York: Crown, 2001), 5.

69. Anne Phillips, *Our Bodies, Whose Property?* (Princeton, N.J.: Princeton University Press, 2013), 97.

70. Nancy Scheper-Hughes, "The Ends of the Body: Commodity Fetishism and the Global Traffic in Organs," *SAIS Review* 22, no. 1 (2002): 61–80, at 65.

71. Emily Kelly, "International Organ Trafficking Crisis: Solutions Addressing the Heart of the Matter," *Boston College Law Review* 54, no. 3 (2013): 1317–49, at 1322.

72. Behrooz Broumand and Reza F. Saidi, "New Definition of Transplant Tourism," *International Journal of Organ Transplantation Medicine* 8, no. 1 (2017): 49–51, at 49.

73. See, for example, John Connell, "Medical Tourism: Sea, Sun, Sand and . . . Surgery," *Tourism Management* 27, no. 6 (2006): 1093–1100; Michael D. Horowitz, Jeffrey A. Rosensweig, and Christopher A. Jones, "Medical Tourism: Globalization of the Healthcare Marketplace," *Medscape General Medicine* 9, no. 4 (2007): 33–59; Leigh Turner, "'First World Health Care at Third World Prices': Globalization, Bioethics and Medical Tourism," *BioSocieties* 2, no. 3 (2007): 303–25; and Dominique Martin, "Medical Travel and the Sale of Human Biological Materials: Suggestions for Ethical Policy Development," *Global Social Policy* 10, no. 3 (2010): 377–95.

74. Marcus P. Adams, "The Ethics of Organ Tourism: Role Morality and Organ Transplantation," *Journal of Medicine and Philosophy* 42 (2017): 670–89, at 670.

75. Broumand and Saidi, "New Definition," 50.

76. Martin, "Medical Travel," 378.

77. Martin, "Medical Travel," 378.

78. Sharon Bolton and Lila Skountridaki, "The Medical Tourist and a Political Economy of Care," *Antipode* 49, no. 2 (2017): 499–516, at 500.

79. Paul D'Amato, *The Meaning of Marxism* (Chicago: Haymarket, 2006), 49.

80. Karl Marx, *Capital: A Critique of Political Economy*, vol. 1, trans. Ben Fowkes (New York: Penguin , 1990), 271.

81. Marx, *Capital,* 1:271.

82. Marx, *Capital,* 1:272 (emphasis added).

83. Mrinalini Chakravorty and Leila Neti, "The Human Recycled: Insecurity in the Transnational Movement," *differences: A Journal of Feminist Cultural Studies* 20, no. 2–3 (2009): 194–23, at 202.

84. Marx, *Capital,* 1:272 (emphasis added).

85. Sharp, "The Commodification," 297.

86. Phillips, *Our Bodies,* 115.

87. Phillips, *Our Bodies,* 116.

88. See Nancy Scheper-Hughes, "Rotten Trade: Millennial Capitalism, Human Values and Global Justice in Organs Trafficking," *Journal of Human Rights* 2, no. 2 (2003): 197–226; Veatch, "Why Liberals Should Accept Financial Incentives"; Sheila M. Rothman and David J. Rothman, "The Hidden Cost of Organ Sales," *American Journal of Transplantation* 6, no. 7 (2006): 1524–28; Debra Satz, *Why Some Things Should Not Be For Sale: The Moral Limits of Markets* (New York: Oxford University Press, 2010); Julian Koplin, "Assessing the Likely Harms to Kidney Vendors in Regulated Organ Markets," *The American Journal of Bioethics* 14, no. 10 (2014): 7–18.

89. Joralemon, "Organ Wars," 344.

90. Rothman and Rothman, "The Hidden Cost," 1524.

91. Koplin, "Assessing the Likely Harms," 7.

92. Joralemon, "Organ Wars," 344.

93. Scheper-Hughes, "Rotten Trade," 204.

94. Donald Joralemon and Phil Cox, "Body Values: The Case Against Compensating for Transplant Organs," *Hastings Center Report* 33, no. 1 (2003): 27–33, at 29.

95. Jenny Slatman and Guy Widdershoven, "An Ethics of Embodiment: The Body as Object and Subject," in *Medicine and Society: New Perspectives in Continental Philosophy,* ed. Darian Meacham (Dordrecht: Springer, 2015), 87–104, at 90.

96. Joralemon and Cox, "Body Values," 30.

97. Geoff Mann, *Disassembly Required: A Field Guide to Actually Existing Capitalism* (Edinburg: AK Press, 2013), 14.

98. Gísli Pálsson, "Biosocial Relations of Production," *Comparative Studies in Society and History* 51, no. 2 (2009): 288–313, at 298.

99. Nancy S. Jecker, "Selling Ourselves: The Ethics of Paid Living Kidney Donation," *The American Journal of Bioethics* 14, no. 10 (2014): 1–6, at 5.

100. Richard A. Demme, "Ethical Concerns about an Organ Market," *Journal of the National Medical Association* 102, no. 1 (2010): 46–50; 47.

101. Joralemon and Cox, "Body Values," 30.

102. Joralemon and Cox, "Body Values," 30.

103. Rothman and Rothman, "The Hidden Cost," 1524.

104. Koplin, "Assessing the Likely Harms," 7.

105. Demme, "Ethical Concerns," 48.

106. Demme, "Ethical Concerns," 48.

107. Debra Satz, "Ethical Issues in the Supply and Demand of Human Kidneys," in *Bioethics: An Anthology*, ed. Helga Kuhse, Udo Schüklenk, and Peter Singer (Malden, Mass.: John Wiley and Sons, 2015), 425–36.

108. Scheper-Hughes, "Rotten Trade," 202.

109. Demme, "Ethical Concerns," 48.

110. Demme, "Ethical Concerns," 48.

111. Leigh Turner, "Commercial Organ Transplantation in the Philippines," *Cambridge Quarterly of Healthcare Ethics* 18, no. 2 (2009): 192–96, at 194.

112. Madhav Goyal, Ravindra L. Mehta, Lawrence J. Schneiderman, and Ashwini R. Sehgal, "Economic and Health Consequences of Selling a Kidney in India," *Journal of the American Medical Association* 288, no. 13 (2002): 1589–93. See also Vivekanand Jha, "Paid Transplants in India: The Grim Reality," *Nephrology Dialysis Transplantation* 19, no. 3 (2004): 541–43. For an opposing view, see Sunil K. Vemuru Reddy, Sandeep Guleria, Okidi Okechukwu, Rajesh Sagar, Dipankar Bhowmik, and Sandeep Mahajan, "Live Related Donors in India: Their Quality of Life Using World Health Organization Quality of Life Brief Questionnaire," *Indian Journal of Urology* 27, no. 1 (2011): 25–29, at 25.

113. See Syed Ali Anwar Naqvi, Bux Ali, Farida Mazhar, Mirza Naqi Zafar, and Syed Adibul Hasan Rizvi, "A Socioeconomic Survey of Kidney Vendors in Pakistan," *Transplant International* 20, no. 11 (2007): 934–39; and Javaad Zargooshi, "Quality of Life of Iranian Kidney 'Donors,'" *The Journal of Urology* 166, no. 5 (2001): 1790–99.

114. Scheper-Hughes, "The Ends of the Body," 78.

115. Jecker, "Selling Ourselves," 5.

116. Gorovitz, "Against Selling Body Parts," 11.

117. Phillips, *Our Bodies*, 106.

118. Sallie Yea, "Trafficking in Part(s): The Commercial Kidney Market in a Manila Slum, Philippines," *Global Social Policy* 10, no. 3 (2010): 358–76, at 367.

119. Mann, *Disassembly Required*, 78.

120. Satz, *Why Some Things Should Not Be for Sale*, 93.

121. Hacking, "Our Neo-Cartesian Bodies," 83.

122. Turner, "Commercial Organ," 193.

123. Scheper-Hughes, "The Ends of the Body," 66.

124. Veatch, "Why Liberals Should Accept Financial Incentives," 20.

125. Veatch, "Why Liberals Should Accept Financial Incentives," 30–31.

126. Veatch, "Why Liberals Should Accept Financial Incentives," 32.

127. Veatch, "Why Liberals Should Accept Financial Incentives," 20.

128. Veatch, "Why Liberals Should Accept Financial Incentives," 33.

129. Quoted in Satz, *Why Some Things Should Not Be for Sale,* 198.

130. See, for example, Arthur W. Frank, "Emily's Scars: Surgical Shapings, Technoluse, and Bioethics," *Hastings Center Report* 34, no. 2 (2004): 18–29.

131. Rose, *The Politics of Life Itself,* 20.

132. Frank, "Emily's Scars," 18.

133. Hacking, "Our Neo-Cartesian Bodies," 85.

134. Catherine Waldby, "Biomedicine, Tissue Transfer and Intercorporeality," *Feminist Theory* 3, no. 3 (2002): 239–54.

135. Waldby, "Biomedicine," 240.

136. Kaufman and Morgan, "The Anthropology," 330.

137. Scheper-Hughes, "Rotten Trade," 197.

138. John P. Lizza, *Persons, Humanity, and the Definition of Death* (Baltimore, Md.: Johns Hopkins University Press, 2006), 178.

139. Lizza, *Persons,* 178.

Postscript

1. Karl Marx, *Economic and Philosophic Manuscripts of 1844,* trans. Martin Milligan (Amherst, N.Y.: Prometheus, 1988), 85.

2. Joseph Choonara, *Unravelling Capitalism: A Guide to Marxist Political Economy,* 2nd ed. (London: Bookmarks, 2017), 44.

3. Choonara, *Unravelling Capitalism,* 44.

4. Michael Dillon and Luis Lobo-Guerrero, "The Biopolitical Imaginary of Species-Being," *Theory, Culture and Society* 26, no. 1 (2009): 1–23, at 2.

5. Karl Marx, *Capital: A Critique of Political Economy,* vol. 1, trans. Ben Fowkes (New York: Penguin, 1990), 274.

6. Marx, *Capital,* 1:274.

7. Marx, *Capital,* 1:275.

8. Marx, *Capital,* 1:275.

9. Marisela Montenegro, Joan Pujol, and Silvia Posocco, "Bordering, Exclusions and Necropolitics," *Qualitative Research Journal* 17, no. 3 (2017): 142–54, at 143.

10. Zohreh Bayatrizi, *Life Sentences: The Modern Ordering of Mortality* (Toronto: University of Toronto Press, 2008), 5.

11. Bayatrizi, *Life Sentences,* 53.

12. Emma W. Laurie and Ian G. R. Shaw, "Violent Conditions: The Injustices of Being," *Political Geography* 65 (2018): 8–16, at 15.

13. Marx, *Capital*, 1:275.

14. Robert Albritton, *Let Them Eat Junk: How Capitalism Creates Hunger and Obesity* (New York: Pluto, 2009), 147.

15. Katharyne Mitchell, Sallie A. Marston, and Cindi Katz, "Introduction: Life's Work: An Introduction, Review and Critique," *Antipode* 35, no. 3 (2003): 415–42, at 418.

16. Laurie and Shaw, "Violent Conditions," 12.

17. Laurie and Shaw, Violent Conditions," 15.

18. James Tyner, *Violence in Capitalism: Devaluing Life in an Age of Responsibility* (Lincoln: University of Nebraska Press, 2016), 209–10.

19. Tom Koch, "Let's Speak Less of Death and More About Care," *The Star*, July 2, 2013, thestar.com/opinion/commentary/2013/07/02/lets_speak_less_of_death_and_more_about_care.html. See also Tom Koch, *Ethics in Everyday Places: Mapping Moral Stress, Distress, and Injury* (Cambridge, Mass.: MIT Press, 2018).

20. See, for example, Ian Hay, "Making Moral Imaginations: Research Ethics, Pedagogy, and Professional Human Geography," *Ethics, Place and Environment* 1, no. 1 (1998): 55–75; David M. Smith, *Moral Geographies Ethics in a World of Difference* (Edinburgh: Edinburgh University Press, 2000); Susan J. Smith, "States, Markets and an Ethic of Care," *Political Geography* 24 (2005): 1–20; Victoria Lawson, "Geographies of Care and Responsibility," *Annals of the Association of American Geographers* 97, no. 1 (2007): 1–11; Sarah Atkinson, Victoria Lawson, and Janine Wiles, "Care of the Body: Spaces of Practice," *Social and Cultural Geography* 12, no. 6 (2011): 563–72; and Sarah M. Hall, "Personal, Relational and Intimate Geographies of Austerity: Ethical and Empirical Considerations," *Area* 49, no. 3 (2017): 303–10.

21. Linda McDowell, "Work, Workfare, Work/Life Balance and an Ethic of Care," *Progress in Human Geography* 28, no. 2 (2004): 145–63, at 146.

22. McDowell, "Work," 147.

23. McDowell, "Work," 156.

24. Clare Madge, "Creative Geographies and Living On from Breast Cancer: The Enlivening Potential of Autobiographical Bricolage for an Aesthetics of Precarity," *Transactions of the Institute of British Geographers* 43, no. 2 (2018): 245–61, at 255.

25. Paul Cloke, "Deliver Us from Evil? Prospects for Living Ethically and Acting Politically in Human Geography," *Progress in Human Geography* 26, no. 5 (2002): 587–604, at 597.

26. Lawson, "Geographies," 1.

27. Cloke, "Deliver Us from Evil," 598.

INDEX

absolute surplus value. *See* value
Agamben, Giorgio, 13
Albritton, Robert, 84
Andrews, Lori, 114
autonomy, 12, 14, 27, 32, 94, 118–19

bare life, 13, 79, 83
Barkan, Joshua, 31
Bauman, Zygmunt, 9, 85
Bayatrizi, Zohreh, 92–93, 110, 129
Bernat, James, 6–8
biocapital, 101, 103, 116, 118, 124
bioeconomics, x, xiv, 107, 114, 128–29
biofinance, 92, 95, 101, 105
biopolitics, x, 101–2, 114
body: laboring, 3; living, 23, 33, 39, 103, 117; material, 2–6; natural, 3; organ trade and, 114–26; relational, 3; scientific knowledge of, 106–14
Bonefeld, Werner, 56
border: management, 64–83, militarization, 52, 79, 82
Bracero Program, 67–68, 77–78
brain death, 112–14
Butler, Judith, 10, 15

capital: accumulation, 15, 27, 31, 38, 53, 66, 72–73, 86, 88–89, 95, 129; constant, 24, 28, 40, 61, 73, 83, 87, 91; fictitious, 89, 92, 97–100; finance, 86–92, 130; organic composition of, 28, 87; variable, 1, 24, 59, 87, 91
capitalism: biologics of, 126; commodities and, 20–23; defined, x, 18–19; finance, 90–101; labor and, 23–30; necrocapitalism, xiii–xiv, 16, 125–26, 129–30, 132; subjectivity and, 30–36
Castro, Robert, 78
Chang, Ha-Joon, 20
Chin, William, 22
Choonara, Joseph, 127
citizenship, x, 35, 45, 52–53, 61–62, 75, 77, 80, 82, 94, 123, 131
Cleaver, Harry, 57–58
Cloke, Paul, 131–32
Coleman, Mathew, 73, 81
colonialism, 12, 42, 57–58, 106, 120
commodity: fetish, 23; finance capital and, 92–100; labor as, 23–36; production of, 36–40

JAMES TYNER is professor of geography at Kent State University.

CPSIA information can be obtained
at www.ICGtesting.com
Printed in the USA
BVHW040303090319
542207BV00006B/49/P